COMPUTER
BOOK SERIES
FROM IDG

Computer Security For Dummies®

Cheat Sheet

Top Ten Security Measures

✔ **Back up your files.**
We can't stress this point enough. It is only a matter of time ~~...~~ you're able to recover it.

✔ **Pick proper passwords.**
If you use passwords in word processors, online services, ~~...~~ aren't easy to guess. String two or three words and numbe~~...~~

D0809223

✔ **Never divulge your password.**
Not to anyone. Change it on a regular basis, such as every 30 days.

✔ **Use an antivirus program.**
You are at risk if you use other people's diskettes or download files from the Internet. Protect yourself by running virus protection software against these diskettes and files.

✔ **Buy a tape backup device.**
Diskettes are great, but using them to back up your files is time and labor intensive. A tape backup device makes life much simpler. These devices enable you to back up your entire hard drive, making recovery from a disk failure much easier than using hundreds of diskettes.

✔ **Don't violate copyrights.**
Buy your own software; don't copy it from your friends. Vendors are realizing that they need to let people evaluate programs before buying them, and many companies offer evaluation copies that expire after a certain time or perform limited functions. After you try the program and know that you like it, go out and buy it!

✔ **Use a surge protector.**
These devices protect your computer from power fluctuations and lightning strikes. Even if you believe that using a surge protector is not necessary where you live, your machine can be affected if it is on the same circuit breaker as your power tools, refrigerator, or other energy-intensive appliances.

✔ **Keep food and drinks away from your computer.**
If you spill a drink on your desktop keyboard, you might be able to get away with rinsing it under a tap (unplugged!) and drying it off, but if you spill liquid on a laptop, the monitor, or the CPU, you're in big trouble.

✔ **Use a screen saver or turn off the monitor when you're not using it.**
Most monitors do not like being left on for extended periods of time. If you do not need to use the monitor for three or four hours, turn it off. You can leave your machine powered on without the monitor being on.

✔ **Place your computer on a sturdy table.**
We often cringe when we visit friends and find that they have placed their new $2,000 computer on a rickety old table that they dug up from the basement. Trust us: You don't want your computer to drop to the floor when someone bumps the table or the table collapses from old age.

. . .For Dummies: #1 Computer Book Series for Beginners

COMPUTER
BOOK SERIES
FROM IDG

Computer Security For Dummies®

Cheat Sheet

Acronyms and What They Mean

Use this list to impress your friends and family. They'll think that you're an expert if you drop a few of these gems into your conversation:

CISSP	Certified Information Systems Security Professional
CISA	Certified Information Systems Auditor
COPS	Computer Oracle and Password System
DEA	Data Encryption Algorithm
DES	Data Encryption Standard
DCE	Distributed Computing Environment
GSSP	Generally Accepted System Security Principles
IDEA	International Data Encryption Algorithm
ISACA	Information Systems Audit and Control Association
(ISC)2	International Information Systems Security Certification Consortium
ISSA	Information Systems Security Association
PGP	Pretty Good Privacy
PIN	Personal Identification Number
RSA	Rivest, Shamir, and Adleman
SAC	Security, Audit, and Control
SANTA	Security Analysis Network Tool for Administrators
SATAN	Security Administrator Tool for Analyzing Networks
SSL	Secure Sockets Layer
SSO	Single Sign-On
TCB	Trusted Computer Base
UPS	Uninterruptible Power System (or Supply)

Those Old Familiar Tunes: Security Terms

Denial of service: The loss of access to your personal computer or to the network you're using. Simply put, denial of service occurs when some other person's actions keep a legitimate user from using the computer or network.

Disclosure: Not the movie, but that someone who should not have read the information has read it.

Identification: The process of a computer recognizing who you are, typically through the use of a userid or account.

Modification: To change something.

Password: Secret. Secret. Secret. A collection of characters and numbers that you assign and *never* tell to anyone. You use passwords to prove that *you* are signing on the computer, not some stranger.

Risk: The likelihood that a vulnerability or threat will be exploited or cause harm; the potential for something bad happening.

Separation of duty: The principle of dividing important transactions so that at least two people are needed to finalize the transaction.

Userid: This term has so many brothers and sisters that it's hard to keep up; also called *username, Logonid, account,* or *sign on.* They all mean the collection of characters assigned to you that identify you to the computer.

...For Dummies: #1 Computer Book Series for Beginners

 ®

References for the Rest of Us! ®

COMPUTER BOOK SERIES FROM IDG

Are you intimidated and confused by computers? Do you find that traditional manuals are overloaded with technical details you'll never use? Do your friends and family always call you to fix simple problems on their PCs? Then the *...For Dummies*® computer book series from IDG Books Worldwide is for you.

...For Dummies books are written for those frustrated computer users who know they aren't really dumb but find that PC hardware, software, and indeed the unique vocabulary of computing make them feel helpless. *...For Dummies* books use a lighthearted approach, a down-to-earth style, and even cartoons and humorous icons to diffuse computer novices' fears and build their confidence. Lighthearted but not lightweight, these books are a perfect survival guide for anyone forced to use a computer.

> *"I like my copy so much I told friends; now they bought copies."*
>
> **Irene C., Orwell, Ohio**

> *"Quick, concise, nontechnical, and humorous."*
>
> **Jay A., Elburn, Illinois**

> *"Thanks, I needed this book. Now I can sleep at night."*
>
> **Robin F., British Columbia, Canada**

Already, hundreds of thousands of satisfied readers agree. They have made *...For Dummies* books the #1 introductory level computer book series and have written asking for more. So, if you're looking for the most fun and easy way to learn about computers, look to *...For Dummies* books to give you a helping hand.

IDG BOOKS WORLDWIDE ™

COMPUTER SECURITY FOR DUMMIES®

by Peter T. Davis
and
Barry D. Lewis

IDG Books Worldwide, Inc.
An International Data Group Company

Foster City, CA ♦ Chicago, IL ♦ Indianapolis, IN ♦ Braintree, MA ♦ Southlake, TX

Computer Security For Dummies®

Published by
IDG Books Worldwide, Inc.
An International Data Group Company
919 E. Hillsdale Blvd.
Suite 400
Foster City, CA 94404

Library of Congress Catalog Card No.: 96-76246

ISBN: 1-56884-635-5

Printed in the United States of America

10 9 8 7 6 5 4 3 2 1

1O/TR/QV/ZW/IN

Distributed in the United States by IDG Books Worldwide, Inc.

Distributed by Macmillan Canada for Canada; by Contemporanea de Ediciones for Venezuela; by Distribuidora Cuspide for Argentina; by CITEC for Brazil; by Ediciones ZETA S.C.R. Ltda. for Peru; by Editorial Limusa SA for Mexico; by Transworld Publishers Limited in the United Kingdom and Europe; by Academic Bookshop for Egypt; by Levant Distributors S.A.R.L. for Lebanon; by Al Jassim for Saudi Arabia; by Simron Pty. Ltd. for South Africa; by Pustak Mahal for India; by The Computer Bookshop for India; by Toppan Company Ltd. for Japan; by Addison Wesley Publishing Company for Korea; by Longman Singapore Publishers Ltd. for Singapore, Malaysia, Thailand, and Indonesia; by Unalis Corporation for Taiwan; by WS Computer Publishing Company, Inc. for the Philippines; by WoodsLane Pty. Ltd. for Australia; by WoodsLane Enterprises Ltd. for New Zealand. Authorized Sales Agent: Anthony Rudkin Associates for the Middle East and North Africa.

For general information on IDG Books Worldwide's books in the U.S., please call our Consumer Customer Service department at 800-762-2974. For reseller information, including discounts and premium sales, please call our Reseller Customer Service department at 800-434-3422.

For information on where to purchase IDG Books Worldwide's books outside the U.S., contact IDG Books Worldwide at 415-655-3078 or fax 415-655-3295.

For information on translations, contact Marc Jeffrey Mikulich, Director, Foreign & Subsidiary Rights, at IDG Books Worldwide, 415-655-3018 or fax 415-655-3281.

For sales inquiries and special prices for bulk quantities, write to the address above or call IDG Books Worldwide at 415-655-3200.

For information on using IDG Books Worldwide's books in the classroom, or ordering examination copies, contact the Education Office at 800-434-2086 or fax 817-251-8174.

For authorization to photocopy items for corporate, personal, or educational use, please contact Copyright Clearance Center, 222 Rosewood Drive, Danvers, MA 01923, or fax 508-750-4470.

 is a trademark under exclusive license to IDG Books Worldwide, Inc., from International Data Group, Inc.

About the Authors

Peter T. Davis

Peter is the founder and principal of Peter Davis+Associates, a management consulting firm specializing in the security, audit, and control of information systems. He has served on the board of the Computer Security Institute and the Information System Security Association. In addition, he is a member of the committee formed to develop Generally Accepted System Security Principles (GSSP), an international security methodology. Peter has written, cowritten, or edited four other books.

Barry D. Lewis

Barry Lewis got started with computers way back in the Dark Ages in 1969, working for a major financial institution with whom he stayed for the next 18 years. His first personal computer was, by today's standards, less functional than a cheap calculator. In 1980, he got his first exposure to computer security when he joined the team developing the bank's security program. Barry has been hooked ever since.

In 1987, Barry moved from the financial field into consulting, joining one of the world's largest audit firms. Shortly after, he joined a second international audit firm and over the next five years provided security consulting to organizations across North America. He went into private practice in 1992 and joined a small consulting firm called Cerberus Information Security Consulting Inc. in 1993, where he currently serves as president. You can check out their Web page at www.cerberus.com/~cerberus.

Barry has delivered training courses and seminars across North America to a wide variety of organizations, including the Computer Security Institute (CSI), the annual Computer Associates Enterprise-wide Security and Audit Conference (ESAC), and the EDPAA. In 1994, he won the Best Speaker Award at ESAC, one of the largest security conferences in North America.

Barry is a prolific author and has published articles in *Auerbach, Computing Canada,* and the *Journal of Systems Management.* He is coauthor of a book on client/server security due out in spring 1996.

ABOUT IDG BOOKS WORLDWIDE

Welcome to the world of IDG Books Worldwide.

IDG Books Worldwide, Inc., is a subsidiary of International Data Group, the world's largest publisher of computer-related information and the leading global provider of information services on information technology. IDG was founded more than 25 years ago and now employs more than 7,700 people worldwide. IDG publishes more than 250 computer publications in 67 countries (see listing below). More than 70 million people read one or more IDG publications each month.

Launched in 1990, IDG Books Worldwide is today the #1 publisher of best-selling computer books in the United States. We are proud to have received 8 awards from the Computer Press Association in recognition of editorial excellence and three from Computer Currents' First Annual Readers' Choice Awards, and our best-selling ...For Dummies® series has more than 19 million copies in print with translations in 28 languages. IDG Books Worldwide, through a joint venture with IDG's Hi-Tech Beijing, became the first U.S. publisher to publish a computer book in the People's Republic of China. In record time, IDG Books Worldwide has become the first choice for millions of readers around the world who want to learn how to better manage their businesses.

Our mission is simple: Every one of our books is designed to bring extra value and skill-building instructions to the reader. Our books are written by experts who understand and care about our readers. The knowledge base of our editorial staff comes from years of experience in publishing, education, and journalism — experience which we use to produce books for the '90s. In short, we care about books, so we attract the best people. We devote special attention to details such as audience, interior design, use of icons, and illustrations. And because we use an efficient process of authoring, editing, and desktop publishing our books electronically, we can spend more time ensuring superior content and spend less time on the technicalities of making books.

You can count on our commitment to deliver high-quality books at competitive prices on topics you want to read about. At IDG Books Worldwide, we continue in the IDG tradition of delivering quality for more than 25 years. You'll find no better book on a subject than one from IDG Books Worldwide.

John Kilcullen
President and CEO
IDG Books Worldwide, Inc.

IDG Books Worldwide, Inc., is a subsidiary of International Data Group, the world's largest publisher of computer-related information and the leading global provider of information services on information technology. International Data Group publishes over 250 computer publications in 67 countries. Seventy million people read one or more International Data Group publications each month. International Data Group's publications include: **ARGENTINA:** Computerworld Argentina, GamePro, Infoworld, PC World Argentina; **AUSTRALIA:** Australian Macworld, Client/Server Journal, Computer Living, Computerworld, Digital News, Network World, PC World, Publishing Essentials, Reseller; **AUSTRIA:** Computerwelt, PC TEST; **BELARUS:** PC World Belarus; **BELGIUM:** Data News; **BRAZIL:** Annuário de Informática, Computerworld Brazil, Connections, Super Game Power, Macworld, PC World Brazil, Publish Brazil, SUPERGAME; **BULGARIA:** Computerworld Bulgaria, Networkworld/Bulgaria, PC & MacWorld Bulgaria; **CANADA:** CIO Canada, ComputerWorld Canada, InfoCanada, Network World Canada, Reseller World; **CHILE:** Computerworld Chile, GamePro, PC World Chile; **COLUMBIA:** Computerworld Colombia, GamePro, PC World Colombia; **COSTA RICA:** PC World Costa Rica/Nicaragua; **THE CZECH AND SLOVAK REPUBLICS:** Computerworld Czechoslovakia, Elektronika Czechoslovakia, PC World Czechoslovakia; **DENMARK:** Communications World, Computerworld Danmark, Macworld Danmark, PC World Danmark, PC World Danmark Supplements, TECH World; **DOMINICAN REPUBLIC:** PC World Republica Dominicana; **ECUADOR:** PC World Ecuador, GamePro; **EGYPT:** Computerworld Middle East, PC World Middle East; **EL SALVADOR:** PC World Centro America; **FINLAND:** MikroPC, Tietoverkko, Tietoviikko; **FRANCE:** Distributique, Golden, Info PC, Le Guide du Monde Informatique, Le Monde Informatique, Reseaux & Telecoms; **GERMANY:** Computer Business, Computerwoche, Computerwoche Extra, Computerwoche Focus, Electronic Entertainment, GamePro, I/M Information Management, Macwelt, PC Welt; **GREECE:** GamePro, Macworld & Publish; **GUATEMALA:** PC World Centro America; **HONDURAS:** PC World Centro America; **HONG KONG:** Computerworld Hong Kong, PCWorld Hong Kong, Publish in Asia; **HUNGARY:** ABCD CD-ROM, Computerworld Szamitastechnika, PC & Mac World Hungary, PC-X Magazine; **INDIA:** Computerworld India, PC World India, Publish in Asia; **INDONESIA:** InfoKomputer PC World, Komputek Computerworld, Publish in Asia; **IRELAND:** ComputerScope, PC Live!; **ISRAEL:** PC World 32 BIT, People & Computers; **ITALY:** Computerworld Italia, Computerworld Italia Special Editions, Lotus Italia, Macworld Italia, Networking Italia, PC Shopping, PC World Italia, PC World/Walt Disney; **JAPAN:** Macworld Japan, Nikkei Personal Computing, SunWorld Japan, Windows World Japan; **KENYA:** East African Computer News; **KOREA:** Hi-Tech Information/Computerworld, Macworld Korea, PC World Korea; **MACEDONIA:** PC World Macedonia; **MALAYSIA:** Computerworld Malaysia, PC World Malaysia, Publish in Asia; **MEXICO:** Computerworld Mexico, GamePro, Macworld, PC World Mexico; **MYANMAR:** PC World Myanmar; **NETHERLANDS:** Computable, Computer! Totaal, LAN Magazine, Macworld, Net Magazine; **NEW ZEALAND:** Computer Buyer, Computerworld New Zealand, MTB, Network World, PC World New Zealand; **NICARAGUA:** PC World Costa Rica/Nicaragua; **NIGERIA:** PC World Africa; **NORWAY:** Computerworld Norge, Computerworld Privat, CW Rapport Klient/Tjener, CW Rapport Nettverk & Telecom, CW Rapport Offentlig Sektor, IDG's KURSGUIDE, Macworld Norge, Multimedia World, PC World Ekspress, PC World Nettverk, PC World Norge, PC World's Produktguide, Windows Spesial; **PAKISTAN:** Computerworld Pakistan, PC World Pakistan; **PANAMA:** GamePro, PC World Panama; **PARAGUAY:** PC World Paraguay; **P. R. OF CHINA:** China Computerworld, China Infoworld, Computer & Communication, Electronic Product World, Electronics Today, Game Camp, PC World China, Popular Computer Week, Software World, Telecom Product World; **PERU:** Computerworld Peru, GamePro, PC World Profesional Peru, PC World Peru; **POLAND:** Computerworld Poland, Computerworld Special Report, Macworld, Networld, PC World Komputer; **PHILIPPINES:** Computerworld Philippines, PC Digest, Publish in Asia; **PORTUGAL:** Cerebro/PC World, Correio Informático/Computerworld, Mac•In/PC•In Portugal; **PUERTO RICO:** PC World Puerto Rico; **ROMANIA:** Computerworld Romania, PC World Romania, Telecom Romania; **RUSSIA:** Computerworld Rossiya, Network World Russia, PC World Russia; **SINGAPORE:** Computerworld Singapore, PC World Singapore, Publish in Asia; **SLOVENIA:** MONITOR; **SOUTH AFRICA:** Computing S.A., Network World S.A., Software World; **SPAIN:** Computerworld España, COMUNICACIONES WORLD, Dealer World, Macworld España, PC World España; **SWEDEN:** CAP&Design, Computer Sweden, Corporate Computing, MacWorld, Maxi Data, MikroDatorn, Nätverk & Kommunikation, PC/Aktiv, PC World, Windows World; **SWITZERLAND:** Computerworld Schweiz, Macworld Schweiz, PCtip; **TAIWAN:** Computerworld Taiwan, Macworld Taiwan, PC World Taiwan, Publish Taiwan, Windows World; **THAILAND:** Thai Computerworld, Publish in Asia; **TURKEY:** Computerworld Monitör, MACWORLD Turkiye, PC WORLD Turkiye; **UKRAINE:** Computerworld Kiev, Computers & Software Magazine, PC World Ukraine; **UNITED KINGDOM:** Acorn User, Amiga Action, Amiga Computing, Amiga, Appletalk, CD Powerplay, CD-ROM Now, Computing, Connexion, GamePro, Lotus Magazine, Macaction, Macworld, Open Computing, Parents and Computers, PC Home, PC Works, The WEB; **UNITED STATES:** Cable in the Classroom, CD Review, CIO Magazine, Computerworld, Computerworld Client/Server Journal, Digital Video Magazine, DOS World, Electronic, InfoWorld, I-Way, Macworld, Maximize, MULTIMEDIA WORLD, Network World, PC World, PUBLISH, SWATPro Magazine, Video Event, WebMaster; **URUGUAY:** PC World Uruguay; **VENEZUELA:** Computerworld Venezuela, GamePro, PC World Venezuela; and **VIETNAM:** PC World Vietnam   10/17/95a

WINNER
Eighth Annual
Computer Press
Awards 1992

WINNER
Ninth Annual
Computer Press
Awards 1993

IDG
BOOKS
WORLDWIDE

Dedication

Authors' Acknowledgments

A special thanks is given to:

Megg Bonar, Mary Corder, and Gareth Hancock for helping us get started with the book. We couldn't have done this without your help.

Pam Mourouzis, our Project Editor, for her candid comments and professionalism in this project. The success of this project is owed in many ways to her.

Everyone at IDG Books who helped with the finished product, especially Mary Bednarek. We would also like to thank Sam Faulkner, our technical editor — wherever you are.

Everybody who encouraged us to compile the book — and those who said they would buy it.

Peter Davis also would like to thank Janet and Kelly for their support and understanding. Sorry about the Easter long weekend.

Barry Lewis adds his thanks to Peter. It's been fun.

Publisher's Acknowledgments

We're proud of this book; please send us your comments about it by using the Reader Response Card at the back of the book or by e-mailing us at feedback/dummies@idgbooks.com. Some of the people who helped bring this book to market include the following:

Acquisitions, Development, & Editorial

Project Editor: Pamela Mourouzis

Assistant Acquisitions Editor: Gareth Hancock

Product Development Manager: Mary Bednarek

Permissions Editor: Joyce Pepple

Copy Editors: Robin Drake, Rebecca Whitney

Technical Reviewer: Samuel Faulkner

Editorial Managers: Kristin A. Cocks, Seta K. Frantz

Editorial Assistant: Chris H. Collins

Production

Associate Project Coordinator: Regina Snyder

Layout and Graphics: Brett Black, Todd Klemme, Jane E. Martin, Anna Rohrer, M. Anne Sipahimalani, Angela F. Hunckler

Proofreaders: Henry Lazarek, Jenny Overmyer, Christine Meloy Beck, Michael Bolinger, Nancy Price, Dwight Ramsey, Carl Saff, Robert Springer, Carrie Voorhis, Karen York

Indexer: Sherry Massey

General & Administrative

IDG Books Worldwide, Inc.: John Kilcullen, President & CEO; Steven Berkowitz, COO & Publisher

Dummies, Inc.: Milissa Koloski, Executive Vice President & Publisher

Dummies Technology Press & Dummies Editorial: Diane Graves Steele, Associate Publisher; Judith A. Taylor, Brand Manager; Myra Immell, Editorial Director

Dummies Trade Press: Kathleen A. Welton, Vice President & Publisher; Stacy S. Collins, Brand Manager

IDG Books Production for Dummies Press: Beth Jenkins, Production Director; Cindy L. Phipps, Supervisor of Project Coordination; Kathie S. Schnorr, Supervisor of Page Layout; Shelley Lea, Supervisor of Graphics and Design

Dummies Packaging & Book Design: Erin McDermitt, Packaging Coordinator; Kavish+Kavish, Cover Design

♦

The publisher would like to give special thanks to Patrick J. McGovern, without whom this book would not have been possible.

♦

Contents at a Glance

Cartoons at a Glance

By Rich Tennant • Fax: 508-546-7747 • E-mail: the5wave@tiac.net

page 63

page 289

page 157

page 5

page 221

Table of Contents

Introduction

⦁ ⦁

*I*n the constantly changing, modern world, computers have become a valuable tool used not only by computer technology professionals, but also by the average person: you. Today's computer handles everything from your family's financial history to your children's homework to Grandma's recipes. Because we know that this information is important to you, we want to help you become familiar with the concepts of security.

This book can help you — the average noncomputer professional — plan, implement, and, above all, understand the need to back up your system and secure your data so that, if a hardware or software malfunction occurs, you can recover your data. Or if someone tries to get at your personal data, the intruder does not get access or reads unintelligible garbage.

About This Book

Computer Security For Dummies helps you figure out how to protect your valuable data and system resources. This book serves two purposes. First, we explain the security issues. Second, we provide some proven techniques for protecting yourself. Using this book, you see how to do the following:

- Identify threats to your system and your data.
- Recognize the risks associated with those threats.
- Control your environment.
- Avoid common mistakes such as spilling drinks on your system or suffering from power problems.
- Find useful stuff on the Internet and other commercial online services.
- Purchase security hardware and software.

Who Are You?

In writing this book, we think that you are

- ✔ Definitely not a dummy, or you wouldn't be concerned about personal computer security.

- ✔ Interested in protecting your data and system from accidental or intentional harm.

- ✔ Using a personal computer (PC) running either Apple's Mac OS or Microsoft Windows (any flavor, really).

- ✔ Not interested in becoming a security academic, but want practical advice.

- ✔ Interested in continuing to use your computer for fun or profit.

How This Book Is Organized

This book is divided into five parts. You don't have to read the parts in order, but doing so helps. However, you can start wherever you want and read only the parts that interest you. Please at least familiarize yourself with the contents of Part I to get acquainted with the inevitable security jargon.

Part I: The Basics

Part I lays the foundation for your understanding of security. You can read about the goals of security — confidentiality, integrity, and availability. In addition, we introduce you to threats, risks, vulnerabilities, and controls. The material in this part includes a discussion of well-known threats and also covers preventive, detective, and corrective controls. After you get the terminology down pat, you can apply it to your environment. This part also shows you how to perform a risk analysis to determine your level of risk.

Part II: The Methods

After you understand individual threats and vulnerabilities, you can select and implement specific compensating controls. Read about getting access control, picking good passwords, using built-in security features, making backups, and recovering data in Part II.

Part III: The Places

Part III exposes you to some of the places where *you* may be exposed. Because many people are connecting to online services and using electronic mail, we tell you about securing your e-mail, encryption, filtering, true file erasure, access control, and replication.

Part IV: The Part of Tens

As the name implies, Part IV provides you with a collection of valuable nuggets that we compiled while writing this book. This part supports the other chapters. For example, we talk about viruses, but in this part, we tell you about ten of the most prevalent ones. You can also find ways to back up your system and protect DOS, Windows, and Macintosh computers.

Part V: Appendixes: Real References for Real People

In Appendix A, we talk about purveyors of useful security hardware and software and security-conscious organizations. We also provide you with the names of hard copy resources such as books and periodicals.

Appendix B tells you where to find computer security resources online.

The glossary, Appendix C, defines all security-speak. Each profession and quasi-profession has its own lingo and jargon that only insiders know. We let you in on the special words and handshakes used in the computer security profession.

Finally, the security abbreviations appendix provides the English for all those TLAs (three-letter abbreviations) used in this book and in the industry.

Icons Used in This Book

We use several icons throughout the book. These icons point out useful, important, or interesting matters. Here's what they look like and what they stand for:

These icons point out critical information. You should definitely read this stuff. Occasionally, we use a Remember icon to remind you that additional information is in another chapter or appendix.

This icon lets you know that we couldn't explain the topic easily, so we had to resort to "technobabble." You can skip the sections marked with Technical Stuff icons and not lose anything. On the other hand, you may want to read them — they give some interesting background information.

If you're looking for labor- or money-saving advice or tricks, you can find them next to these icons.

Watch out! People have learned lessons about securing their systems the hard way. We hope you won't have to learn them, too. Follow the advice next to these icons to avoid repeating these lessons.

Conventions Used in This Book

In this book, we use `monospaced` fonts for Internet addresses, on-screen messages, and basically anything that looks like it should come from or be put into a computer.

When we introduce a term for the first time, you see it in *italics*.

We also use standard Uniform Resource Locators (URLs) for Internet addresses, where we suggest that you use the following:

- **ftp:** File transfer protocol, such as your Fetch or Chameleon client, or your Web browser, such as Netscape
- **http:** Web browser

Feedback, Please

If you want to contact us, please feel free to do so in care of this address:

IDG Books Worldwide, Inc.
7260 Shadeland Station, Suite 100
Indianapolis, IN 46256

Or even better, send us encrypted e-mail to `feedback/dummies@idgbooks.com`.

Part I
The Basics

"SOMEONE KEEPS GOING INTO MY PERSONAL FILE. I'D SURE AS HECK LIKE TO FIND OUT WHO USES THE PASSWORD 'PEANUT-BREATH'."

In this part...

Before you know which measures to take to secure your data and your personal computer, you need to know what security is all about. This part gives you the lowdown on computer security concepts and terms and explains the types of threats and controls that you need to think about. Finally, Part I tells you how to assess your own situation to determine your personal security needs.

Chapter 1

The ABCs of Security

"Security is mostly a superstition. It does not exist in nature, nor do the children of men as a whole experience it. Avoiding danger is no safer in the long run than outright exposure. Life is either a daring adventure, or nothing."

— Helen Keller

Well, you're obviously no dummy. The fact that you bought this book proves that! Only dummies would *not* be concerned about the security of their personal computers.

Throughout history, humans have been much better at gathering information than controlling it. But information is a valuable commodity that needs protection. Is your data important to you? Like millions of computer owners, you probably answered a resounding and emphatic *yes!* Not only is your data important to you, but some of it may be irreplaceable.

For this reason, you need to know how to defend yourself against unforeseen situations. Lots of events are unforeseen:

- Have you ever finished typing or keying in data only to find that your computer didn't save it?

- Have you ever started your computer to find that someone changed your system configuration without your approval?

- Have you ever lost data because of a power failure?

- Have you spent hours, days, or even weeks working on something, and then sometime during the night, gremlins ate that work, and you had to start all over? (And of course, you never feel quite right about the second document.)

✔ Has your notebook computer ever failed to warn you about the status of your battery and shut down in the middle of some work? Have you lost all the information that you entered on the five-hour flight from New York to Los Angeles?

✔ Have you ever turned on your computer and found no hard disk icon?

Looking at the preceding list, you can see that most of the events are not really unforeseen and actually can be avoided. For example, you can turn on the Autosave feature in many programs to save data as you enter it. You can apply access control to your personal computer or use encryption to make your data unintelligible to foil individuals from reading or changing files. In addition, you can use (or install) battery-saver software to warn you when laptop power levels are critically low. Performing preventative maintenance can help you preserve your hard disk. If you don't take preventative measures, you had better practice your recovery procedures.

Not practicing safe hex (or is it safe text?) can lead to disappointment. How many countless hours have you wasted recovering or retyping data? Is your peace of mind worth all the hours you spend in aggravation? After all, security is a state of mind. If we stopped 20 people on the streets of San Francisco and asked them to define security, we would get 21 different definitions. (Someone is sure to offer more than one definition to hedge his or her bets.) So with this book, we hope to help you sleep better at night. And we know that the best way to sleep better at night is to know as much about your problem as possible. That's where *Computer Security For Dummies* comes in handy. Security is not glamorous, but it is very much a necessary function in the computing world.

We created this book for the many people who are using computers for work, research, fun, education, or exploring cyberspace — also known as the Internet. Many people now using personal computers are not trained computer professionals. They use their computers for different reasons, without knowledge of the security basics that many computer professionals take for granted. This book is a primer of techniques that professionals have used in mainframe, minicomputer, and PC networks for years.

Security Exposed

Personal computer security has several definitions. Simply put, personal computer security lets you accomplish the tasks that you want to accomplish without interference. The goal of genuine security is to protect the confidentiality, integrity, and availability of information stored within a computer — and provide that protection at an acceptable cost.

Confidentiality involves protecting information from people whom you don't want to read your information. You may want to stop the cleaning service from seeing a copy of your stock portfolio, for example.

Integrity of data means that the information hasn't been changed by anyone whom you don't want to change the information. You probably want to stop your children from getting into Quicken and changing your household expenses at budgeting time.

Availability concerns itself with making sure that your data and your personal computer are available when you want them to be available. You don't want to "sweat blood" for three days as repair people try to copy your valuable data from your hard drive that won't spin anymore. Chapter 2 gives you a detailed explanation of these terms.

Personal Computers Unmasked

Your concern for security suggests that you feel that something on your personal computer is worth protecting. But before you figure out what that something is, you should understand what we mean by a *personal computer.* Today's personal computers blur the line between the definitions of mainframe, minicomputer, and personal computer. The best way to understand personal computers is to contrast them with minicomputers and mainframes.

Typically, people think of mainframes as large, host-centric systems that primarily process batch jobs. IBM has been making and selling mainframes for a long time. Large corporations know the value of mainframes: They provide centralized control and good integrity features.

After mainframes came the development of *minicomputers,* which are used for mid-level computing. Though not as small as PCs, minicomputers are smaller than mainframes, although the original minicomputers would dwarf today's mainframes. Organizations still use minicomputers for transaction-processing applications and as interfaces between mainframe computer systems and PC networks.

The term *personal computer* was coined by IBM in 1981 and rapidly became a standard in the computer industry. Personal computers were designed for use by one person at a time. Microcomputers that use microprocessors became known generically as *PCs.* Microcomputers allow you to take charge of the entire computing process. On your system, you are the system programmer, production control, application development, client, user, operations support, operations, performance and capacity planning, hardware planning, change control, and storage management. PC users do not need to share processing cycles, disk storage, or a printer with another computer to make the system work, although they may. These attributes make security important —and scary.

Note: In this book, we deal with personal computers in general. So when we talk about PCs, we don't mean just systems sold by IBM. Instead, we mean any system (you can say *clone*) that can run PC-DOS, MS-DOS, Windows 3.*x*, Windows 95, Windows for Workgroups, and Windows NT, in addition to Mac OS, OS/2, and UNIX systems. Our examples, however, focus mainly on Windows and Mac OS systems because they are the most common.

Measuring the Value of Your Information

What is the value of your data? Only you know what your data is worth to you. To place a price on your data is not our purpose at this time; however, we'll try to establish some parameters to give you an idea that what resides on your computer is more valuable than you realize. Think about the following things:

✔ Do you keep your financial records on the computer?

✔ Do you do your banking by using a computer?

✔ Do you file your income tax return by computer?

✔ Do you keep track of your investment portfolio online?

✔ Do your children use your home computer for their school work?

✔ Do you keep personal information on the computer, such as addresses, phone numbers, and important dates?

✔ Do you use the computer for a side business or work-at-home endeavor?

✔ Do you keep an inventory of everything you own on the computer?

✔ Do you keep a catalog of your videotapes, compact discs, albums, and cassettes on your computer?

✔ Do you have your favorite games and leisure activities loaded on the computer?

✔ Do you have address books for your online services — for example, America Online, CompuServe, or Prodigy — on the computer?

✔ Do you keep your recipe, hobby, or bowling team records on the computer?

✔ Do you use your home computer to keep in touch with your work computer system or network?

✔ Do you keep things on the computer that aren't covered in this list but that are important to you?

Good news and bad news

It won't happen to me, you say. Sure, it happens to other people, but it can't happen to me. Well, that line of thinking may not be the most prudent for many reasons. Look at some of the security-related events that occurred in 1995:

- In January, a British teenager hacked into sensitive U.S. government computers, where he could monitor secret communications over the North Korean nuclear crisis in the spring of 1994. He tapped into several defense computers for over seven months in what officials called the worst breach of security in recent years.

- In February, crackers planted a Trojan horse on the CapAccess Internet provider in the Washington area. The rogue software grabbed userids and passwords for over 12,000 users, which caused two days of downtime as the system operators worked feverishly to fix the problem.

- March went out like a lion as U.S. Marshals raided the Assassin's Guild, one of the world's largest pirate bulletin boards. The bulletin board was home to Pirates With an Attitude (PWA) and Razor 1911 and provided current pirated software.

- Instead of May flowers, the month brought a furor over Microsoft's Registration Wizard for Windows. Rumor had it that the wizard would automatically forward a system's configuration to Microsoft, whereas you really had the option of sending the information.

- Also in May, the FBI announced that it had broken a computer chip theft ring in San Jose, California. They arrested 15 people at Prestige Computer Inc., alleging that they planned to break into the warehouse at the Intel Corporation, where saleable, untraceable chips were stored.

- Someone at Great American Insurance Company of Cincinnati, Ohio, had a rather unpleasant Father's Day in June. The company agreed to pay $266,436 to legitimize software found on its computers during a Business Software Alliance investigation.

- Randal Schwartz of Portland, Oregon, found July very hot. He was convicted of hacking Intel Corporation's computer networks in what he claimed was an effort to point out security weaknesses while he was working as a consultant. Hackers went on vacation in August and made their way to Las Vegas for DefCon III, a hacker convention. Attendees reprogrammed hotel televisions to scroll "Hackers Rule" across the screen.

- While the kids were returning to school in September, news broke of Russian hackers attacking Citibank's cash management systems. Apparently, the hackers stole $10 million but bungled attempts to withdraw the money.

- In October, the Internet community was less than bewitched by the security flaws in HotJava 1.0 alpha 3 release, which allowed people to capture all traffic between a client and a Web site.

- November saw Christopher Pile convicted under Britain's Computer Misuse Act of 1990 for creating and spreading the Pathogen and Queeg viruses.

- At year's end, America Online made headlines for attempting to clean up its network. AOL's automated screening program blocked the word *breast* in its attempt to clean up pornography on its network. Unfortunately, AOL forgot about legitimate uses of the word, such as by a breast cancer support group.

Most of these incidents did not affect personal computer users directly. But you're wrong if you think that these examples have nothing to do with your PC.

Now imagine that your personal computer was stolen or destroyed by a natural disaster; the hard drive sounds like a coffee grinder; or you just deleted all your files by accident. How much trouble would you have in replacing the data? How much time would you have to spend in rebuilding the databases, applications, or files? Would you worry about what someone might discover on your system?

With that in mind, decide how much your data is worth to you in lost time, money, or disclosed information. We're willing to guess that it has greater value than you first thought. Security is a necessary evil that you must endure to make sure that anything that happens to your data is recoverable in the shortest amount of time with the least amount of expense. It is also a little-used function by the average computer user. Too often, people take a reactive approach to security. This book is designed to help you take a proactive approach instead. The intent of this book is to make you a little more aware of what choices you have to defend yourself from losing valuable information and your business if you use the computer for your SOHO (that is, your Small Office/Home Office) that is your retirement fund or primary revenue stream.

Asking the $128,000 Question

At this point, you still may be wondering whether you need to implement security controls on your system. If you have a personal computer at home or at work, consider these questions:

- Are you using password protection on your system?
- Do you have a surge protector for your system? Alternately, do you have a line conditioner between your computer and the power supply?
- Could you re-create all your records if your system were stolen or damaged?
- Do you back up changed files daily?
- Do you have original diskettes for all the software on your system?
- Do you have a written record of the serial numbers of all your hardware and software?
- Would you know whether a diskette that you inserted into your PC had a virus?

Answering no to any of these questions means that you are reading the right book. But the point of this book is not to cause undue alarm but to raise awareness. When we increase awareness, we can change attitudes. The proper security attitude leads to the proper security posture.

Taking the Security Path to Enlightenment

To help you develop the proper security awareness, we present information without much of the "technobabble" that computer professionals use to describe processes in their field. So if you suffer from "acronymophobia," don't despair; this book uses a common sense approach to security that will help you keep your data safe, complete, and available to you no matter what happens. Also, Appendix C is a glossary of common security terms that you can use to look up anything that might throw you for a loop.

This book is very economical. How much do you think it would cost to hire a professional to show you how to protect your data? Hundreds or thousands of dollars? We hope that you enjoy the information and use it to insure your data. Instead of relying on a professional, you can increase the security of your personal computer yourself. With these thoughts in mind, we begin our tour through the world of computer security.

Chapter 2
Security Lingo and Australian Dingoes

"Science and technology multiply around us. To an increasing extent they dictate the languages in which we speak and think. Either we use those languages, or we remain mute."

— J. G. Ballard, English novelist, from the Introduction to the French edition of *Crash*.

All businesses have their own buzz words, special abbreviations, and particular phrases. If you are a bean counter (oops, we mean accountant), for example, you deal in words such as *debit, credit,* and *Return on Investment (ROI).* Over time, the number of acronyms in use has increased so much that many have the same letters but mean different things, depending on whom you talk to. Quickly now, what does ATM stand for? If you said *automated teller machine,* you're right! Of course, if you said *asynchronous transfer mode,* you're not only a technical weenie, but you're also correct. As Mom always said, it depends on your upbringing! So in this chapter, we take some of the mystery away from security and challenge everyone to speak and write clearly.

After you get through this chapter, will you be inaugurated into the secret society of computer nerds? We hope not! You need to keep some things to yourself, after all. What you can read about here are some of the terms in use, what they mean, and how they may apply to you. If you already know all that anyone can know about the subject, skip this chapter. You can refer to it later if you run across some arcane term that baffles you.

What Is Security?

First, we need to discuss some of the more basic terms that come to mind when you're dealing with security. You may often hear the words but have no idea what they mean. We include a glossary of terms at the back of this book; for clarity, however, we need to define some of the basic terms here.

So what do we mean by the term *security?* (How many books do you read that include a definition for one of the terms used in the title? Are we good or what?) Perhaps you think of a large dog or armed guards when you think of security. And you're right. But not for this book.

Webster's Dictionary defines security as a) "freedom from danger, fear or anxiety"; and b) "measures taken especially to guard against espionage or sabotage." Freedom from fear or anxiety sums it up. With sound security, you are assured that your data and information remain safe and are always available to you.

The Business of Threats

You may be thinking of cement shoes, dark alleys, and other nefarious things when you think about threats, but you're wrong. (Don't watch so much television.) No, the world of computer security is far more mundane and really consists of understanding the threats and taking the appropriate actions. In this section, we deal primarily with those things that apply to the workplace more than to the home, so if you are a home computer user and not a business user, you may want to skip this section.

Who and what are you trying to protect yourself from? In other words, what are some of the *threats?* Most experts believe that the primary source of threats to computers is . . . well, quite frankly, you! The largest number of problems are caused accidentally by the computer user. (So does this mean that we don't trust you? We plead the Fifth Amendment on that question.)

Take a minute to explore the concepts. You can consider security in a cyclical fashion that starts with a *threat* (such as dropping the laptop on your way to the office) that exploits some weakness or *vulnerability* (all your data exists only on the laptop) and thus exposes your *assets* (the computer or information you have stored on it) to a loss. This loss is typically categorized by three terms — *confidentiality, integrity,* and *availability* (in this example, the loss is an availability issue) — and produces some sort of business or home impact. This impact may consist of losing a contract because the proposal that you painstakingly worked on until midnight to present at 8 a.m. the next day existed only on the laptop that you dropped and damaged. To protect against this impact, you hopefully implement the necessary safeguards, or *controls,* against all the threats you think could occur, such as copying the proposal onto a floppy disk for safety as soon as you finish it.

Now that you have an understanding of these concepts, we can move to some of the terminology related to threats. Chapter 1 talks about the three categories of confidentiality, integrity, and availability. This chapter explains other terms that the people in the information security business use.

Some of the most common terms that you might hear being bandied about are *denial of service* and, typically preceded by the word *accidental* or *intentional,* the following:

- ✔ Disclosure
- ✔ Modification
- ✔ Destruction
- ✔ Misuse

So what do we mean by these terms?

Denial of service

People in the industry use the term *denial of service* to describe the loss of access to your personal computer or to the network you're using. Simply put, denial of service occurs when the legitimate user of a computer is kept from using the computer or network through some other person's actions. In other words, some other person makes the computer or network unavailable to the legitimate user.

Follow a simple scenario: Your home computer resides in the spare bedroom on a small table near the bed. (Don't laugh; I know a consultant who has his primary computer sitting on a table at the end of his bed. Perhaps he and his wife play games on it?) Anyway, you invite guests over for the weekend. After a few days of frolicking and fun, you say goodbye to your guests and retreat to the spare room to send a letter to beloved Aunt Mabel before you retire for the night. You press the power-on button and wait the obligatory few minutes for the darn thing to go through its contortions. You are ready to settle in and begin work when you notice a problem: The machine doesn't respond. At all. What's going on? The computer is mumbling something about the F1 key, whatever that is, but nothing happens when you press it.

Out come the manuals. After dubious minutes spent finding what you want (wouldn't it be nice if manuals were well written?), you discover that those keys on the front of the machine turn a keyboard lock on and off. So that's what they're for! Simple solution. Obviously, they got turned accidentally, and all you have to do is — where are the keys? After some frantic searching, you recall that *those* guests visited for the weekend — you know, the practical jokers. Could they have done something? A quick call confirms that they thought it would be fun to see what happened if they turned the key lock and hid the keys.

Note: Not all computers use key locks in the same way. Some locks are for show and do nothing, and others merely lock the case. Check your computer to see what happens after you lock it.

You may find this story amusing, yet we regularly visit organizations that have no policy concerning these keys. They are typically left in a desk drawer or, worse, right in the lock. You can create temporary havoc at any firm by walking around collecting keys and locking the machines. Now, before you rush out, please realize that we are *not* suggesting that you do this; only that you should be aware of the risk and take the appropriate (and simple) action.

Accidental or intentional

Now look at the terms *accidental* and *intentional.* Fairly simple, really. Did you mean to drop your coffee on the keyboard, or was it an accident? Did you intentionally borrow the payroll records to give to your friend in a competing business who just happened to offer you that big new job at his firm?

Usually, these terms are fairly straightforward to understand and recognize; however, things have gotten more complex over the last few decades with the proliferation of lawyers and activists. (We promise that this is the only lawyer joke — you have to read on to see about activists, though.) What seems straightforward can often be hard to determine. For example, if you are in the middle of intense negotiations with your eldest child about curfews, and things are not going well, is it accidental or intentional that he spills cola on the keyboard? Of course, it's accidental from his viewpoint, but the fact that he is facing unpopular curfews makes the determination less clear to you.

Making these determinations can be easier with a clear set of policies that everyone understands. In this example, the policy, *Do not place any liquids near the computer at any time,* would eliminate the need to question the person's intent; the act is clearly wrong, because no drink should have been close to the keyboard in the first place. You should write a clear, well-defined policy document and make sure that everyone reads and understands it.

Disclosure

No, we're not talking about the movie starring Demi Moore and Michael Douglas. This fancy term exists so that consultants can collect big bucks and sound important. All *disclosure* means is that someone who should not have read the information has read it. (It's been *disclosed,* get it?)

So is this a problem? Well, that depends on what the information consists of and how important it is. If you're talking about your mother's favorite recipe on the home computer, the world is probably still safe. However, if you're talking about your latest medical results or the company's secret recipe, your world may be collapsing around you. If you think not, ask KFC, Nabisco, or Pepsi whether this problem would concern them.

The fundamental issue of disclosure, then, is this: What is the information, and how much do you care about it? The main problem lies in defining all the data and then deciding whether the information is important and to what degree.

Think about your personal information. What data do you have? Where is it? Is it safe from prying eyes? Can you even get at it? Who is allowed access to your data, and what can they do with it after they access it? On many home computers, for example, people store sensitive information so that it is available if they lose their wallets or purses. You have a driver's license, credit card numbers, PIN numbers, bank records, love letters, unlisted telephone numbers, and where you have hidden the spare door key and car key.

Just deciding what information you have and where it resides is the first problem; then you must take each piece of data, assess it, and assign it some level of importance. The industry calls this process *data classification,* and it is an art to itself. Because entire books are devoted to this subject, we stop, but we hope you understand that one of the primary show-stoppers to securing information properly is understanding its relative importance.

Modification

This term is also reasonably straightforward. *Modification* means to change something. Changing data, such as rewriting portions of a letter to a friend, requires write access, whereas you need only read access to view, but not change, the letter. Security software typically enables you to control access to files by granting or refusing the associated right. For example, if we give you read access to this book on our computers, you could read it, but you could not change any of it because you are not permitted write access. You need to purchase special security software (or obtain shareware or freeware) to get this capability for your home computer. We tell you how to do so in Chapters 17 and 18.

Although the concept seems simple, determining who changed what can be very complex. For example, determining what may have changed is very hard if the letter you and your spouse (who really is a practical joker) wrote to Grandmother is 50 pages long, and you aren't sure who had access to it on the computer before you mailed it. Just the thought of someone making a slight word change in such a letter brings tears to our eyes.

Companies face the same problem, only on a larger scale. With perhaps hundreds of people accessing a file, knowing who made a particular change is very difficult, hence the company tries to limit who has access in the first place.

Destruction

This term requires little definition. If it ain't there and it should be, you may have a case of intentional or accidental destruction. Again, the simple solution is to limit the number of people who can delete the file in the first place.

Think of your home computer and your budget records. Perhaps you use a financial software program to manage your finances. This software creates files and stores all your sensitive information in them. With a typical home computer, anyone who can access the computer (parents, children, neighborhood kids, and so on) has access to these files. Aha! you say. The program enables me to assign a password so that no one can get into my files, so they are safe. Well, not really. They are reasonably safe from disclosure and modification, but now we are talking destruction.

Can someone delete the file even though that person can't read it in the program? Yes! All you have to do is run any of a large number of utilities programs that "clean up" your system for you; run the FORMAT command *(don't!),* which destroys everything on your hard drive; or run a DOS command to clean up a directory, and enter the wrong command. You get the picture? Data on a personal computer is not safe.

Now before you go panicking, you can find ways to protect yourself in later chapters of this book. For now, realize that companies face a similar problem; to ensure that staff can perform their jobs, the company must grant them access to all the files and programs they need. Often, such access leaves the company vulnerable to losing those files and programs if a staff person accidentally or intentionally destroy them. Balancing the risk of allowing people to access a file against the threat of losing it through accidental or intentional means is one of the many problems that both businesses and security professionals face.

Misuse

This term is not used as often as you may believe it would be. Here, we are referring to using information or resources for your own purposes. For example, one child might read her sibling's personal letters and spread the information around school, possibly embarrassing the writer.

Think of it this way: You buy a computer for the home to manage your finances and play games. Then someone in the home puts a modem on it and begins to dial up NASA and attempt to get into its computers. Is this why you bought the machine? No. In fact, you followed our earlier advice and wrote down a list that you placed on the refrigerator specifically stating that the computer was only to be used for managing your finances and playing games. Moreover, you stated that only games that you purchased and installed were allowed on the machine. You told everyone that you did so for two reasons. First, you wanted to know whether the games were suitable for the family, and second, you wanted to ensure that there was little risk of being infected by those virus things you'd heard about. (More on viruses in Chapter 22.)

So now you have a misuse problem. Someone not only attached a piece of hardware called a modem, but they likely also added appropriate software to run the modem. Finally, that person is using your machine to illegally gain access to NASA. How do you determine who is doing it? What actions do you take against the culprit?

Corporations face this threat each day. People run their small businesses by using the companies' machines to do their word processing, for example, which takes resources away from the legitimate users of the system, possibly forcing the company to buy more powerful machines before they really need to.

An easier and more obvious misuse may consist of playing games on the company computer during office hours. Some companies allow the use of games and trust their staff not to abuse the privilege; others have strict policies against playing games; and many have not formulated a response and turn a blind eye to the practice. Playing computer games when the company has specifically stated that it is not permitted is considered misuse. Although explaining misuse is relatively simple, getting companies and individuals to recognize it and take some action (such as posting what's allowed and what's not on the refrigerator!) is much harder.

Vulnerability: Being a '90s Kind of Person

What do we mean by *vulnerability?* Are we talking about how you feel walking down a very dark alley in a big city late at night? We certainly feel vulnerable then, but then again, we're not 6'5" and 250 pounds, and perhaps you are.

In the book *Computers at Risk — Safe Computing in the Information Age*, the authors describe vulnerability as follows:

"A weakness in a system that can be exploited to violate the system's intended behavior. There may be security, integrity, availability and other vulnerabilities. The act of exploiting a vulnerability represents a threat, which has an associated risk of being exploited."

Whew! That's quite a mouthful. Just think of walking down that dark city street, and consider your computer doing the same thing. A number of vulnerabilities come to mind. First, not having a backup copy of your report on paper or on a floppy disk certainly leaves you in a vulnerable position. Perhaps you back up the file onto another area of the computer's hard drive. That's nice, but what good does that do if you drop the machine or it is stolen?

Next, the relative strength of the computer case is certainly a vulnerability. Even though laptops are designed for travel, few manufacturers build them strong enough to survive a drop of over a foot or so in height. (This is probably one of those risk versus cost issues that vendors must make when designing and pricing laptops.) Finally, you may be the ultimate weakness if you have a predilection for stumbling (remember President Ford?), forgetfulness (such as leaving the laptop where it may be stolen), or anger (have you ever punched your machine?). Other risks exist, but you get the picture.

Controls: For Control Freaks Only

Controls are a necessary part of civilized life. People take many controls for granted because they grew up with them and likely never gave them much thought. For example, without air traffic controllers managing who flies at what height and speed and which plane can land first, would you fly on a commercial airliner? So you can consider controls to be those actions or steps taken after evaluating the risks and threats to reduce your chances of being affected.

These key principles are typically associated with controls:

- Individual accountability
- Identification
- Authentication
- Auditing
- Separation of duty

Accountability

What do these words mean? *Individual accountability* essentially means that you take responsibility for your acts. (It seems that no one wants this anymore; everyone wants to blame someone else.) To help ensure your accountability, you need such things as *user authentication,* which provides a way to audit the things you do and, therefore, makes you responsible for those actions. How does this work? On an individual PC, it's difficult to do unless you make use of the features of some of the newer operating systems such as Windows 95 that enable you to sign on to the computer or use special access control software.

Use your home computer as a simple example. Suppose that you come home from work and head up to the spare room to use the machine to finally get that letter off to Aunt Mabel. You find that the word processor isn't functioning because it can't find any of its critical files. After some trial and error (you really are getting the hang of these things now, aren't you?), you discover that someone has removed several files that the word processor needs. How do you determine who did it? One way is to call an inquisition, get out the rack, and . . . well, perhaps not. You can ask the family who changed anything, but you are at the mercy of their memories and their willingness to 'fess up. However, if you use identification and authentication, you may be able to determine who changed the files.

Identification

Identification is the process of a computer recognizing who you are, typically through the verification of your "userid" or account. In a typical situation, each person signs on to the computer by using a special, unique name (called an *account* or *userid*) that the system uses to control your access to data and programs. That name can also be used to track your activities. To be effective, all the accounts on a system must be unique. No two can be the same.

For example, an identifier on CompuServe consists of a long string of numbers; Barry has an account consisting of the character string 73521,771. Change one digit, making a number such as 73521,772, and you have some other person's account. To sign onto CompuServe, Barry must enter this number. CompuServe then tracks the time that he spends online and bills him appropriately.

Personal computers using DOS or Windows 3.*x* do not have the capability of distinguishing one user from another. Macs and Windows 95 have a rudimentary system that a user can set up if he or she wants to. In Chapters 17 and 18, we point you to some software that gives you this capability.

Authentication

Using identification by itself is not enough to manage access to your computer. If someone knows what your identifier consists of, that person can use it, too. In the example of the CompuServe account in the preceding section, Barry would be billed for the time if someone took his identifier and used it to browse through CompuServe. Not good! So you need a method of proving that it is really you when you use your account. To accomplish this task, you assign a secret password to the account that you must use before the system enables you to perform any work. The combined use of an account and a secret password is called *authentication*.

Keeping your password secret is essential for good authentication. You can now verify the identity of the person signing on because only that person knows the secret password associated with his or her unique account.

Auditing

Auditing essentially ensures that established procedures and management directives are being carried out. An audit trail provides a means of tracking activities and using that information to know who has performed a particular action, such as signing on to the computer. Audit services make and keep these records, which they then use to help provide accountability. Our intent is not to get into this area, because we would need an entire book or two to go over the fundamentals of auditing. Suffice it to say that you need some minimum level of auditing if you are to properly assign and enforce individual controls.

Separation of duty

Finally, the *separation of duty* principle divides important transactions so that at least two people are needed to finalize the transaction. This concept is highly embedded in banking, and when used properly, it helps to prevent debacles such as the Waring bank fiasco, where one person appears to have been able to perform huge transactions without anyone else verifying them, subsequently losing the bank so much money that it went bankrupt.

Most bank tellers employ this principle all the time with a supervisor override needed to enable a teller to accept a check for more than a certain limit. This principle is less applicable within the PC arena. (Why do you think they call it a *personal* computer?)

What's This Risk Thing?

We conclude this chapter with a definition of *risk*. If you just bet the lot on Willie's Edge coming in first in the fourth race, skip this section. You know all about risk and the resulting potential for loss. What is risk to the computer security professional? As we mention throughout this chapter, one of the key components of a security program is managing the risk of something happening against the cost of preventing it. The traditional cost-benefit-versus-risk approach, however, is not really what we propose that you use.

Defining risk

So what do we mean by *risk?* Basically, the likelihood that a vulnerability or threat may be exploited or cause harm, or the potential for something bad happening.

To ascertain risk, you must have access to information — lots of information. In the new world of computing, that's a tough call. More information than you could ever read is available. Additionally, a lot of the information is highly subjective — it depends on your point of view. So now what? If you consider eliminating risk, you need to remember that you can only reduce risk; you can never completely eliminate it. You can manage it, reduce it, retain it, or transfer it to someone else, but you cannot eliminate it.

Managing risk

That brings us to risk management. This concept can be defined simply as the science associated with identifying, measuring, controlling, and minimizing vulnerabilities or threats, or making an effort to ensure that your exposure is minimized. For example, as authors, we perform rudimentary risk management when we take a contract to our lawyer to review before we sign it.

A risk management program identifies the potential threats, tries to predict the companies' exposure to each threat, rates the threats by priority, cost-justifies each control, and then implements them. For the PC owner, this process may consist of reviewing all the threats that we identify in this book, deciding which ones may apply to you, rating them according to cost (a significant priority consideration) and according to their likelihood of occurring, and finally, spending the money to put the appropriate controls in place.

For example, one risk consists of losing your data if your hard drive goes belly-up. Many people may consider the risk low. (In more than ten years, we have never lost a hard drive — of course, we upgrade every couple of years, which limits the risk.) But those who have experienced the risk may consider it high. An effective control, apart from upgrading every couple of years, would be to purchase a tape backup unit and use it regularly. The cost is reasonable compared with the cost of losing your data. Check out what we say about these devices in Chapter 23.

See Chapter 5 for a more detailed discussion about risk managment.

Chapter 3

Viruses, Password Grabbers, Trojan Horses, and Other Threats

• •

In This Chapter

▶ Intentional threats

▶ Unintentional threats

▶ Stupid human tricks

• •

*T*he preceding chapter lets you in on some security lingo so that you can talk knowledgeably about threats, risks, vulnerabilities, and controls. This chapter introduces you to some of the pitfalls, pestilence, and vermin lurking in the computer world.

A discussion of security would be incomplete without mentioning the widely misunderstood concept of threat. In your everyday life, you face threats all the time. If you do not bring your umbrella with you, the skies may threaten rain. Should the economy go flat, you face the threat of losing your job.

To understand the concept of risk, you can use these same examples. For instance, if you do not bring your umbrella, the threat of rain concerns you only when your local weather forecaster tells you that there is a chance of precipitation. Also, your job is at risk if your company or organization lets people go or your performance is poor.

For our purposes, people or events that exploit system vulnerabilities are aptly named *threats*. Actually, they are called *threat agents* — that is, someone or something that carries out a threat. So the big guy on the street who threatens to punch your lights out should you not give him your wallet is a threat agent, and the threat is physical pain (and the likelihood, or *probability,* is high because he has done time for battery). And you can figure out the vulnerability. Every place on your body is vulnerable, and you could hurt all over. Your *exposure,* or what you stand to lose, could be two front teeth.

Intentional Threats

Most experts believe that the biggest threats to information security are errors by honest people, followed by malicious attacks by dishonest or disgruntled people you know. These facts probably surprise you because external threats such as acts of God and hackers get more press. Not often do you read in the paper that someone pressed the wrong key and caused $50,000 worth of damage. But realistically, it happens quite frequently.

Hacker is not a pejorative term. The term *hacker* was originally applied to members of MIT's model train club. Apparently, they had a big train layout, and every time they got it to work, they would decide to move a switch, mountain, or station. They would "hack" out that piece and move it.

When these same people started playing with minicomputers, they took that same methodology and applied it to programming. Someone would write some code that took 32 bytes, and someone else would say, "I can code that routine in 28 bytes." Another person would say, "I can write that code in 24 bytes," and the others would say, "Write that routine."

Yesterday's hackers are today's bastions of the computer industry. For this reason, we shall henceforth label what most people call hackers, *crackers. The Hackers Dictionary* defines a cracker as "one who breaks security on a system. Coined ca. 1985 by hackers in defense against journalistic misuse of hacker." Therefore, a cracker is an unauthorized person who tries to penetrate computer systems for fun or profit.

Crackers can get you in many ways. If someone figures out your Windows screen saver password, for example, that person can look at your data. He or she can view information on your hard disk or floppies that you allow him or her to access. The intruder can load programs on your system. Your information or data can be changed or deleted while stored on your hard drive. All these threats are very real to you.

Disclosure

Disclosure is the threat that most people intuitively associate with security. Fundamentally, disclosure happens when someone gains access to your information without your authority. In other words, disclosure occurs when you do not protect the information on your system and someone reads the data.

Masquerading

Masquerading is the reuse of validated messages by an unauthorized individual. For example, someone could intercept a message to your stock broker that says, "Please purchase 1,000 shares of Netscape Communications." That person can replay (or basically resend) the intercepted message to your stock broker, which you might not realize until he or she phones up and inquires whether you really want to buy 100,000 shares of Netscape.

You masquerade by assuming the identity of a legitimate user or process after getting proper identification through wiretapping or other means. You can get the identity in several ways. Frequently, people obtain identities by guessing passcodes that authorized users create.

Wiretapping involves placing a tap (just like the Feds) and listening to the traffic. You can pick out the important information, such as userids and passwords. Read more about this topic in Chapters 15 and 16.

Denial of service

Denial of service occurs when someone or something prevents you from accessing your system or delays critical operations. It can consist of a variety of natural or man-made events that have the potential to deny operations. Denial of service is potentially very costly to you. For example, you may go to file your income tax return on April 15 (or April 30 in Canada) and find that someone deleted your Intuit Quicken or Microsoft Money files.

Computer crime

Lawmakers generally define *computer crime* as any crime accomplished through special knowledge of computer technology. Computers have been used for most kinds of crime, including fraud, theft, larceny, embezzlement, burglary, sabotage, espionage, murder, and forgery, since the first cases were reported in 1958. With the advent of personal computers, enabling the manipulation of information and access to computers by telephone using a modem, an increasing number of computer hobbyists or crackers, displaying a high level of technical expertise, have perpetrated mostly simple but costly crimes, such as electronic trespassing, copyrighted information piracy, and vandalism.

No valid statistics about the extent of computer crime exist. Victims often resist reporting suspected cases because they can lose more from embarrassment, damaged reputations, litigation, and other consequential losses than from the acts themselves. Limited evidence indicates that the number of cases is rising each year because of the increasing number of computers in business applications, where crime traditionally occurs. The largest recorded crimes involving insurance, banking, product inventories, and securities have resulted in losses of tens of millions to billions of dollars — all facilitated by computers.

Recent U.S. legislation, including laws concerning privacy, credit card fraud, and racketeering, provide criminal-justice agencies with tools to fight business crime. As of 1988, all but two states have specific computer crime laws, and a 1986 federal computer crime law deals with certain crimes involving computers in different states and in government activities.

Password grabbers

You may have read about password grabbers or sniffers. These threats fall into a class of threats called *spoofing*. Spoofing occurs when someone other than you deceives your correspondent into believing that he or she is you. This threat is similar to masquerading in nature; however, masquerading usually involves the reuse of messages. One method of spoofing involves monitoring an insecure communications line, sending back a false logoff message to the user, and then using the line as your own.

Suppose you leave your PC logged in to e-mail while you go for coffee one day. The social misfit in the next office decides to get even and uses your system to send inflammatory mail to the boss. Your boss is so incensed that she fires you before she realizes that someone impersonated you. This is spoofing.

America Online customers were spoofed by an unknown individual. While logged into AOL, several customers received a message supposedly from the AOL *sysop,* or system operator, requesting the customers to re-enter their passwords so that they could be re-authenticated. Some people unwittingly gave out their passwords!

A similar trick made its rounds several years ago. An individual would write a program to fake a sign-on screen. When a user entered his or her userid and password, the program informed the user that the maximum number of users was logged on and asked the user to try later. Meanwhile, the perpetrator had captured the userid and password and the associated privileges. Tricksters tried this one on every platform, including mainframes and minicomputers.

A *threat scenario* — another fancy security term for an illustrative example — may help explain how these programs work. In your organization, you may have a large local area network that you use to develop database applications. Now, if we want to access or read all the data on your network, we need permission or privilege. However, we can get privilege fairly easily. We just download a shareware program called GETIT.COM from the Computer Freaks and Geeks bulletin board.

Then we start a workstation and install the program on the hard disk. Then we load the program and call over the network administrator with a request for help. The network administrator, always willing to help, logs on to the micro-computer. After helping, the system administrator excuses himself or herself to attend the weekly problem-resolution meeting.

The administrator doesn't realize that he or she has unwittingly become an accomplice. The program was a password grabber, and we now have the network administrator's access code and password. This scenario sounds complicated, but it isn't. Furthermore, Windows and other operating systems come with a free key capture utility that enables someone to do the same thing to you! Chapter 8 provides information on protecting your passwords.

Viral attacks

Everyone understands viruses. As we write this book, the winter weather in North America has been particularly bizarre. We have seen plenty of snow and cold weather. People have complained about having the flu for weeks on end. The cold weather also has fostered the growth and transmittal of cold and flu viruses.

Viruses are extremely small parasites that reproduce within the cells of their hosts, upon which they depend for many of their fundamental life processes. They are the causal agents of many infectious diseases. Hundreds of virus types exist, each normally growing in a restricted range of hosts, different viruses, however, have a very wide variety of hosts, including bacteria, plants, and animals.

It's not chance that computer experts chose to name rogue computer programs after viruses. A *computer virus* is computer code designed to insert itself into an existing computer program, alter or destroy data, and copy itself into other programs in the same computer or to programs in other computers. Its name was coined because of its parasitic nature and its capability to replicate and infect other computers.

A computer virus can spread through shared computer software — those disks you get from your neighbor, for example — through an online service, or through a network. Often, programmers who design computer viruses are hackers or crackers who do so as a prank. A typical virus may cause a message to appear on a computer's video screen, such as `Vote for Mike Dukakis`. Other programmers, however, design viruses with the deliberate intent to destroy data. In one well-publicized 1988 incident called the *Internet Worm,* a rogue computer program crippled or slowed down 6,000 computers on the Internet overnight. Experts estimate the damage from the incident at some-where between $6 million and $100 million.

Since computer viruses emerged in the early 1980s, many countries, such as the United States and England, and many U.S. states have passed laws making it illegal to introduce viruses into the computers of unwitting users. Computer software companies also provide safeguards against computer viruses, but the safeguards are not foolproof. These companies specialize in *virology,* the study of viruses, and the damage they cause. Just as in the biological world, virology in the computer world includes the investigation of virus particles, viral growth within hosts (your computer), and the spread of viruses from host to host. Chapter 11 looks at viruses and other pestilence in more detail, and Chapter 22 lists ten common viruses and what they do.

Trojan horses, cuckoo eggs, and time bombs

You have probably heard of the Trojan Horse. But do you remember where it came from? In Greek mythology, the Trojan War pitted a coalition of Greek principalities against Troy, a city located on the coast of what is now Anatolia, just south of the entrance to the Dardanelles.

Odysseus, a Greek commander and Ithacan king noted for his cleverness, suggested the stratagem of the Trojan Horse. The Greeks feigned retreat; their fleet sailed out of sight, leaving behind the Trojan Horse as a "gift." Concealed inside the large wooden horse was a squad of Greek soldiers who, after the horse had been dragged into the unsuspecting city under cover of darkness, emerged and opened the gates. After the Greek fleet quietly returned, the soldiers entered Troy and great slaughter followed. Many Trojan women, including members of the royal family, were carried off into captivity. The phrase "beware of Greeks bearing gifts" comes from this incident.

So, you ask, what does this have to do with my computer and security? Well, sometimes viruses are spread as Trojan horses. You get a neat game from your neighbor, which really is only a vehicle to transport a virus. You install the game on your system only to discover a week later, on Friday the 13th, that the game is a virus.

Similarly, you may be nurturing a *cuckoo's egg* on your system. The name *cuckoo* is used for some of the 127 species of birds of the cuckoo family. Some cuckoos are known to be brood parasites — birds that build no nests of their own but leave their eggs in the nests of other birds, which then rear the young. So a cuckoo's egg is software that you nurture and raise and then one day turns on you and bites you. For example, someone may create a program titled "logni" and leave it on your system. This program sits around until one day you mistype your login. Then the logni program is executed.

A *time bomb* is a program that will go off at some time in the future. When it goes off, it may delete your data or remove records from your system. The code usually hides as a Trojan horse. Many viruses are time bombs. For instance, the Friday the 13th virus is programmed to go off on, you guessed it, Friday the 13th. You may come across viruses also on January 5 (Joshi), March 6 (Michelangelo), July 13, July 26, June 12, and June 26.

Theft

A growing threat is the theft of computer chips. Thieves are opening up personal computers and stealing the memory within. This practice turns out to be almost as profitable as dealing crack (not to be confused with crackers). You can take a bag of SIMMs and resell them with little risk. The chips do not have serial numbers, so they cannot be traced.

Other components of your computer also might grow legs and walk away. For instance, someone might liberate your new sound card or fast Ethernet card.

Stories about computers being stolen from airports and hotel rooms abound. The nature of these thefts would lead you to believe that these acts are not random. Reportedly, gangs pick up target personal computers for about $10,000. A person accidentally spills mustard on you, and while you and this person fuss over the mess, an accomplice steals your computer. In another scenario, someone with a metal plate in his head cuts in front of you at the airport metal detector while your PC is being scanned. While security fusses with this person, an accomplice grabs the PC and runs, long before you walk through the detector. Because most PCs and their software are not worth $10,000, you should assume that they want more than the hardware and software — they want the data as well!

Unintentional Threats

But intentional threats are only one type of threat. Your system faces unintentional threats as well. Some unintentional threats are

- ✔ Electrostatic energy
- ✔ Spikes, surges, or brownouts that cause equipment malfunctions
- ✔ Natural disasters, such as typhoons, hurricanes, tornadoes, and earthquakes
- ✔ Major accidents, such as chemical spills or train derailments
- ✔ Human error, such as a dropped device or a deleted file

 ✔ Carelessness, such as inattentiveness when connecting or disconnecting devices from your personal computer

 ✔ Damage from accidents, such as tripping over a cable or spilling coffee on your keyboard

If you are like most individuals, you believe that these things won't happen to you. This phenomenon is natural; people believe a threat only when it has happened to them or someone they know. But you can be proactive instead of reactive and prevent many threats up-front. You only can *mitigate* — a fancy security term for *lessen* — against some other threats. For example, presently there is no way to prevent an earthquake; however, by erecting strong buildings and tethering equipment, you can lessen an earthquake's impact.

Now we'll look in depth at some of these threats.

Zapping your data

Static electricity, the oldest known form of electricity, is generated unintentionally and is considered a nuisance. It makes the air crackle and your hair stand up.

Under ideal conditions, the static charge accumulates when the scuff of your shoes on the carpet exceeds 20,000 volts. Although this amount may cause a painful shock, it is not harmful to you because low current is involved. However, 20,000 volts is enough to zap your PC when you aren't properly grounded. At one organization where Peter worked, an employee kept complaining about losing data. Although technicians could recover the data from the hard drive, this problem was perplexing until they determined the cause. The air in the building was extremely dry, and the owners of the portable computers didn't properly ground themselves before touching their keyboard. Sparks literally flew from the person's hand to the computer, zapping open files.

Spikes, brownouts, and blackouts

Not only can too much electricity cause a problem; but a lack of electricity can likewise cause serious problems. The term *blackout* has become synonymous with both accidental power failures and planned interruptions, such as rotating area blackouts to limit loads during power shortages. Most severe blackouts are associated with storms, sudden failures of generating or transmission equipment, or human error. In general, the pattern of such disturbances is the loss of some power-system element followed by rapid development of unstable or overload conditions, resulting in the automatic disconnection of other generating or transmission elements and a cascading, widespread loss of electrical service.

A *brownout* is a curtailment, or reduction, of power. A *spike* is a sudden increase in current to high levels. Too little or too much power can damage or destroy your computer equipment.

Serious blackouts cause losses of industrial production, disturbances to commercial activities, traffic and transportation problems, disruption of municipal services, and extreme personal inconvenience. Your computer system won't function very well without a backup power supply.

You can read about ways to protect yourself from these harmful power fluctuations in Chapter 6.

Acts of God

Security experts lump a class of threats together and call them *acts of God*. An act of God is an inexplicable happening or natural phenomenon. A tree crashing through your roof during a thunderstorm, for example, is an act of God — that is, assuming that your neighbor wasn't out there with a chainsaw.

Every region has its natural disasters or calamities. People in the Atlantic and eastern Pacific areas face hurricanes. People in the Western Pacific area face equally devastating typhoons. Those who lived through Hurricane Andrew can attest to the destructive nature of these storms.

Most people who have lived on the West Coast for any amount of time have experienced an earthquake. Earthquakes are among the deadliest of natural catastrophes. Although buildings located along a fault may be torn apart, more damage is caused by the shaking, which can topple structures far from the actual fault. The force of this shaking has been known to approach the force of gravity during the few seconds that the earthquake lasts.

Earthquakes also cause indirect damage through landslides, fires, and the collapse of dams. The civil disorder that follows can lead to disruption of food and water supplies and sanitation systems, causing starvation and the spread of disease.

The effects of floods, both beneficial and destructive, have been recorded for at least 5,000 years, serving as the basis for myth, religious beliefs, and scientific study. (Most people watched in awe as CNN reported on the havoc created by the Mississippi River flooding.)

Tornadoes, also popularly called *twisters* or *cyclones,* are characterized by rapidly rotating columns of air hanging from cumulonimbus clouds. At ground level, they usually leave a path of destruction only about 170 feet (50 meters) wide and travel an average of only about 5 to 15 miles (8 to 24 km). Ground contact is often of an intermittent nature — lasting usually less than a couple of minutes in any particular area — because the funnel skips along. Wind speeds of approximately 500 mph (800 km/h) have been inferred from the resultant damage.

The greatest incidence of tornadoes is generally assumed to be in North America, especially in the Mississippi Valley. Within the United States, Texas records the greatest number, usually about 15 to 20 percent of the nation's annual total of about 1,000. On an area basis, however, Texas ranks ninth, far behind Oklahoma, Kansas, and Massachusetts. A rather steady increase in the annual total has been observed, probably as a result of the improving reporting system.

Maybe your region is hit by more than one of these types of natural disasters. Any one of them can destroy your home and all its contents. You can't do much to stop acts of God, so you need to soften their effects by protecting yourself and your possessions.

Stupid human tricks

Of course, the biggest threats to your system are accidents caused by you, your family, or your coworkers. You have probably heard some of the urban myths surrounding security. You must have heard of the one where a computer user was asked to make a copy of a diskette and send it to the head office, so the user photocopied the diskette and sent the photocopy. Maybe you've heard the one in which someone stapled a cover letter to a diskette when returning it to the head office. Now, we don't expect you to believe the story about correction fluid on the computer screen, but other real stories are almost as hard to believe. Following are some other things that after you do them you might say, "Well, that was stupid."

- ✔ Drinking coffee near your system is asking for problems.
- ✔ Shuffling down the hall in leather shoes in a dry environment and then touching your computer without properly grounding yourself is dangerous.
- ✔ Not backing up your system from time to time also tempts the fates.

Many security pundits jokingly say that the only secure system is a system that isn't turned on. Well, consider this item reported in the *Toronto Star* (April 6, 1996): In January, county controller Judith Kraines complained at a Reading, Pennsylvania Commissioners' meeting that she had to type letters and do other business on an old typewriter. She claimed her computer was so old that no one had gotten it to work in the last two years. "If we had a computer," Kraines reportedly said, "letters would go out faster." A red-faced Kraines announced three days later that the computer she complained about had not been plugged in, and that when it was plugged in and turned on, it worked just fine, thank you. At least her accounting data was secure!

This book suggests many simple things that you can do to protect yourself. The fact that individuals and organizations do not suffer these exposures every day proves that you can control them. The next chapter presents an in-depth discussion of controls.

Chapter 4

Controlling the Threats

· ·

· ·

*I*n Chapter 2, we discuss a few of the terms associated with management controls. In this chapter, we talk about what controls consist of and explain how they work. We also discuss methods of preventing problems from occurring, detecting and correcting problems, and several other general control issues. Read this chapter to see what you need to do to help keep your risk to a minimum.

Understanding How Controls Work (For Type A Personalities)

Controls are always directly related to objectives. They provide the direction for the organization, the path toward achievement. As Barry's spiritual guru once said, "If you do not know where you are, you cannot know which way to go." You need a path to follow, a direction to move toward, and controls help to provide this direction.

Control is an essential phase of the management function and is basically cyclical in nature: You plan the steps needed to achieve an objective, act to achieve it, and finally evaluate your actions bringing forth new plans as needed to manage new expectations or reach new objectives. The cyclical nature of controls can be shown in three steps:

1. **Plan your objective.**

   For example, establish which programs each user can run and where his or her data resides (on a diskette that each user can physically manage or in separate directories on the hard drive, where access is limited to each user's own directory).

2. **Act to achieve that objective.**

   You might install security software that helps you to provide controls over each user when he or she uses the computer.

3. **Evaluate your actions.**

   Over time, your original objectives may change. One child user may become old enough to access to additional areas, such as the Internet or AOL. You may decide to add further restrictions, such as restricting the days that each child can use the computer to prevent one child from spending all his or her time at the computer. Evaluating these things and deciding to amend them finishes the cycle and sends you back to the beginning — planning a new objective.

No discussion of controls is complete without mentioning that preventative, detective, and corrective controls exist. Because no one aspect of control provides everything you need, you have to use each aspect in concert with the others.

Preventative

You use *preventative controls* to stop an event from happening. Because computers are constantly changing with new hardware, software, or users, controls are not likely to remain perfect. You fight a constant battle to manage risk against changing threats. Following are two examples of preventative controls:

- ✔ **User authentication:** Influences who can sign on to the computer.
- ✔ **Access control:** Manages what information authorized users can access.

Detective

You use *detective controls* to identify, record, and report the occurrence of an event after it happens. You need to use these controls in concert with a review of the reports that they issue. Organizations often record millions of events but do little with the data they collect, but detective controls are virtually useless unless you act upon the information that they provide. A typical personal computer includes no such controls.

One could argue that the date field that is assigned to each file is a small example of a detective control. This rudimentary control, if used, lets you know when a file was last changed.

A simple example of a detective control is looking into your son's room to see whether he cleaned up after you told him to do so.

Corrective

After you determine which preventative and detective controls to use, you need to put one or more corrective controls in place to cause a remedial action. What do we mean by *corrective controls?* This type of control typically takes the stage after an undesirable event occurs and attempts to bring forth some action that prevents the event from recurring.

A corrective control might consist of the audit department notifying senior management of deficiencies in the way security is being administered. In your home, you might consider as a corrective action Dad's response to finding out that your oldest child ignored what her mother asked her to do all day.

Distinguishing the Types of Controls

We have talked about preventative, detective, and corrective aspects of controls; now we need to discuss the kinds of controls that exist. All controls can pretty well be lumped into a few categories, but it is important to realize that these categories do not operate in a vacuum. Each depends on the other for overall security to be effective. For example, you can place the tightest logical access controls ever devised upon a computer, but if a lack of physical controls allows someone to steal the computer, you still suffer a loss, regardless of whether your data remains secure.

The different types of controls are the following:

- **Management controls** are those things that everyone hates: directives from superiors! In the computer security world, they consist of policy statements, standards, and procedures that are written to reflect management's objectives.

- **Physical controls** are comprised of physical equipment such as computer tie-downs and power line protection devices.

- **Logical access controls** are programmable and reside on the system. You can change these controls easily to reflect changing realities, such as new management objectives.

> ✔ **Operational controls** consist of backup strategies or decisions to imple-
> ment new operating system software (such as Windows 95 or Macintosh
> System 7.5).
>
> ✔ **Communication controls** protect data transmissions, such as those that
> take place when you sign on to CompuServe or The Microsoft Network.

You can implement all these controls formally or informally. For example, an informal standard might suggest that young children go to bed at 7:30 p.m. each night. A formal list of chores for your children specifically states exactly what each child must do each day.

In the second example, the children have little excuse not to get the chores done because the chores are formally documented and clearly explained. And verifying the results against the expectations (objectives) is simple. See how easy implementing controls can be? The following sections look at each type of control in more detail.

Note: This list of controls is not complete. We concentrate our discussion on those controls that are more mainstream, leaving the more esoteric types of controls, like application, system, and network, for another book. This chapter provides an introduction to control basics and covers those aspects that we believe the home user needs to know about.

Management controls

Management controls are those policy documents that you write and place near the computer or on the refrigerator for everyone to see. Determining what needs to be done and ensuring that required tasks are reasonable are some of the things people expect from the management team. In the home, Mom and Dad are considered the management team. Their job is to assess whether the infrastructure in place supports the goals they have in mind.

You probably use management controls every day but don't realize that you can put a fancy title on the actions. You design the proper level of control that you want over your computer. How often can each user use the computer? How do you handle more than one user and the resulting conflicting schedules? Who can surf the Internet? What happens if the hard drive breaks and you lose all your data? To manage these questions, you need to decide what procedures should be followed, such as backing up the data once per week on Friday evenings and giving each user a certain time frame for computer use. In addi-tion, you create the policy document that everyone must follow, and you try to make sure that no one damages the computer.

Business management controls can be condensed into the cycle of planning, organizing, ensuring appropriate staffing, directing activities, and controlling those activities through audit reports and performance evaluations.

Organizations need to manage the same issues that home users do, only many companies have dozens or even thousands of computers and tens of thousands of employees to manage. Although they can't post the policy on the refrigerator, they *can* ensure that the policy is posted where all staff can see it. Better yet, they can deliver a copy to every employee and have each person sign something indicating that he or she received, read, and understands the policy. This way, no one can complain that they didn't know that what they were doing was against company policy.

Controls are just one aspect of management. If you're a manager, you need to remember the human side and consider the feelings of those people you manage, whether they are your children or your office mates.

Physical controls

To a certain extent, this type of control is self-explanatory. That is not to say that exercising control in this realm is a simple task, but it points to the "physicality" of these controls.

Physical controls include the measures taken to protect buildings and computers from the following:

- ✔ **Natural threats,** which include things like earthquakes and floods
- ✔ **Human threats,** such as interception of electronic transmissions and burglary
- ✔ **Other threats,** such as chemical spills and fires

These controls also consider items like electrical power, air conditioning, and telephone lines. Problems with these items can cause service interruptions or physical damage to your computer or data.

So what threats do you have to deal with when managing physical security? They include the following:

- ✔ **Availability:** A threat may interrupt your work and stop you at a time when you really must get something finished. For example, a flood in your basement, where you keep your computer, could prevent you from finishing that report you brought home that is due the next morning. Even though your computer may not be damaged, you may not want to use the power in the basement until you clean up all the water.

During a storm, avoid sitting and working at your computer — why tempt fate? Anyway, it can be a good opportunity to enjoy the show and watch all the lightning strikes.

Finally, homes sometimes lose electrical power when a car hits a transformer or some turkey digs a hole and ruptures the lines. Though these events may not cause you any real loss, you're out of luck until the power returns unless you use a battery-operated computer.

✔ **Physical damage:** If your computer becomes damaged or is destroyed, you have to have it repaired or replaced. Barry's neighbor built a room in the basement for her computer. However, she forgot to turn off the outdoor water taps last winter, and her pipes froze and eventually broke, spilling water all over her computer. She had to replace her machine.

✔ **Unauthorized access:** Sometimes the locks on your doors are all you have to prevent access to your computer (especially if you haven't installed logical access controls, which we describe in the next section). What do you do when you go on vacation and leave your home to a housesitter? How do you ensure that the files on your computer remain safe? One way is to lock the door to your computer room and tell the housesitter that the room is off-limits.

✔ **Theft:** Your computer may be stolen. For most homes, house insurance may not completely cover replacement of the machine — some home policies have limits on these "luxury" items. Your loss also includes any software that is taken along with the computer. And the loss of data and files may be the biggest problem. You can purchase a new computer, but can you recover all the work that you did on the old one? (Make sure that you read and follow our advice about making backups in Chapter 10.)

We may have scared you to death, but not to worry! We have answers to all your fears. For all problems, there are solutions. Some may be too expensive to implement, and you may decide to chance the risk. As Chapter 5 explains, some solutions are not worth doing relative to the potential for the problem to occur and the cost of trying to avoid the problem.

The weather is one thing that you can't do a heck of a lot to prevent. You are not likely to take expensive actions in your home to counter the threat of floods, tornadoes, or earthquakes. You can build a storm cellar or an earthquake-proof house, but doing so isn't very cost-effective. But you *can* do the following things to help minimize physical risks:

✔ Always keep your computer on a desk or table, not on the floor.

✔ Anticipate water damage and place the computer away from ceiling water pipes.

✔ Cover the computer with an inexpensive cover when you're not using it.

✔ Ensure that the desk or table on which you place the computer is sturdy enough and cannot be jarred easily. Unsteadiness can cause your computer to fall to the floor.

✔ If you really need that computer to be available at all times, consider buying a laptop, which gives you two to three hours' work when the house power fails.

> ✔ Put a door lock on the room in which you keep the computer.
>
> ✔ Back up your data regularly and keep a copy at a friend's house.
>
> ✔ Consider some of the safeguards against theft that we discuss in Chapter 6.

One issue that most home users do not need to be concerned with is air conditioning failure, unless you keep your computer in a tiny room next to huge windows that always get direct sunlight, which is a different issue. (Direct sun that is too strong can damage your diskettes and may overheat a computer that is left on.) Modern computers can handle the same heat that people can (or perhaps even more).

Remember, physical security is one of the easier aspects to grasp, and you can do a number of things to protect yourself. Don't wait until disaster strikes.

Logical access controls

This term applies to those controls that are based on the use of computer software. The capability to touch a microcomputer to turn it on and use it are the domain of physical controls.

After you are permitted physical access to the computer, you must log in with your account and password. This act allows the logical access controls on the computer to recognize you; permit or deny access to resources such as data, files, or programs; and track your activities while you are logged in. As Chapter 2 explains, your account (or username, userid, or whatever) provides the computer with a means to identify you, ensure that *you* are actually signing on, and control your actions.

Identification is the means by which you provide your claimed identity to the computer, and *authentication* is the means of establishing the validity of your claim. Your password is a combination of secret characters that only you know, thus providing authentication. Passwords are slowly being augmented and sometimes replaced with newer techniques such as smart cards and to a lesser extent, *biometrics,* which uses some physical part, such as a fingerprint or eye retina, to identify you.

Logical access controls are typically based on the *principle of least privilege,* which means that you should have access to everything you need but nothing more. This principle is often thought of in the negative — what you are not allowed to access. However, the principle sounds better when you apply it positively, stating what you *can* do instead of what you can't do.

So how is this principle applied? You might use this concept in your home when you tell your young children that they can use the computer whenever you are there to supervise. In the business environment, you might use it to suggest that staff members can have access to any data or files that they need to do their jobs, but no more. Employees usually know what they need (or they ask a supervisor), and this principle enforces the positive — that security is not present to hinder but to allow them to get their work done. Staff members know that they are not allowed to look at the boss's paycheck or peek at personal data (unless, of course, they are in charge of maintaining this information).

Logical access controls provide varying levels of access. Table 4-1 gives a simple set of levels.

Table 4-1	Types of Control
Setting	**Description**
Execute	You can run a program but cannot do anything else. This setting cannot always be used, because some programs open a file automatically before they start. You need to experiment if you plan to use this level of control to see whether the intended program runs properly.
Read	You can read the contents of a file but cannot change anything or delete it. This setting does allow you to copy the file to a new filename.
Write	You can add data to an existing file. In most software programs, this setting also allows you to read the data.
Create	You can create new files. You cannot see what is in the file, modify it, or delete it, even if you created the file.
Delete	You can delete files that already exist, but you cannot do any of the above.
None	You can't do diddly to the file.

As you can appreciate, these settings allow for a wide variety of options. For example, you can let Dad read, write, create, and delete his recipes while allowing the rest of the family only to read them. Mom can give herself read and write access to the novel she is writing and restrict everyone else with the None setting so that she doesn't accidentally delete the novel and doesn't have to suffer any unwanted editorial comments from the rest of the family.

Finally, a good logical access control program needs the capability to produce an activity log. Because such a log can be huge if it records all activities on a computer, a bunch of options usually let you decide what should be written to the log. Audit logs can be very detailed, providing you with a list of every person who logged in, how many incorrect passwords they typed before remembering the proper one, what programs they ran, and what files they accessed. Most people are unaware of the hundreds of files that are opened in order to use System 7.5, DOS, or Windows. Logging files that you are allowed to access is usually not necessary, so the log options let you decide to log only unauthorized file access attempts.

Logging options sound great because they allow you to know everything that happens on your computer. However, they can easily and quickly take all the available space on your hard drive if left unchecked. Using the logging option and then never referring to the logs is one of the most common security problems. Unless you intend to check on Junior each week to see what he's doing, or plan to review unauthorized access and invalid password attempts, don't turn on the logging option. It fills up your hard drive and is wasted effort.

Operational controls

Operational controls refer to all the things that are done to run your computer. In most homes, these controls are not nearly as significant as they are in the business environment; however, you need to be aware of some issues and act upon them.

Operational controls consider the things you do to maintain and secure your computer. These things include making sure that you have up-to-date operating system software, fixing hardware problems, and loading and managing the new software you purchase.

To be effective, you need to consider the security aspects of your day-to-day operation of the computer in conjunction with all the other aspects of control. Does this mean that you need to spend years determining risk, managing your hardware, and doing backups? Not at all. If you follow the guidelines we present throughout this book, you need not spend much time and can rest easier knowing that your data and computer are probably safer than your neighbor's computer.

For the home, operational controls consist mainly of user support (your children or spouse, for example), media management (hard drive backups and useful directory-naming structures), and maintenance of hardware and software. We discuss backing up your computer's hard drive in some detail in Chapter 10. Here, we have one piece of advice: Back it up!

Operational controls are minimal for the home user, as you do not need sophisticated procedures for user support or heavy maintenance manuals. Find a knowledgeable friend to provide you with support when you have trouble and use the free (and quickly vanishing) support provided by vendors when you purchase their products. For example, Corel offers technical support for the first 90 days after you buy WordPerfect. The 90 days begin following your first support call. Additional support following those 90 days costs you. Each vendor's support differs, so read your manual for more detailed instructions.

Communications controls

At home, this area consists of managing the one telephone line that three teenage children and Mom and Dad might share. It used to be that all you worried about was getting a boyfriend or girlfriend off the telephone so that someone else could make a call. Now, when you pick up the extension to make a call, you may simultaneously hear a child's scream and a weird racket that hurts your ears. The first is your child not-so-nicely telling you that the file she was downloading and that was almost finished after an hour is now toast because you picked up the telephone and interrupted it. The second is the modem noise that indicates that the file is dying as you listen. (In many cases, the modem can recover from the interruption if you're quick enough in hanging up. However, you can also wreck the transfer. It all depends on the mood of the modem gods.)

You need to consider a number of communications control issues. We touched on one issue in the preceding paragraph: Is one telephone line sufficient? How many users are there? What ages are they? How often do they monopolize the line? How often do the parents need to use the telephone? Are you operating a small business out of the basement and using the house telephone? You may need to set up special software on your computer to enable you to dial into other computers, and you need to manage the account names and passwords that each system requires.

Other issues to consider consist of the damage you can cause when moving from using a telephone to talk to people to using the telephone to talk to other computers. If you think that teenagers talk for a long time, wait until you see what happens when they discover the Internet! So now you need to review what your online policies are. How long can someone use the modem? Can others access your computer through that modem? (Yes, but it's not likely and isn't a great cause for concern.) Do you need to restrict access to parts of the online world, and how can you accomplish that?

When you review all these concerns and begin to develop solutions, you are performing the same tasks that are required in the business community. Only businesses may have to worry about hundreds of telephone lines in addition to the special lines that they lease for computers. Additionally, management must control who can purchase dial-up lines and regular telephone lines.

In your home, you may want to follow some of these suggestions:

- ✔ Consider a second telephone line for computer use. Have it terminate only near the computer with no other extensions so that it cannot be interrupted.

- ✔ If you use one line, consider a special gadget that prevents interruptions from another extension. You can get these gadgets from your local telephone company.

An example of bad controls

In one instance some years ago, an employee was running a small business by using the computer and dial-up lines of his employer. This individual had control over purchasing of all telecommunications lines, and no one monitored his purchases. So he added a few lines, told no one, and offered other companies cheap computing power. Sure, that computing power was cheap for him; he was stealing the time from his employer's computer. The scam was eventually uncovered — not through proper management, communications, or other controls, but by the need to buy a new computer because the one in use was too busy. When technicians checked the system, they found programs running that they were unaware of and investigated, eventually tracking down the culprit. Good controls help to prevent such situations from occurring in the first place.

✔ Be careful in providing children with access to online services. Some services, such as CompuServe and America Online, are expensive to use after the initial few hours, and you can rack up a sizable bill very quickly. If you let children use these services, make sure that they know that it is very expensive, and closely monitor usage. (See Chapter 12 for more information about implementing parental controls with online services.)

✔ Impress upon all users the need to keep passwords secret. Tell the kids never to give out a password to friends. If your password is posted on an underground bulletin board for one evening, your bills will be astronomical.

✔ Pay attention to what is happening at home. That quiet child on the computer could be trying to break into government computers. You don't want the FBI or RCMP knocking on your door.

Preventing Problems

Wouldn't it be nice if you never had any problems? Utopia! However, it is very unlikely that you will never run into them in your lifetime. (Besides, life would be awfully boring if you didn't.) Again, as Barry's guru is wont to say, "There are no problems, only opportunities." How you look at a situation invariably intensifies or diminishes the issue. So start by repeating after us:

"This is an opportunity, not a problem; this is an opportunity, not a problem."

There, you feel better already, don't you?

So how can you prevent an opportunity (or problem) from occurring? We have already determined that if you are clear in your expectations, the results may be more to your satisfaction. So begin with a clearly stated objective. It need not be overly complicated, either. Use the KISS principle: Keep it simple, silly.

Formal or informal controls?

There are two schools of thought on the need to document everything. On one side are those who believe that informal controls work just fine, thank you very much. These people inherently trust everyone and believe in each person's competence and shared values. With strong leadership, a high degree of openness, and high ethical standards, this approach works just fine. Just don't try it in law firms or with politicians.

Most organizations are too large to share these informal values, however. You do not always know who you're working with; ask anyone who worked next to someone they thought they knew but who ended up being charged with espionage. Formal controls work better here. They work on the principle that people act appropriately when they know what is expected and understand what they need to do.

To implement formal controls, you need to put together a set of policies that set the direction toward which the organization is moving. Then you need to implement standards to back up those policy statements and follow them up with the procedures necessary to perform the required actions. It's simple, when you think about it.

Additionally, you might think about the laws and regulations that can impact your particular industry and decide whether to use a centralized form of controls or to decentralize these functions. We do not intend to get into a hissy-fit over centralized versus decentralized controls. Whatever management style your organization uses generally sets the tone for which method you use. If your organization is fairly autonomous and manages in a centralized fashion, guess which style you will likely follow? Yup! Centralized.

So what's the best way to minimize problems in your organization or your home? Set clear policies and procedures and make sure that everyone understands them. Make sure that you involve the people you plan to have follow the controls. Their buy-in is critical to the success of the controls. Finally, make sure that the highest person in authority actively supports the controls. Nothing works better than seeing the big boss approve and follow the same controls you are stuck with. If you think that senior management (or parents) can ignore passwords yet enforce their use throughout the organization (or home), think again! We visit too many organizations in which this attitude exists and watch them struggle with staff indifference to security.

Correcting problems

So you have a clear set of objectives that everyone is following. But your security system is still not air-tight. Now what? Did you think that everything would go away and leave you in peace after you set up the formal stuff? Not a chance. Remember that we mentioned that management controls are a cycle? One thing leads to the next and so on, back to the start?

So you're back at the start again. What do you do? Evaluate the problem. Were existing controls ignored, or are they ineffective? If they were ignored, take corrective action. Taking some action, any action, is important here, as long as the rest of the organization (or home) can perceive that these controls mean something and are not to be taken lightly. Believe us, enforcing compliance pays off; not acting when they are ignored destroys the entire program's effectiveness. If you do nothing when your infrastructure is ignored, you're wasting everyone's time.

If your controls are ineffective, evaluate the effectiveness of the controls in place. Have you uncovered a weakness, or has something new come up? Create and implement appropriate new controls to cover this situation, and make sure that everyone is aware that new controls exist. Finally, continue to monitor the controls until the next time you need to review them.

Notice that throughout this example we stayed away from mentioning risk analysis. That is not to imply that risk analysis does not have its place. It is an industry unto its own. Additionally, the information security field is very young, and most decisions are based on qualitative analysis rather than quantitative analysis; that is to say, it's mostly educated guesswork. More important, the field is moving so fast that you really have little time for expansive risk analysis techniques. You gotta fly by the seat of your pants sometimes.

Some experts in the industry believe that a 30-minute risk analysis is sufficient and that more is a waste of time. The insurance industry uses extensive risk analysis techniques, yet look how slow adapting to new risks like home computing or business computer security coverage can be. These things are not simple to evaluate. Adherents of the quickie analysis eschew the use of extensive analysis, replacing it with standard security baselines. These baselines furnish an organization with the minimum standards needed to provide a reasonable degree of protection over their corporate assets, quickly and efficiently. Chapter 5 gives you enough information about risk analysis to perform all the analysis you need.

Detecting Problems

If you can't prevent problems from occurring (which you can never do), you must ensure that you can detect a problem quickly — preferably before any damage is done. Detecting problems in the personal computer environment is tough. On the one hand, detecting theft may be simple. But what if a thief takes some of the memory from your computer, leaving it with sufficient memory to continue working? How long would it take you to acknowledge the problem? Weeks? Months? Forever?

So detecting a problem is a problem. What can you do? The primary and most effective way is usually through an effective audit program. Oooh, auditors. Doesn't the thought send a shudder down your spine? Like it or not, these friendly characters (and most of the ones we know certainly are characters!) are the best answer. Or if you're really up in arms, the audit process is the most effective way to detect problems. There, feel better?

Perform an audit on at least an annual basis. Listen to staff and follow up when they indicate that a problem may exist. Use checklists occasionally to verify that actions follow proper procedures or that equipment remains intact. If you are a home user, list all the settings that the computer uses — you know, all those IRQs, communication ports, and serial gizmos. Forgetting what you're using and for what purpose is easy, and a list can help you re-create the settings after Junior spoils it all by trying out that new hardware device.

Putting the Control Issue to Rest

The biggest issue with controls is that no one likes them. Humans have an inherent dislike of being told what they can or can't do. Control is usually something that is forced on people as children: Go to bed, don't do this, don't do that. Perhaps that is why some people rebel as they get older. Hmmm, maybe that's why Timothy Leary did all that tripping.

Nonetheless, this issue is a major one. After you perform all the necessary work to analyze, create, and implement your controls, they still often fail. Why? Because you do not get the necessary buy-in from the users of your system. For example, while your kids are young, control is less of a problem. You tell them what you expect and take away TV rights if they do not do what is expected. As they get older, though, this strategy doesn't work (especially as they become bigger than you). So you need to find a way to get them to agree: through compromise. Through discussion. Through buy-in to the need. This chore, as any parent knows, is not easy.

Dealing with people at work is just as difficult. If you implement a set of controls and neglect to obtain agreement from your staff, you end up with problem. Now we can hear all the autocrats (all our old bosses!) screaming about this namby-pamby attitude. But that's too bad. It's also why managers are the very ones with the biggest problems. Staff need to know *why* you are adding controls. They need to know that *everyone* is following them, including management. You need to introduce your staff to the controls gradually, giving people time to adjust to them.

Nobody questions the need for door locks on automobiles. One day, no one will question the need for security controls in computer systems, either. Give people time.

Chapter 5

Analyzing and Managing Risks

*S*imply put, risk management is really a cost-benefit analysis. You shouldn't implement a control unless it makes economic sense. This chapter looks at risks from a cost-benefit viewpoint. What are the potential costs if you don't implement a control? What does the control cost to implement? Do you gain any benefits from implementing the control?

You can manage risks if you understand the cost relationship between threats and controls. One difficulty in implementing controls is that people generally don't believe that the threat is real or don't believe in the exposure from the threat. (For example, some people who are caught without insurance didn't know all the facts about the threats and risks.) Resisting costs that offer uncertain payback — or payback that is difficult to quantify — is understandable; however, security is important, and a well-thought-out program actually can *save* money.

When you choose to ignore threats, don't recognize exposures, inaccurately quantify loss potentials, and overlook risk control and financial opportunities, you may not achieve your objective (for example, to finish your income taxes before the deadline), and you may even lose money. You can measure, budget, and control the net cost of risk. Where you can reduce this cost, you can save money.

This chapter presents an overview of risk analysis, which includes a description of a method you can use to perform your own assessment of risk.

Prudence or Paranoia?

In psychology, *paranoia* is a state of mind characterized by delusions of grandeur, by an unfounded belief that one is being persecuted by others, or both. Although even healthy individuals occasionally are subject to mild forms of paranoia, and even paranoids have enemies, people with chronic cases of paranoia tend to form rigid belief systems, often misinterpret the behavior of others as confirming their delusional views, and exhibit a great deal of anger.

To the casual observer, most security professionals suffer from an unhealthy level of paranoia. They firmly believe that people are out to get them, and they look for spies in every closet and bugs on every computer. The majority of security practitioners we know don't fit this description, however. The ones who do often just misinterpret the actions of others. A case in point: One well-respected security professional is so "paranoid" that he believes all telnets to his site from the Internet are an attempt to breach his security and abuse his system. If he detects an unauthorized telnet, he sends a message to the system administrator at the perceived offending site. The telnets may be accidental, but he doesn't want to see it that way — or can't.

A *telnet* is a remote log in. If someone on one machine wants to use the resources of another system, he or she telnets to that system and logs in. The logged session looks local to that system and can use resources on the system.

Many security professionals have rigid belief systems. They see a perfect world where everyone embraces security with the same passion they do. Unfortunately, they can't see that some situations require compromise. With most paranoids — and some security professionals — no one knows what causes the escalation to paranoia from the natural "vigilance" with which most people regard their sometimes hostile environment.

The best way to deal with this hostile environment is to develop an effective control program, where the cost of setting up protective mechanisms is balanced against the reduction in risk. Implementing security without a control program is like rearranging deck chairs on the *Titanic* — it looks better, but it provides little long-term relief. The process of attempting to achieve a tolerable level of risk at the lowest possible cost is called *risk management.*

Risk management is an element of managerial science concerned with the identification, measurement, control, and minimization of uncertain events. Managers must address risk management from a multidimensional as well as a multidisciplinary perspective. Risk management must be recognized as a continuing, formal, planning technique that includes a whole range of existing management tools — for example, budgets. The multidisciplinary perspective stems from the security levels we explore in the following chapters. The interrelationship between the different levels creates the multidimensional perspective. (Wow, that's a mouthful.)

Costs, Benefits, and Risks

Many decisions in life involve the assumption of risk — the chance that the result will be different than you hoped. When you take a new job, you assume the risk that the job won't turn out as you planned. Rain may fall during your whole annual winter pilgrimage south — not exactly what you had in mind. Decisions made in spite of uncertainties — and in recognition of them — are generally accepted as essential to growth. Simply put, if you don't take chances, you won't get ahead.

Usually, the key to your success lies not in the willingness to accept uncertainty or assume risk, but in the ability to recognize and quantify risk and deal with it in an objective way. As in any self-help program, recognizing problems is half the battle. Using our rain example, you can log in to CompuServe before you go on vacation and check the current weather for your destination. You may get a five-day forecast, so you know the predicted weather for the start of your vacation. In addition, you can look at the weather history for the month you intend to be at that location. During your research, you may determine that it does rain in southern California in the wintertime. Armed with this knowledge, you bring an umbrella and decide to check out the museums and other inside activities, just in case it does rain. "Forewarned is forearmed," as they say; or "Be prepared," as the Scouts warn.

Likewise, as a computer owner, you can find out from your vendor's manual the likelihood that your hard disk may stop working. (They call this *mean-time-to-failure* or *mean-time-between-failures*.) Knowing that your hard disk may fail, you can buy a disk drive to back up your data so that, if your drive fails, you don't have a catastrophe, but a copy.

Everyone must come to grips with and manage risk in some form. You can reduce risk considerably, or in some cases substantially eliminate it, by learning how to use your system and the environment in which you live. These decisions call for good information. But the costs of obtaining this information can be enormous. Increasingly, you confront uncontrollable factors that affect the desired results. To some extent, you can reduce this risk by calculating statistical probabilities; however, increasingly substantive limitations exist.

The overall result is that total certainty is impossible, due to both practical and absolute limitations. Seeking a level of no risk is impractical; therefore, you must reach a level of acceptable risk. Your actions must reflect the level of risk that you deem acceptable. The capability to survive failure and operational losses varies. Some people like to take chances, whereas others may wake up in a cold sweat whenever they think about the loss of data or a system. However, everyone intuitively understands the need to protect important information. The difference is just how much protection different people feel is cost-justified.

The inclination to take risk varies. Psychologically, risk perception differs widely from one person to another. Some people are risk averse; others are risk seekers. People are more sensitive to increased loss than to increased gain, and therefore are risk averse. Simply put, some people are gamblers and take chances; others suffer distress from taking chances. To convince yourself of this fact, ask yourself how much you would be willing to pay to play the following game:

Someone flips a coin. You get $10 every time a head comes up. How much would you pay: $1, $2, $5, $8, $10, or some other value? You should be willing to pay $5, because this is the expected value ($10 times the probability of a head coming up, or 50 percent). You must therefore make your evaluations based on your experiences and preferences. You may have different risk sensitivities — willing to take more chances than your friend or neighbor — from other people, but you need not have different methods for quantifying risk.

The increased awareness of the need for security has caused the need for a method to quantify threats. Risk management provides a cost-effective program for reducing risk to an acceptable level. The program provides you with much-needed information on which to base questions and allocate your precious dollars. Based on the information provided, you decide whether to accept a loss by controlling the threat or accepting the risk. The most important part of managing risks is risk analysis.

Analyzing Risk

You need to do a risk analysis of your personal computer and environment to quantify the losses that you would suffer if your information were to be disclosed to unauthorized persons, damaged, or destroyed.

Determine these factors:

- The relative impact of a specific difficulty occurring
- The probability of encountering that difficulty within a specified period of time

Your risk analysis can be quantitative or qualitative. Quantitative methods yield data that describes the cost of potential problems in terms of cost per unit time, such as dollars per year, and qualitative methods help set priorities. Qualitative methods have scientific merit because of the following factors:

- The method is planned.
- Judgment is based on fact.

✔ The measures are reliable.

✔ The calculations are public.

✔ The conclusions follow from the data.

Basically, risk analysis involves the following steps:

1. **Identify assets needing protection.**

2. **Determine the threats to those assets.**

3. **Determine your vulnerability to the threats.**

4. **Analyze your current controls and safeguards.**

5. **Select and implement needed controls.**

Identifying which assets need protection

The first step in any risk analysis — either qualitative or quantitative — is to identify assets needing protection. Assets are identified at the lowest practical level. What assets do you have? You have your personal computer. What costs would be involved in replacing all your hardware? You also have installed software. If you have backups, the only cost would be the time required to reinstall all the software on your system — assuming that you know everything installed on your system. If you don't have backups, you may need to replace the software or take the time to beg new software from your various software vendors. Software and hardware replacement is relatively straightforward. What about all the data or information on your system? What is its value to you?

Regardless of the method, valuing data is the hardest part of the risk analysis. For best results, you should spend a great deal of time and effort on completing the valuation. Taking the time to figure out what your system and all your information is worth can simplify decisions about how much to spend to protect it.

Determining the threats to those assets

After identifying and valuing your system and information, you should collect and document the threats to your environment. As Chapter 3 discusses, a *threat* is one or more events that can lead to intentional or unintentional modification, destruction, or disclosure of data. Physical threats — natural phenomena such as storms or earthquakes — can damage or destroy buildings or stop you from working. Man-made threats can include terrorist attacks, union work stoppages, accidents (whether by you, your children, or your spouse), malicious acts by disgruntled workers, fraud, theft, or misuse of equipment. Occasionally, you need to revisit your threat identification. Threats can change over time, or you may change your system or environment, which changes the threats.

Determining your vulnerability to the threats

Next, you must determine how vulnerable you are to any particular threat. *Vulnerability* is the cost you incur if an event or threat takes place. After collecting the vulnerability data, you compare it to the identified threats to conclude whether these threats can exploit the known vulnerabilities.

Analyzing your current controls and safeguards

Even if you understand the threats and your vulnerability to them, you still don't have the whole picture. You must look at controls or safeguards that you already have in place. Analyze your data concerning existing safeguards and compare it with your threat/vulnerability results to decide whether your existing safeguards are adequate. This process also includes estimating the likelihood and frequency of occurrence of an event, based on statistics, research, and your experience.

For estimation, you probably use your intuition, but you may rely on statistics published in the newspaper or heard on television. You can tap organizations that keep information about particular threats. For example, ask your insurance agent or local police how many break-ins involve the theft of computer equipment. The same insurance agent can give you some information about the probability of fire in your neighborhood (or you can ask the local fire chief). She also may have data on the likelihood of a flood, tornado, or other natural disaster. You can read the manual that comes with your hard disk drive to find out the mean time between failures (that is, how long the engineers think it may last), and predict when you should consider replacing the drive. By gathering estimates in this way, you build up a threat database for your environment.

If the risk analysis is quantitative, usually expressed as annualized loss exposures, you must establish and evaluate threat frequencies. You obtain these calculations by multiplying the replacement cost of an asset (for example, the cost of a new hard drive) by the annual threat frequency occurrence rate (for example, the manufacturer says that your hard drive may fail every five years). If the risk analysis is qualitative, you assign a scale — alphabetical, numerical, or verbal — to each threat/vulnerability combination for each asset. One verbal scale is high, medium, and low. Using this scale, you focus only on the high-risk items.

Selecting and implementing needed controls

The process of selecting a security-control mix should include an attempt to assure that you adequately protect all critical functions of your system. However, you must balance the benefits of the various control measures against the costs of their implementation and continued use. When selecting controls, consider the following factors:

- ✔ **Cost-effectiveness:** You should implement only cost-justified safeguards.

- ✔ **Degree of automation:** Automated controls have a higher probability of success during operation. For example, if you consider viruses a threat, buy some software that automatically scans your system every time you start your computer.

- ✔ **Growth:** The safeguard should grow in response to a change within the operation.

- ✔ **Robustness:** Controls must not rely on secrecy to be effective. If you can buy the safeguard, so can anyone else; you can't rely on secrecy. Don't rely on "security through obscurity."

Reducing, Retaining, Transferring, and Managing Risk

After you analyze your risks, you have a big decision to make — that is, what do you do with the risk? Risks can be any of the following:

- ✔ Reduced
- ✔ Retained
- ✔ Transferred

You reduce risks by taking action and managing the risks. (Chapter 6 describes some controls that help you manage threats.) But before managing the risks, you must understand the extent of the risks. Follow these steps:

1. **Identify the threats.**

2. **Predict exposures to the threats.**

3. **Rank the exposures by priority.**

4. **Implement controls where they are cost justified.**

Your decision involves risk avoidance, risk transference, or risk acceptance. You can

- ✔ Implement selected identified controls to eliminate or reduce the exposure (risk avoidance).
- ✔ Transfer a portion of the cost of the exposure to another agency or organization by buying insurance (risk transference).
- ✔ Acknowledge the risk and its resultant exposure and choose to accept it, based on the information provided by a risk analysis (risk acceptance).

Your trade-off can be simply stated as *collective threat – collective security measures = acceptable level of risk.*

Because adequate security is a relative concept, you must make the decision. To ensure that you make the best decision, you need to use the best information.

Review the results of the risk analysis and select a plan of action based on the analysis. You can accept risk as inherent in life and absorb it. Self-insurance, common in government, is a form of risk acceptance. In other words, instead of purchasing replacement insurance, you decide that, if someone steals your laptop, you buy a new one. However, you also have three other possibilities to consider:

- ✔ You can make changes in the way you operate. Because you can anticipate so many problems, risk avoidance should be at the heart of your plans. You can trace back almost every computer-related disaster to ignorance of environmental threats or to hardware/software design or maintenance deficiencies that allowed minor problems to escalate into major disasters.
- ✔ You can choose to control or limit the risks through the use of protective measures. For example, you can buy an uninterruptible power supply to support your computer, thereby ensuring continuous power. You can buy a surge protector to prevent the disastrous consequences of a power surge or spike. Workstations can check floppy disks for viruses automatically. Duplicate disk drives can bypass a single point of failure.
- ✔ You can decide that you can't change the way you operate, or that controls are cost-prohibitive, and transfer a portion of the risk associated with the operation to others.

The following section talks about some of the others to whom you can transfer risk.

Risk Transference

If you can't reduce or avoid residual risk, you must finance it. You have many ways of financing risk; the most important ways are the following:

- ✔ **Your personal budget or reserves:** You pay for the loss out of your pocket.

- ✔ **External grants:** Your rich maiden aunt (or some other generous soul) leaves you some money.

- ✔ **Credit:** You borrow money to buy new equipment.

- ✔ **Insurance:** You can purchase additional insurance to cover your computer equipment. Your regular policy, however, does not cover all your equipment.

You must evaluate the advantages and disadvantages of each option, based on the effect on your cash flow, taxation, and earnings.

Insurance is a method for transferring risk to another organization — in effect, applied risk management. It's a mechanism for reducing financial risk and spreading financial loss. Buying insurance is a form of risk transference.

Microcomputers are different from cars, photocopiers, and other appliances. Most office insurance policies exclude personal computers. The value of the microcomputer is more than the value of the hardware and software. However, you can buy insurance to cover the loss of your equipment and data. Under the concept of indemnity, which is central to insurance, you have insurance to cover a financial loss. To recover a loss, you must have some way of proving a loss. If you haven't done an analysis of the worth of your data, you can't show your insurer the value. So knowing the true value of your computer system is really important.

When looking for insurance, consider the following coverage:

- ✔ Loss of or damage to hardware, including peripherals

- ✔ Loss of or damage to media, including the cost of restoring or recovering files, software, and other data

- ✔ Business interruptions

Insurance companies offer insurance against computer viruses, software piracy, and toll-call fraud, among other crimes. Safeware (800-822-2345) and The Computer Insurance Agency (800-722-0385) provide this insurance for about $70 to $100 per $5,000 coverage.

Reevaluating Your Choices

You should review controls periodically to identify ineffective, nonfunctioning, or nonessential safeguards. Upgrading your software and hardware or installing new safeguards may also result in changes to your risk environment. So you should evaluate changes to determine the effect of new hardware or software on your previous decisions.

Final Words on Risk Management

Qualitative versus quantitative — which is best? Well, that depends. We have used both. In a small company, employees got together and agreed on the most important assets and the threats to those assets. In addition, they agreed on controls to protect those assets. In a bank, we used a more formal, quantitative methodology. Management liked the formal method and the expected losses we came up with. Both methods were effective, because they focused attention on risks and controls. You should base your decision on your background. For example, engineers or accountants may favor quantitative methods, and artists may choose a qualitative method.

Which methodology you choose isn't important. What's important is that you apply the methodology with consistency.

Part II
The Methods

"OH YEAH, AND TRY NOT TO ENTER THE WRONG PASSWORD."

In this part...

This part describes some of the methods you can use to keep your computer secure. It covers physical security devices, discusses how to control access to your computer, explains how to use the built-in security measures that come with some of the more popular software programs, and talks about how to avoid and get rid of those pesky viruses you may pick up. Most important, Part II talks about two critical things that you need to do: pick good passwords and back up your data.

Chapter 6

Keeping Your Computer Physically Secure

*F*irst, we'll get the obvious out of the way: If you think that this chapter is going to introduce you to exotic, erotic techniques, get a life! Seriously, folks (well, that's what the comics always say), this chapter introduces you to those things that you can buy or do to help ensure that your precious computer doesn't take an unwanted hike. Computer theft appears to be a burgeoning industry these days, with the darn things disappearing like Houdini props.

Why should you take measures to physically secure your PC? A primary reason is to prevent the theft of that equipment. You may also prevent unauthorized access to your precious files (although Chapters 7 and 16 talk more about that), and, finally, keep yourself from unintentionally damaging the PC.

Hardware Restraints

Now that we have established that we're not talking about bedroom games here, we can explain what we really mean. You may not have considered that, as PCs become smaller and smaller, they become easier to move. We remember our first laptops — they were referred to as a *luggables* at that time and weighed in at around 28 pounds. The only people who could have stolen them were professional weight-lifters, who as a rule don't get into that type of profession. So during the years when we lugged them to the office and back home (you've really got to be a dweeb to move something that heavy on a regular basis, don't you?), we were on the lookout for people with biceps bigger than our thighs. Now, of course, even desktop machines probably weigh less, and laptops are really lightweight.

One way to secure laptops against theft is by using restraints. Think about this: In response to consumer needs, the computer industry has made these things portable, making them lighter and more powerful every year. So far, so good. Unfortunately, machines are being stolen with increasing frequency, so you need to consider ways to protect your machine and ensure that it stays where you leave it. How can you accomplish this feat? (Stay with us now; this is where it gets to be fun.) By installing devices that lock your machine to a desktop or other heavy object. Neat, eh?

Other means of helping to protect yourself against the evils of the "it fell off the back of a truck" empire also exist. In addition to tie-downs, which we just mentioned, you might consider labeling the PC. We discuss a couple of ways to do so in a later section in this chapter.

Other tools to consider include key-locks that protect the on/off switch from being used and locks that prevent the floppy drive from being activated. These types of devices help to minimize unauthorized access, but, of course, they do not prevent the machine from being stolen. Depending on how sensitive the data on your machine is, you might consider using a number of these devices in concert. For example, you might use a tie-down device to secure the machine to your desk and an on/off lock to stop anyone from starting the machine when you are not there.

You can use a wide range of other devices to help protect your equipment from theft or unauthorized access. In fact, there are probably too many to list here. (If we have omitted your particular device, please e-mail us and we'll see about adding it to the next version of this book. You can reach Barry at this address: lewisb@cerberus.com. You can reach Peter at 72734.36@compuserve.com.) The following sections describe some of these devices in more detail.

Tie-downs

Tie-downs are devices that attach to the computer and then to a desk, table, or other heavy, generally immovable object, with the intent being that your precious PC doesn't take a walk. Of course, the problem is that you bought the thing for its lightweight portability in the first place. Now you're going to tie it down and lock it up?

But these devices have their places. For example, the Toshiba 410CDT comes with a small connection at the back that permits the quick attachment of a tie-down cable. If you use the machine in an office and on the road, you can attach this cable to your office desk and then detach it when you travel. Vendors reading this book (as well they should, we might add) might consider providing a flexible, tough travel cable that would enable people to wrap it around a hotel room chair or other relatively immovable object. The cable that is available for purchase from Toshiba is relatively short. All these cables are usually made from hardened steel, making them difficult to cut.

For desktop equipment, tie-downs are useful tools. They are especially needed in schools and other public building to help prevent theft. Barry's son's school has suffered a number of break-ins over the past couple of years, and his understanding is that computers are always the target. Because the school has an alarm system, thieves must get in and out quickly. Tie-downs would help prevent these crimes of opportunity, because the thieves would not have time to dismantle the tie-down before the police arrived on the scene.

A similar logic can be used in the business community, where inadequate stairwell protection, poor physical security precautions, and, unfortunately, employee theft leave desktop machines vulnerable. Tie-downs probably don't work well in the home, though, because most thefts occur when no one is at home and the thief has a lot of time to mess around. Some thieves have been known to make a sandwich and drink a beer while robbing the house! Some nerve.

Key-locks

Key-locks prevent unauthorized persons from opening up the computer and stealing stuff from inside it. Little is worse than arriving at work, pressing the power button on your machine, and being told in no uncertain terms that something is amiss. Typically, thieves remove the hard drive or memory modules, which are small, transportable, and apparently expensive enough to be worthwhile.

Most organizations do not bother with the simple precaution of using key-locks. In many cases, the machines that companies buy don't support this type of lock, or the organization views locking as too much of an administrative overhead. Should you use such a device? If you are a home user and a lock for your particular machine is available, a lock might prevent Junior from inserting that new internal modem, high-end graphics card, or additional memory, destroying parts as he mucks around without ridding himself of static electricity first. (And you thought that those commercials for fabric softeners were of no use!)

Audible alarms

You can purchase a card that fits inside your desktop or laptop computer and emits a very high-decibel shriek if the machine is moved before the device is turned off. (Sort of like Aunt Mabel when she caught you letting mice loose in the house so that her cat could learn to hunt.) This card enables you to leave the machine unattended for a while and know that the machine is not likely to disappear on you.

We understand that alarms work quite well with perhaps one minor flaw: What do you think happens when a thief picks up your beautiful new laptop and makes a run for it only to hear a bazillion-decibel alarm go off? Right — he or she drops the offending device and keeps going. Now, we're not sure about you, but the instructions that came with our laptops distinctly discourage us from dropping them. In fact, the vendor suggests that it's a good thing that this new, improved model can survive a drop of about a foot. Yup, one foot. Unless your thief has arms like an orangutan, you can bet that the sound of your machine dropping is going to sound a lot like copious sums of money flowing from your wallet.

Labeling

Labeling your machine so that it may be recoverable if someone steals it is a good idea. One option is to use an engraving tool to add your name, address, and serial number (sorry, we watched too many war movies as kids) to the external cover of the machine. Be careful not to get overzealous and try to engrave sensitive areas, such as the shiny part of a CD or the computer screen.

Another method of protecting your computer is to use self-adhesive labels specially designed for this task. These labels are almost impervious after you install them, so again, make sure that you place them where they do not interfere with any of the machine's functions. Be aware, however, that a determined person can remove the label if they are not concerned about scratching the machine.

A number of companies market various types of labels. These labels make sense for organizations to use, as they can help in tracking equipment as it moves from office to office. Additionally, many organizations use labels as part of an automated inventory, where each label is registered in a database by the department that "owns" the equipment. This practice enables the security and audit staff to validate inventories as they perform an audit. For home users, the labels provide a means of identifying your machine if it is ever stolen. Should the police recover your computer from the thief, they can track down the rightful owner and return the machine to you.

A newer type of labeling consists of spraying a special chemical on the device. The particular chemical makeup is registered to you by the company that provides it, enabling the police (with the help of the vendor) to find the rightful owner of the computer. This type of label can be very effective in ensuring that you are the registered owner but not in making sure that the police realize that the equipment may be so labeled. Therefore, another label warning of the first label is needed. (Whew! Sounds a little like a bunch of lawyers, doesn't it?)

We are not sure that this type of security is of much use on laptops or any device that gets stolen. Assuming that the label has not been forcibly removed, about your only chance of recovery is if the police recover the computer during an arrest. And even then, they are likely to keep it as evidence for so long that you may as well assume that it is gone forever and get a new one.

Cabinets

If your office is small, you might consider using one of the computer cabinets that are available. These cabinets function as work areas until the end of the day, when they enclose all the equipment and allow you to lock it up. Wandering out the front door lugging a massive cabinet is a lot tougher for a criminal than carrying the computer by itself, so this solution is a reasonable one. Of course, if you own a mess of computers, this option gets awfully expensive.

For home users, investigating such a device is a good idea. Most home users need a work area for the computer anyway (the kitchen table is great until breakfast, lunch, and dinner roll around), so this solution kills two birds with one cash outlay.

Floppy drive locks

Floppy drive locks help to prevent persons from gaining access to the computer by using a bootable floppy disk or any number of nefarious programs that enable people to attack your PC. Primarily useful only if you are already using some sort of file control system (see Chapters 7 and 17 for more information about such systems), locks, nonetheless, can provide an additional level of control. In addition to the key-locks that we mentioned earlier, special controls that protect against unauthorized machine access also are available.

One or two vendors (such as Personal Computer Card Corp. and Smartdisk Security Corp.) provide special floppy disks that have extensive security embedded in the floppy disk and work to prevent any use of the machine unless you are in possession of this special disk. Coupled with the security provided in the machine, they leave you, the user, with little to worry about, apart from losing that disk. No passwords, unless you choose to add them. No keys. Just the floppy disk. Mind you, if you lose that disk, you're in big trouble.

Keyboard covers

Make sure that we're straight here: Keyboard covers do not help you keep your computer safe from theft. They do, however, keep it safe from a far greater threat: coffee (or tea) and other drink spills. A keyboard cover is a little thing, but it's a good thing. (Wasn't that a commercial years ago?)

A neighbor of Barry called one day to ask what would happen if she accidentally spilled coffee on her keyboard. Being a major psychic (you haven't read about him in the tabloids?), Barry immediately deduced that she had performed this act already and was now concerned. He told her to either use a hair dryer (as though everyone has a hair dryer at work) or leave the keyboard overnight and see what happened. As it happens, the keyboard was toast. *Finit.* Done in. She purchased a new one for about $30 and went on her way. And never called Barry again. Hmmmm.

Barry's neighbor would have been protected if she had used a *keyboard condom,* which consists of a flexible rubber device that you place over the keyboard. Surprisingly, you can still type over it — it doesn't take much getting used to. Touch-typists may want to try one out first, as we understand that you're a sensitive lot and do not like things interfering with your nubile digits.

These covers are not expensive, and they may save you one day. Barry used one eons ago when his son was small. Those sticky little fingers! You may also want to use one if you insist on eating sticky buns while keying stuff into the computer. Home computer users especially should consider using a cover, as controlling all the little fingers in the house is awfully hard. Make sure to get one that fits your keyboard. Most keyboards are a consistent size, so unless you have one of the newer ergonomic keyboards, you should be able to find a generic cover that fits.

Hardware-driven access controls

We mention these controls here to let you know that we haven't forgotten them. Hardware-driven access controls basically consist of a card (no, not like that cute birthday card that you sent to Aunt Mabel) that fits inside the computer and is used in conjunction with some software to provide user authentication and file-access controls. We consider it a physical control here because it can prevent anyone who steals the PC from signing on or obtaining any of the data on the hard drive, rendering the machine a little harder to sell, or, in street terms, to *fence.*

Because the card is physical, you can remove it, but doing so usually destroys any possibility of your using the hard drive without performing a low-level format. You can read more about formatting a drive in Dan Gookin's *DOS For Dummies.*

UPS, UPS, and Away

What do we mean by this weird term? (Sounds like we're planning on sending a parcel or something, doesn't it?) *UPS* is another in the endless realm of abbreviations and acronyms and is short for *uninterruptible power supply.* It's really a bit of an anomaly, because all power is interruptible. But if you use a UPS device, your computer switches from the wall outlet to the battery assembly provided by the device when your local power goes off. This setup provides you with a couple of things. First, it helps to protect your machine from the "instant off" that a power failure forces, and second, it provides you with a temporary power source until your power comes back on.

How does a UPS device work? The unit consists of an electronic part that senses power fluctuations and a battery. The unit sits between your machine and the wall and monitors the flow of power. Upon sensing a loss of power from the wall outlet, a gizmo inside switches over to the battery.

Unfortunately, these devices do not provide the endless power that your wall outlet does. They typically provide a few minutes, enough for you to save your work and power down the machine gracefully. In addition to providing this sometimes life-saving event, UPS devices act as protection against the spikes and power surges that are so common during the winter or on older electrical grids.

We highly recommend that any *power user* (defined as a person who relies heavily on the use of the machine) obtain and use a UPS unit. They are quite reasonable in price, often costing between $150 and $350, depending on the amount of power you need to run your computer. In your office, large diesel engines may provide your power, so check with the information systems department first.

If you really must use your computer at all times, regardless of storms and lightning, buy a UPS. These devices enable you to continue using the machine by using its internal battery when the power fails. Realize, however, that UPS devices last only from a few minutes to a few hours and get much more expensive the longer you want them to last. In most cases, 15 or 20 minutes is probably long enough for a power failure to be resolved, so you might use that time as a benchmark. If you want a little more accuracy, time a few power outages or ask your local electricity provider to give you some idea of how often power in your particular area is lost and the time of the average outage.

Grounding Your System

As Barry's guru once said, find the center of your being and be one with the earth. Perhaps this is what he meant. Most computers plug into the wall by using a three-prong plug for a reason. In North America, the third prong (the one in the middle) is usually the *ground*. If your electrical cord is a two-prong affair, this does not mean that it isn't grounded; it just does the grounding in a different fashion. As long as you use the cord that comes with your computer and plug it into a wall socket that has been installed by a qualified electrician, you don't need to worry about electrical shocks.

Do not misuse the cord by plugging it into a two-hole extension cord; it needs a three-prong connection. With common sense and normal precautions, you can survive without ever directly meeting those little electrons that run through your home or office wiring.

On a similar vein, static electricity can be considered a grounding problem. Static electricity is the bane of computers; it is to computers what earthquakes are to buildings. Too much destroys. You need to eliminate it. As we mentioned earlier, you can eliminate its effects by grounding yourself before touching the PC.

Locking the Door

If you live in a major city, you may be wondering why we need to state the obvious. Today, few places are left where people feel safe enough to leave their doors unlocked at night. Or at any time, for that matter. So if you live in New York or Detroit, you may want to skip this section; the habit is an ingrained one for you.

For those not used to the concept of locking doors, get used to it. Paying more attention to locking doors and windows is becoming a fact of life today. We don't like it, and you don't have to either, but nevertheless, it is an ugly reality. Never leave your computer (either laptop or desktop) in a room that is not locked unless

  ✔ The surrounding rooms are locked, and only trusted people can enter.

  ✔ Your computer is protected with a physical security device.

  ✔ Someone you trust remains nearby and watches the computer.

  ✔ You no longer like your computer and wish that it would disappear.

Physically Protecting Your PC

Sure, you have a zillion ways to protect your PC from theft, spills, and your curious ten-year-old. But we narrowed it down to seven because we realized that most people don't bother with the majority of the stuff in this chapter. These are the most likely ways to get the best bang for your hard-earned buck. You can read about some dumb things that you can do to a laptop in *PCs For Dummies,* 4th Edition, but here we tell you some neat things you can do to protect yourself!

Plug it in

Your desktop computer needs power. The monitor needs power. All those extra gizmos you bought, such as the modem and printer, need power. That's a lot of power! Actually, it isn't so much the power needs as the place to plug it all in. Protect your considerable investment by following some sound advice. As a general rule, do not use extension cords. They can be pulled out of the wall by people tripping over them or by the cleaners if they need that extra outlet. If you are in the middle of some serious work, you've got a problem. Additionally, some really cheap cords may overheat with everything you plug into them.

Finally, raw power from the wall may be great for toasters, but it's not good for computers. Get a surge protector or at a minimum a line filter to ensure that the power you get is nice and clean. Surge protectors also help protect against brownouts and power spikes. I have a fairly good surge protector that I bought a good ten years ago that protects my desktop computer (which is on 24 hours a day, 7 days a week). I have seen the house lights dim during the winter while my computer remained up and running. As with all else, *caveat emptor* (buyer beware) — there are good ones and there is junk. You've probably spent close to $2,000 or $3,000 on your computer; is another $100 so much?

Never leave a laptop unattended

Laptop computers get lonely and become people magnets — any people. Unfortunately, it always seems to be the bad person who wanders by and relieves the machine of its loneliness. So take it with you. To the washroom. To the telephone. Everywhere! At the office, lock it in a desk drawer if you must leave, even for a few minutes, unless your office is really, really safe. Has anyone ever had a wallet or purse stolen from the office? Yes? Then lock up the laptop.

Eliminate static

This primal force is the scourge of electronics. The insides of your computer are very vulnerable to static electricity, and while making your hair stand on end looks cool, making a computer chip stand on end destroys the chip!

The simplest method of eliminating static is to raise the humidity level. Buy a humidifier and use it in the room with your computer. Be careful that it doesn't get carried away and become too humid, though. Fortunately, most computers can survive a large range of humidity: from around 20 to 80 percent if you're using the PC, and a bit higher if the machine is turned off. If you are at all unsure and feel that there is still too much static, touch a piece of metal to ground yourself before touching the machine, or use one of the special mats that you can purchase.

Manage the keys

What do we mean by *manage the keys*? Most PCs arrive with a set of keys that lock the keyboard or cover. What do you do with these keys? Leave them in the computer for the guests to walk off with as a practical joke. Or lose them. Lose them? How could that ever happen? As we were writing this book, we decided to test our desktop machines to see what the keys do. Unfortunately, neither of us could find the blasted keys. Now, we know we put them somewhere safe so that we wouldn't lose them. But where? Well, as this book goes to print, we have yet to discover where they are.

At your office or in your home, find a safe place for the keys and write down where you put them. If you use them regularly, good for you! But don't leave them where someone can use them against you by locking your machine and throwing away the keys.

Let an orangutan carry the laptop

Okay, so we're running out of ideas to finish off this list. But if you do let an orangutan carry your laptop, the laptop is much more likely to survive the drop than if you were to drop it. If you don't have a favorite orangutan available, consider packing the laptop in a good, well-protected carry case. And don't ever test it by dropping the thing with the laptop inside.

Chapter 7
Controlling Access

• •

• •

*I*n this chapter, we provide you with some background information on why controls are necessary, and what sorts of things you should consider in attempting to control a personal computer. Typically, you want to implement controls to protect your files and information from being deleted or changed without your knowledge. Reading this chapter can help you to ensure that your files and data remain safe.

Why Should You Control Access?

As in most aspects of your life, you need controls to provide a sense of security. Where would you be without the controls that you obey each day when driving a car, such as speed limits, stop signs, and using turn signals? Your computer also needs controls to help keep files safe and keep the system free from viruses.

In the home, you may apply controls because you share the computer and others want to use it. You also may not want your children spending their entire lives in front of the monitor. (Like watching television, spending too much time with a computer can lead to a less active social life and who knows what other horrors.) You also realize that the information on your computer is key to why you might want to provide controls. What's on your computer? Everything from the software you need to do your job to personal mailing lists and recipes. For example, the laptop that we used to write this book contains software like Word, Excel, and PowerPoint for Windows 95. We used Word to write the book, and we use PowerPoint to create and present seminars that we provide to various organizations. (Excel came with Microsoft Office 95 and pretty well just takes up space because we don't use it that much.)

With only these programs on the machine, you probably aren't concerned about who accesses it, are you? But with a little more thought, you realize that a lot of other information is on the machine. Important information. For example, our computers contain all the book chapters we are writing, some financial information, a number of access codes and addresses for our electronic mail accounts, and many documents that we have created for clients across North America. We don't want just anyone accessing our laptops, because they can read or accidentally destroy our book chapters or electronic mail.

But some people don't store any data on their computers. All the data is retained up on the central computer, and nothing remains on the desktop. Others simply store all data on diskettes instead of on the hard drives of their machines. It would be all right for others to access these people's computers, would't it?

Unfortunately, it's not that easy. You still may need to control access. Why? Because although no data exists, you have to consider other things. For example, do you use The Microsoft Network, America Online, or CompuServe? Do you enter your password every time you sign on, or does the program store it for you so that you don't need to be bothered? Do you have special programs in place to provide network access (that thing you sign onto each morning before accessing your day-to-day programs)?

Although you may believe that nothing important is on the machine, we beg to differ. Anyone using your machine can sign on to your online service (CompuServe and so on) at your expense! Access control is one method of minimizing this risk.

The Security Reference Model

No book would be complete without some sort of *model.* We don't mean the kind of racing car or model airplanes that you make with your children; we mean an approach to doing something. A really old version of *Webster's Dictionary* defines a model as "something taken or proposed as being worthy of imitation; to plan or form after a pattern." In this section, we talk about a model that is prevalent in the information security field: the security reference model.

This model has four primary components, and they are arguably the foundation for all security programs. These components are

- ✔ Identification
- ✔ Authentication
- ✔ Authorization
- ✔ Audit

Using any one of these components without the others limits the effectiveness of your security. They are designed to be used as a complete package, an endless circle, an infinite loop. What we mean is that security is not a one-time thing, installed and forgotten; it is an endless process of give and take, as users and applications come and go within an organization. In the home, the security model provides a basis for managing the activities that each family member can do on the computer. Preventing your children from finding adult material, for example, is a classic use. Figure 7-1 represents the model pictorially.

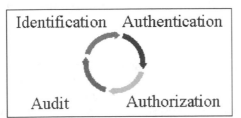

Figure 7-1:
A security
reference
model.

To help ensure adequate security, whether on your personal computer or on a corporation's network, always look at each of these components and put into place those practices that you believe are appropriate. As we say in the computer security business (well, some of us, anyway): "Don't put a $100 fence around a $10 cow!"

Now, you may believe that your cow is very important. But you should spend only the amount of money that you feel is necessary to protect your cow, *based on the level of perceived risk*. So what is the level of risk? As we discuss in detail in Chapter 5, the amount of money you are willing to spend to protect something depends greatly on how much risk you are willing to accept.

For example, continuing the cow analogy, if your cow resides in the backyard, you might put up a fence that is adequate to stop the cow from leaving but not so strong that it prevents wolves from gaining access. After all, the risk of wolves attacking your cow (especially in downtown areas) is extremely remote. On the other hand, you ensure that the cow can be identified, if it is stolen, by branding it. A branding iron and a fence are probably within your acceptable budget relative to the value of your cow.

You have taken some of the essential steps to protect your assets. First, you *identified* the cow with a branding iron. Second, you *authenticated* the cow by ensuring that the brand you put on the cow was easily recognized as your own. Third, you need some city *authorization* papers that permit you to keep your cow in the backyard. Finally, by looking out the back window once in a while, you perform an *audit* — ensuring that the cow is still there and remains unharmed. Of course, the city requires a leash and a license, but that's another story.

The following sections take a closer look at each of these issues.

Identification

Barry has a guru who always asks, "Who are you?" and waits for a response. Naturally, Barry gives him the wrong response and realizes why he needs the guru to begin with. (This trick question is designed to make you realize that you are more, and less, than what you think you are.)

In the information security world, *identification* means recognizing who a user is and using this recognition to make the user responsible for his or her actions. What are some of the ways to identify users? The primary method that a computer uses is to issue you something that it can use to recognize you and track your actions.

A number of terms for tracking and identifying users are in use. All of them mean the same thing: *you.* These terms developed over time and in different technical environments to describe the item that a computer uses to identify each person on the computer. When you sign on to your computer, you tell the computer who you say you are and provide a way for the computer to know that you are who you say you are. For example, Barry has an electronic mail account called `lewisb`. Peter has one called `pdavis`. This account name is our identifier.

An identifier is not enough security, however. Now that you know our electronic mail identifiers, you can get access to our accounts. So we need something more: *authentication.*

Authentication

Authentication works hand in hand with identification. It describes the piece of information you have that clearly lets the computer know that it is talking to Barry, Tom, or Sally. First, you tell the computer who you are by entering your

Computer identification terms in use

You may hear any of the following terms used to describe computer identification:

- ✔ Account
- ✔ User ID (userid)
- ✔ Logon ID (Logonid)
- ✔ Identifier
- ✔ Username (user name)

As you can see, we can't even agree on how to spell something within this profession.

Note that some of these terms are considered proprietary to some vendors. For example, Computer Associates has registered the term *Logonid.*

account, userid, or Logonid. (Remember, these terms all mean the same thing.) Next, you prove who you are by authenticating that access in some way. In order to authenticate yourself, you need something that no one else has — typically a password.

 When you type your account name and your password, you are identifying and authenticating yourself to the computer. Remember that this piece of information proves who you are. That is why you should never give out your password to any person: not to your mother, the security officer, your manager, or the stranger on the street. And never let anyone see it as you type it or use something simplistic, like your name or birthdate. (See Chapter 8 for more details about choosing and using passwords.)

Authorization

After you properly identify and authenticate yourself, the system needs to know what you are allowed to do. This task is called *authorization.* Another way to put it is to ask what you are authorized to do. Can the children access the Internet without your permission? Can anyone in the family add software? At home and in business, people often place emphasis on what you *can't* do rather than what you are *allowed* to do.

 We believe that explaining authorization in terms of what you are allowed to do is better. For example, tell the children that they are allowed only to play games or use the word processor. To access CompuServe or the Internet, they need a parent with them. Trying to access Dad's files or do anything else on the computer is not allowed, or, as they say in the business community, is an *unauthorized activity.* The emphasis is on what they *can* do.

What do we mean by the term *unauthorized?* Well, before something can be truly unauthorized, someone needs to know that the action is unacceptable. Set up specific areas on your computer for each family member to use for storing personal files and explain to everyone that they can access only their own files. Even better is to write down everyone's personal list of directories and files, add a line or two explaining that everyone can access only their own files, and post it near the computer. Doing so helps to ensure that everyone sees it and cannot say that they didn't know that they weren't supposed to delete your favorite recipes to free up some space for their files. You might add that browsing around other people's files to see what can be found is also unacceptable.

 Authorization depends heavily upon *access controls* in order to work. Access controls are specialized tasks that use your identifier as a keyword to control the programs and data you can access. Access controls are used primarily on large computers (mainframes and servers) and rarely on personal computers.

You can use a number of access control programs on your personal computer, however, should you want to add this functionality. The home user typically wants to control access to only a few files, so a simple program is best.

Chapters 17 and 18 discuss a number of simple control programs that you can use.

Audit

The final part of the security model is auditing. My trusty *Webster's Dictionary* provides the following description for the word *audit:* " . . . to examine with intent to verify." If you imply that people can access only certain data, from time to time you should verify that only authorized people are accessing those files, shouldn't you? This is the essence of auditing. Verification typically requires some sort of reporting and logging system to provide details on who has done what. Most access control packages allow you to log certain events, such as who accessed Dad's business files or how often a game is played. You can then use these reports to see whether everyone is following the rules set out earlier and posted near the computer.

Note: This book does not get into a lot of detail on auditing. We emphasize that this aspect is necessary to complete the circle, to close the cycle. The events discovered during an audit lead you to re-examine aspects of identification, authentication, and authorization, making your security program stronger each time.

Using Screen Savers for Security

What do screen savers have to do with security? Well, in a nutshell, not much. People buy screen savers for desktop computers because, according to vendors (we called a very helpful technical support person at Viewsonic for the latest information), screens today still rely on phosphorus to project an image. What does this mean? Simply put, you need to turn down the lighting on the screen until it shows all black, or turn it off if you are not using it for long periods of time. Doing so saves you money in the long term, because that phosphorus stuff wears out after a while, turning your once-bright image darker and darker until it is useless. Additionally, if you leave the same image on-screen for a really long time, it burns into the monitor, and you will be stuck looking at that favorite picture of Aunt Mabel you once thought was a cool idea to use as background image.

Screen savers do have a password option, and we often see them in use. But you cannot rely on these passwords to protect the files and programs on your hard disk. Why? Because they are poorly implemented and were never designed (in our humble opinion) to provide real protection. In Windows, all anyone has to do to defeat a screen saver password is perform the infamous three-finger salute: Ctrl+Alt+Delete. Or power off the computer. After that is done, he or she can bypass the Windows screen saver and proceed to do whatever nefarious thing he or she chooses to do. Darn!

Screen saver passwords do provide a little protection for your network connection. The three-finger salute terminates all open connections to your network. As long as you are always forced to enter your network password before being reconnected, you have a bit of protection.

Why only a bit? Because a whole bunch of programs give away the password that you thought was safe and secure. Run the program called SCRNLOCK.EXE, and it tells you the current screen saver password on any Windows 3.1 system. So all anyone has to do is insert a diskette into your machine and run Scrnlock, and he or she knows your password. That person does need to stop the present screen saver first, but, as we have mentioned, that isn't a problem. And just how many times do you walk away from your workstation, knowing that the screen saver will kick in within a few minutes? In case you are feeling somewhat smug, knowing that you have Windows 95, we are sure that similar programs for this system also exist.

Use the screen saver to provide protection for your monitor, but do not depend on the password option for any real security protection. As a final note, if you are using a laptop, the screen saver really is unnecessary, because these machines for the most part use liquid crystal displays (LCDs) and have no phosphorus, so they cannot burn in.

Logging into Your Personal Computer

You may never need to log in to a personal computer. The login that you perform at the office is probably giving you access to some other computer that is attached to yours via a network. Why would you want to log in to your own computer? Being careful with your data isn't nerdy. Everyone needs to be concerned about who can access their files and data, and providing login controls on your personal computer is one method of accomplishing that control.

Before we begin discussing the login process, a few notes:

- First, if you use a DOS computer without Microsoft Windows (like a friend we know), you are still living in the technology dark ages and therefore this section is of no use to you; DOS includes no sign-on provisions.

- Next, when we discuss logging on to your computer, we don't mean entering the password you type when you first power on the computer — these are probably power-on passwords. We discuss power-on passwords in Chapter 8.

✔ Finally, if you are still using an Amiga or Commodore 64, well, what can we say? Finding resources is tough, because personal computer security is a relatively new field and is concentrated within the Windows and Mac environments.

Logging into Windows 95

Windows 95 allows you to set up passwords for each user of your system. Most people do not use this option, however. In the home, it really isn't necessary; at the office, well, Windows 95 has not made a big impact in the workplace yet, so it isn't used much there, either.

However, you are asked at setup whether you want to use a password, and perhaps you said yes. Now each time you power on the machine, Windows 95 dutifully asks for your password and allows user access only if you type the password correctly. Does this mean that Windows 95 security protects your files and programs? No, it offers no protection against someone getting at any files or programs on your computer.

Why? For the same reason that Windows 3.1 doesn't protect your files and programs. It has to do with both programs being dependent on a thing called DOS. Even though Windows 95 hides it better, it still uses DOS in order to keep running all the older programs that are around. DOS doesn't have the smarts to prevent anyone from accessing files; in fact, it was designed for exactly the opposite task — to let people get access.

First, you can always get to files without Windows being present, simply by using DOS on a diskette. Or you can run Windows 95 in Safe mode. *Safe mode* is a special Windows 95 facility that makes sure that you can get into Windows regardless of silly things like passwords or the fact that you messed around with some files that you shouldn't have messed with.

Second, try adding a different name in the space provided next to the words *User name* when Windows 95 shows you the Welcome to Windows screen and asks for a user name and password.

Note: You see this Welcome window only if you are using user password security.

Does Windows 95 say, "Heck, no! You can't use that name because it's not registered"? No, it doesn't. It says, "Gee, you've never used this name before. Still want to sign on?" You reply yes, and up pops Windows. This simple bypass strategy is why these passwords are useless for security over files and programs on the computer.

So why does Windows 95 come equipped with these password things? They are helpful in two areas:

✔ They allow you to set different views of the desktop for each person who uses the computer.

✔ They are useful when used in context with network sign-ons and their passwords, enabling you to manage all your passwords from one place.

Check out Andy Rathbone's *Windows 95 For Dummies* (IDG Books Worldwide, Inc.) for additional details.

Setting up a password in Windows 95

If you decide that you want to add password security so that Aunt Mabel can't log in to your computer and see what you really think of her, here's what to do. In this scenario, we assume that you didn't choose to use a password when you installed Windows 95 and are choosing to add one now.

To assign a password, follow these steps:

1. **Double-click your left mouse button on the My Computer icon.**

   If you cannot find this icon, click on Start, choose Settings, choose Control Panel, and skip step 2.

2. **Now double-click on the Control Panel icon.**

3. **Find the icon called Passwords and double-click on it.**

   After you double-click on the Passwords icon, Windows may display a screen asking whether you want to change your Windows screen saver password at the same time. This screen appears only if you are already using the screen saver option. The intent is to make both the Windows sign-on password and the screen saver password the same.

   If you are using a screen saver password, we recommend that you keep it different from the sign-on password. While remembering two passwords requires a little more effort, you may give out the screen saver password to let someone onto the machine and wouldn't want them to know the sign-on password also. So leave the small check box called Windows Screen Saver blank and click on the OK button.

4. **Click on the Change Windows Password option.**

   The Change Other Passwords option primarily refers to network passwords and lets you manage all your passwords. This option is beyond the scope of this book, so don't change anything there without consulting with an expert.

5. **Enter a new password in the New Password box.**

See Figure 7-2 for an example of the Change Windows Password screen.

Use the information in Chapter 8 to select an acceptable password. Don't worry about the Old Password box; it should be blank. (If you want to change an existing password, type the old password and then the new one. Windows updates the password to the new one you specify.)

6. **In the Confirm New Password field, enter the password that you typed in step 5. Then click on OK.**

Windows responds with a message indicating that the password change was successful.

All good security programs require the user to type a password twice when changing it. This requirement serves a very important purpose. By typing the same word again, you confirm that you didn't accidentally mistype the word. If you mistyped the password, how would you get into the computer the next time you powered it on? This problem happened so often in the golden oldies days of computing that someone decided that users should be forced to type a new password twice. The method works.

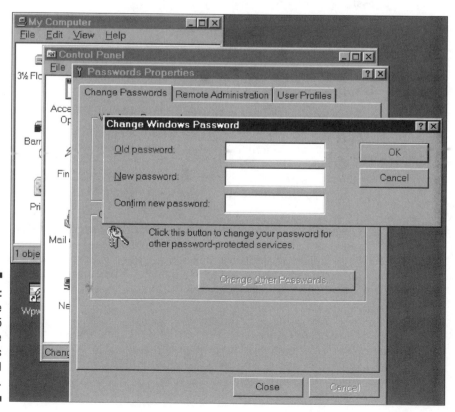

Figure 7-2:
The Windows 95 Change Windows Password screen.

7. Click on the Close button to close the Password Properties dialog box.

You added a password!

From now on, Windows asks you to enter that password each time you start Windows. Don't forget the password. You can change it at any time by following the same steps and including the old password as requested.

If you decide that maintaining the password is too much of a pain, go through the steps required to change the password, enter the old password, and leave the New Password and Confirm Password fields blank. Windows then stops asking you for a password.

Again, you should know that programs that can find these passwords are available, because the passwords are not very well hidden. (Windows uses a protection system called *encryption* that you can read about in Chapter 13.) Microsoft has created a program fix that enhances the level of security for the password file, but you need to get the file from Microsoft and install it. We'll have to see whether this latest update provides better security. At the time of this writing, it appears that the new fix will work well, but who knows?

You can add a number of users and give each person a separate password. Windows 95 automatically sets them up if you enter a new login name and password at startup. You can then use custom options for each person so that he or she has a unique view of the desktop. This is a good way to give your young children a screen showing only games and a word processor, for example.

Logging into Windows 3.1

This section is fairly straightforward. You can't log in to Windows 3.1. Windows 3.1 provides no provision for passwords except for the screen savers mentioned earlier.

Logging into Windows 3.11 or Windows for Workgroups

This section is also fairly straightforward. Like Windows 95, Windows 3.11 has a provision for a login password; however, the password is used only if you are networking with other computers. No provision exists for signing on and restricting access to the files and programs you have residing on your computer's hard drive. This is not to say that this password is meaningless — merely that it performs a useful function only if you use other networks and want to retain passwords for those networks on your Windows desktop. The login password cannot protect your files and programs.

Note: When you see or hear about Windows for Workgroups, you might think that it's a new product. Wrong. It's good old Windows 3.1 souped up to include some basic networking functionality. Confusing, huh?

If you really need security over any of the Windows platforms, a bunch of third-party products provide solutions from the simple to the complex. See Appendix B for more details.

Logging into Windows NT

This is the latest and greatest from our friends at Microserf. It is highly unlikely that you have it on your machine, as it has yet to gain wide acceptance. This product is great, however. It also does security. Well. Very well, in fact. So why hasn't it gained global acceptance? Probably because running it requires a big machine.

One thing you notice immediately with Windows NT is that you must either power on your machine to get a password screen or perform a three-finger salute. In this way, Windows NT forces you to relinquish control and go through its internal security processes, helping to prevent anyone from running a password-stealing program. In fact, a cool little welcome window prompts you to log in. After you press Ctrl+Alt+Delete, NT presents another welcome window with a couple of fields for you to use. Earlier, we discussed the terms *account, userid,* and *Logonid* and how they all mean the same thing. Well, Windows NT uses *Username.* Sigh. Username means the same as account, Logonid, and userid.

So you must enter a valid Username and enter a valid password to get Windows NT to talk to you and let you do your work. This is good security. If you type the Username or password incorrectly, you get a `User Authorization Failure` error message. NT doesn't tell you which part of the login sequence was wrong. Very annoying — but very good security. This scheme helps to stop people from trying various combinations until they guess a login sequence, because they never know whether they have a correct Username and a wrong password, the reverse situation, or have both wrong. Cool!

After you log in to the system, you can do a whole mess of really neat security-related things. For example, you can allow Aunt Mabel to log in but not access your library of letters or see those weird games you like to play.

There really are many sound, practical reasons for having this level of security, and we will not be surprised to see much more of this type of security as businesses begin to choose between Windows NT and a product that is not as stable, has little security, and needs the same resources (that is, Windows 95). Especially when Microsoft ports the user-friendly interface of Windows 95 to Windows NT. Some of the Windows 95 features are present now, and Microsoft is promising the same look entirely in the near future.

Windows NT

We mention earlier that Windows NT needs a big machine to run. Now, when we say *big,* this concept is relative. To have 8MB of memory was luxury only a short while ago. And regardless of those big PC magazine writers who get stuff free and think that everyone has a spare $500 bucks for every little toy that comes along, most people we know have a hard time justifying anything, let alone a 16MB or 32MB Pentium with gigabytes of disk storage. So a lot of 4MB machines are out there. Windows NT Workstation really doesn't like that level of memory. It prefers at least 16MB of memory, or it gets cranky and slows drastically. Are you beginning to see a trend? Everyone has small machines. NT likes big machines. NT hasn't made a big hit yet.

But machines in the last year or so are increasingly including a minimum of 8MB of memory, and businesses are putting in 16MB as a standard. Why? Is memory getting cheaper? (Not where we live. Send us some if it's inexpensive where you are.) No, again, it is because businesses realize that Windows 95 and Windows NT need at least 16MB to really move. So people are purchasing new machines with this in mind. Look for an explosion in the NT market over the next couple of years.

Logging into your Mac

The Mac does not have any login requirements when you first use it. You need to install additional software if you want security and control. Several file- and folder-locking programs are available for the Macintosh. When you buy a new Macintosh, Apple normally gives you At Ease for free. (If you don't have it, you can buy it for about $37.) To use the software, you must install it and set up the necessary parameters, such as adding users and passwords.

At Ease offers the following features:

- ✔ A simplified desktop for young or inexperienced users
- ✔ A restricted Finder interface for limited-access users
- ✔ A normal Finder interface for authorized full-access users

You can support up to 40 different users with At Ease. Each user has his or her own account and password, allowing you to control what each person sees and can access. Useful security features allow you to control access to specific applications and documents; specify privileges for opening, copying, deleting, and renaming selected files; assign individual user passwords; block access to the hard disk; prevent other users from launching applications from floppy disks; and protect system settings, control panels, and the Chooser.

Finally, several vendors sell software that provides Mac security. These packages typically offer a more granular level of security and control. For example, most vendor software offers improved audit trails that let you know what each person is doing when he or she is on the system. We provide names and addresses for these firms in Appendix B.

These Macintosh products typically change the hard drive's directory; that is, they write to it. Your virus software may not like this, especially software that doesn't rely on scanning. So you might have to disable virus-checking to use At Ease, which may not be such a great idea. If you can wait until the second half of 1996, Apple will deliver its new Mac operating system, code-named Copland. Copland has real security built-in — and will be worth the wait.

Personal Computer Security Products

All is not lost if you want really good security on your personal computer. A number of vendors provide more robust systems that offer an increased degree of security and control over your machine.

Most of these vendors supply software for DOS, Windows, Mac, and OS/2, so regardless of which you are using, you should find a product that works for you.

Product name:	OmniGuard/EAC
Vendor:	Axent Technologies
Internet:	www.axent.com
Telephone:	800-262-8296

Product name:	PC/DACS
Vendor:	Mergent International
Internet:	www.mergent.com
Telephone:	203-257-4223

Product name:	Watchdog PC Data Security
Vendor:	Fischer International Systems Corp.
Telephone:	813-643-1500

Product name:	Folderbolt
Vendor:	Kent Marsh Ltd.
Internet:	www.kentmarsh.com
Telephone:	713-522-5625

Product name:	Stoplight
Vendor:	Safetynet Inc.
Telephone:	800-851-0188

Secure Single Sign-On

Secure single sign-on is the Holy Grail of the '90s. Can it be done? Is it being done? (If you're a home user, you should probably skip this section, because it is not likely to contain one iota of meaningful material for you.) This section may interest anyone who must log in to more than one computer each day to do work.

Many people have to log in to a number of different computers each day to perform their jobs. They might log in to their *workstation* (essentially a business term for a personal computer), then log in to another computer in another department, and finally log in to a third computer to get their electronic mail. In most businesses today (and a few homes from which a small business runs), all these computers are connected by a network. A *network* is a bunch of wires (some are like your cable TV wire, and others are more like your telephone wiring) connecting all the computers and special software that tells each computer where the other computers are. This setup allows you to "talk" to the other computers and get data and files from them, but you have to log in to each one first.

What do we mean by *secure single sign-on?* If you use only one machine, like your home computer or office workstation, and never use any other computers, single sign-on means exactly that: You sign on only once and begin your work. If you sign on at all, that is. As discussed earlier, perhaps you merely turn on your computer and get to work. For you, single sign-on is a benign, almost meaningless term. For others, however, the story is different.

Secure single sign-on is also known as just plain *single sign-on,* or *SSO* for short.

If you implement the Windows 95 password option and also use America Online, The Microsoft Network, or some other online service, then you have to enter at least two passwords. Other users go to work each day, power up their workstations and begin the sign-on process:

- ✔ They may start with Windows 95.

- ✔ Then they sign on to their corporate network to get access to their day-to-day application programs, such as accounting or payroll systems.

- ✔ Next, they probably sign on to the corporate mail system to see what electronic mail they have received. That's three sign-ons so far.

- ✔ During the course of the day, they may have to access a *database* (a fancy term for a collection of data). They likely have to sign on to this database to get access to the information they need. That's four sign-ons.

✔ Now they travel across the network in search of some data to add to a report for the vice president about how many staff members have a company dental plan. This information resides in yet another database on a separate computer over in the Finance department. First, they have to sign on to this computer, and then they sign on again to the new database. That's six sign-ons.

As you can see, this process can go on and on and on. We know computer administrators and technical staff who must sign on to 5, 10, or 15 different machines.

Managing all the passwords and account names is a major problem for these people, hence the search for the Holy Grail. (We often think that the search is progressing much like the Monty Python movie — in obscure, indecipherable ways.)

You might think that having a person sign on once and being done with it would be a simple matter. However, you have to know a little about the history of computing and the almost diabolical lack of concern for the average user.

Over the last 20 years, computers have exploded in speed, capacity, and capability to handle data. Vendors have rushed to address the needs of businesses and appear to have spent most of their attention in a tunnel-vision approach to providing solutions. By this, we mean that most vendors responded to concerns about security by chucking all kinds of security into their products. This way, they could market the new whatchamacallit by touting its extensive security. At around the same time, the operating systems that ran the computers began to gain security functions. The operating systems for these big computers can be thought of as the DOS or Windows NT of PCs. Although they're far larger and more complex, they essentially perform the same function — allowing you to run the programs you actually use, such as games or word processors. In business, they allow the company to run the payroll program or the program that manages all those ATMs that you use to get your money from the bank.

So big computers had some level of security. Now corporations had some control over who could access their computers and what they could do after they signed on. But other vendors jumped onto this security bandwagon. Major software vendors decided to offer security within their applications. In their zeal to please customers, they began to duplicate some of the security features that corporations already had. Doing so was fine at the beginning of this revolution; security was a good thing. However, as companies purchased more and more applications, they began to question the need for all this duplication.

This point came before the latest revolution — the personal computer. Over the last ten years, the proliferation of *networks* (collections of computers that can talk to each other over a bunch of wires) has exacerbated the situation. Of course, all these new vendors developing new operating systems like NetWare, Banyon VINES, and Windows NT began to realize that they better follow those mainframes and include security. What a novel concept. As companies rushed to purchase these new, fast, efficient, and very effective networks, the sign-on problem grew into a major calamity. Instead of having one or two big mainframe computers and only a few technical staff members with more than one account and password, companies now have dozens, hundreds, and even thousands of computers that need to be signed onto by staff members. Big problem.

So what's the solution? Well, happily, as we stated earlier, other vendors have jumped into the fray (ain't free enterprise grand?), and a whole slew of potential saviors exist. Be warned, however, that no one has found the single sign-on Holy Grail. So many *platforms* (another word often used — perhaps incorrectly — to refer to computers and their particular operating systems) exist that no one has developed a solution for single sign-on that works with all of them. In addition to actual operating systems, you can sign on to hundreds of other applications, such as electronic mail, payroll systems, and databases.

So if your organization uses some of the more popular platforms, a solution exists. If you use an odd variety of UNIX or Banyon VINES, however, your chances of finding a solution diminish, as most vendors are concentrating on larger markets. You'll have to wait a while before a solution for all platforms is available.

Chapter 8

Picking Perfect Passwords

*A*s Chapter 7 discusses, access control systems involve authentication and authorization. Typically, an access control system tries to identify and authenticate you; then, knowing who you are, it attempts to restrict you to accessing only authorized information. Normally, identification involves an access code, sometimes called a *username* or *user access code*. User authentication, supplied by a password or passnumber, can be anything you have, know, or are — for example, a key, access code, or biometrics. *Biometrics,* as the name implies, measures one of your unique characteristics: for example, a fingerprint or lip print. Each item is described as a *factor*.

In a one-factor security system, for example, a password is something you know. When you use an automated teller machine, you use a two-factor access control system. You have the bank card with the magnetic strip — something you have — and you enter your personal identification number (PIN) — something you know.

For the purposes of this book, a *password* is composed of a word, whereas a *passnumber* is only numbers, such as the personal identification number that you use for getting money out of the bank machine. A *passcode* is a combination of letters and numbers (or alphanumeric, should you prefer) that is not a word.

You probably think that access control is necessary only in a business environment, where you're trying to protect secrets from prying eyes. Well, you may have personal information on your computer at home that you also want to protect, such as income or tax information that you don't want your five-year-old daughter finding and telling everyone. More likely, you want to protect your valuable data from accidental destruction by a well-meaning but bungling family member. Access control can provide peace of mind by protecting important data and files.

The correct use of passwords and passnumbers is an essential first step in establishing effective access control. A password or passnumber can be composed of anything associated with you — for example, fingerprints or a signature — and has an extremely low probability of discovery or duplication by an unauthorized individual.

The Need for Strong Passcodes

For years, security practitioners have stressed the need for good password systems. The use of the term *password* is unfortunate because it focuses on the ordinary terms *pass* and *word*. Using ordinary words limits the number of potential personal identification codes you can create. Even if math isn't your strong point, you probably understand that just adding a number to a word increases the potential number of codes you can generate.

The *Oxford Unabridged Dictionary* contains approximately 100,000 words; the abridged *Webster's Dictionary* contains about 10,000. However, in common, everyday English, people tend to use about 2,000 words. This number is the length of standard dictionaries that come with some operating systems. If your password system allows only four-letter words, people use four-letter words. When you use only four-letter words as passwords (including "four-letter" words — most eight-year-olds know exactly how many of those exist!), you significantly limit the potential passwords you can create.

Always avoid the use of words of any length. You should also not use English words in English-speaking countries, French words in French-speaking countries, Spanish words in Spanish-speaking countries, and so on. To discourage the use of just words, in fact, we refocus the terminology and call these authentication keys *passcodes*. A good passcode has the traits described in the following list:

- The passcode isn't easy to guess.
- Generally, the passcode has sufficient letters and numbers to thwart a brute-force attack.
- You keep your particular passcode for a reasonable length of time. Change your passcode frequently to be safe.
- Passcodes aren't visible when you type them.
- Passcodes that are stored and transmitted aren't available for reading by anyone.

Creating Good Passcodes

A *passcode* is a sequence of characters selected or generated from a possible *password space,* which encompasses all the possible passcodes. For example, if you allow only letters and the password length is one character, the password space is the set of letters from A to Z. (It may be 26 or 52, depending on whether you distinguish between uppercase and lowercase.) The password space may include some passwords that are not acceptable. A good password system has a very large space of acceptable passwords. The space should be large enough to make a brute-force attack unprofitable. (A *brute-force attack* occurs when the attacker breaks the system by trying all possible passwords. Discovering the password through a search of all passwords should cost more than the value of the information being protected.)

Composition is the set of acceptable characters that you can use in a valid passcode. The password composition is affected by the way you enter it, the way you store it, and the way the system verifies it.

When creating your passcode, generate it randomly to minimize the possibility that someone can guess it. You can derive passcodes by transforming a chosen expression, as shown in Table 8-1.

Table 8-1	Passcode Transformations	
Transform	**Illustrative Expression**	**Resultant Passcode**
Transliteration	photograph, schizophrenic	FOTOGRAF, SKITSOFRENIK
Interweaving of characters in successive words (or numbers)	database, Peter Davis	DBAATSAE, PDEATVEIRS
Interweaving vowels and consonants	password	PASESIWORUD
Translation	strangers	ETRANGES
Replacement of letter by decimal digit (modulus-10 index of letter in natural order)	babbage	2122175
Replacement of decimal number by letter (with corresponding position, in natural order)	10/12/1492	JABADIB
Insertion of a special character	Barry Lewis, database	BARRY$LEWIS, DATA&BASE
Shift from "home" position on the keyboard	personal, computer	OWEAIBIK, XINOYRWE

(continued)

Table 8-1 *(continued)*

Transform	Illustrative Expression	Resultant Passcode
Actuation of keyboard 'shift'	6/6/1944, 1/1/2000	^?^?!($$, !?!?@)))
Substitution of synonyms	coffee break	JAVAREST
Substitution of antonyms	stoplight	GODARK
Substitution of abbreviations	relative humidity	RELHUM
Use of initials	Internal Revenue Service, Security Audit & Control	IRSSAC
Repetition	tom	TOMTOM
Imagistic manipulation (180 rotation of letters)	swimshow	SMIWSHOM

Of course, *crackers* (those nasty individuals trying to break into your systems) have a copy of these transformations, and you can bet that they will try them — so be careful how you use this list!

Avoid the following passcodes:

- ✔ Words in the dictionary
- ✔ First and last names
- ✔ Street and city names
- ✔ Valid license plate numbers
- ✔ Room numbers, Social Security numbers, social insurance numbers, and telephone numbers
- ✔ Beer and liquor brand names
- ✔ Athletic team names
- ✔ Days of the week and months of the year
- ✔ Repetitive characters
- ✔ Software default passwords

For example, never use passwords such as the following:

- ✔ **peter:** It's based on a user's name.
- ✔ **blewis:** Again, it's based on a user's name.
- ✔ **retep:** A user's name, backwards.

 ✔ **qwerty:** A common keyboard sequence.

 ✔ **asdfgh:** A common keyboard sequence, shifted one key down.

 ✔ **aaaaaa:** Repetitive characters.

 ✔ **password, secret, keepout:** Hey, these are the first ones we'd try.

 ✔ **plane1:** Dictionary word with a random number appended.

 ✔ **1plane:** Dictionary word with a random character prepended.

 ✔ **gandalf:** Nice try, but it was in Robert Morris Jr.'s list of passwords. (See Chapter 11 for more information.)

You probably think that by eliminating certain passcodes, you're reducing the password space. Obviously, you are, but is it a concern? How many possible passwords exist? Sooner or later, most people want to know the answer to this question — worried that password brute-force attacks eventually work, given advances in computer programming and processing power. Well, assume that

 ✔ You use 62 characters (A to Z [capitalized], a to z [lowercase], and 0 to 9) to create your passwords; and

 ✔ All passwords have more than five and fewer than eight characters.

Then the size of the valid password space is 222,000,000,000,000, or more than 8,000 passwords for every man, woman, and child in the United States, or approximately 400 passwords for every person on Earth. (A figure far too large to undertake in a realistic, exhaustive brute-force attack with current technologies.) Don't forget, however, that you can make up passcodes with even more characters; you can use a <space>, punctuation marks, and symbols (~<>|\#$%^&*), too. Using the 95 noncontrol characters in passwords increases the search space for a cracker even further.

Sufficient length

Length is closely associated with passcode strength. The length of a passcode determines the potential security of your data. A passcode length of one reduces the potential passcode space to the number of characters in the composition set — for example, 0 to 9 for numeric and A to Z for alphabetic characters. How long do you think cracking a one-character password with a Pentium computer would take? About one nanosecond? But what is a nanosecond? A nanosecond is the length of time it takes New York cabbies to honk after the light turns green. Now that's fast!

Increasing the length of a random passcode can make it drastically more difficult to discover. With each additional character, both the number of possible combinations and the average time required to find the passcode increases exponentially. A length of two characters squares the number, a length of three cubes the number, and so on. However, passcodes made up of truly random combinations are harder to remember as they increase in length. See Table 8-2 to see the effect of passcode length on randomness.

Table 8-2	How Passcode Length Relates to Time to Detect	
Number of Characters	*Possible Combinations (Rounded Up)*	*Average Time to Discover (Rounded)*
1	36	6 minutes
2	1,300	4 hours
3	47,000	5 days
4	1,700,000	6 months
5	60,000,000	19 years
6	2,000,000,000	630 years
7	78,000,000,000	25,000 years
8	2,800,000,000,000	890,000 years
9	100,000,000,000,000	32,000,000 years
10	3,700,000,000,000,000	1,200,000,000 years

Using combinations of seven letters and numbers (exactly 78,364,164,096) gives you enough characters for more than 314 passwords for every man, woman, and child in the United States.

Even a computer that would enable the attacker to test 1 million passcodes per second would require, on average, close to 60 years to figure out a random 10-character passcode. However, say that the passcode is not random but is a 10-letter word from a 60,000-word spell checker; then the attacker could figure out the passcode in an average of only 7 days. A significant difference from 1.2 billion years!

Reasonable time period

You can improve passcode security by changing the passcode frequently to minimize compromise. *Lifetime* is the time during which a passcode is valid — in other words, how long you should keep the passcode. The useful lifetime of a passcode depends on the following issues:

✔ Cost of passcode changes; creating good passcodes and changing old passcodes takes time.

✔ Risk associated with information disclosure, which you need to calculate. (Refer to Chapter 5 if you forget how to calculate this factor.)

✔ Probability of guessing the passcode — for example, if the passcode is in a dictionary.

✔ Number of times you use the passcode.

✔ Susceptibility of passcode to a brute-force attack.

You should change your passcodes regularly to reduce the risk of compromise. The passcode's lifetime should fit both your security and operational requirements. The maximum period for passcode usage should not exceed one year. However, you should keep your password for only 30 days if you really want to be safe.

Entering a Password Securely

Entering a passcode securely is often a difficult task. Observers can easily detect passcodes as you enter those codes into an automated authentication system. Unauthorized individuals can "shoulder surf," or steal access codes by reading the numbers or letters over your shoulder. Do you ever get nervous when someone is standing too closely to you at the automated banking machine? You should get nervous when entering your calling card PIN at either Penn Station or Grand Central Station in New York. A devious criminal with binoculars may be watching you enter that PIN to record and sell it!

You should enter passcodes into an automated authentication system only if you can prevent their compromise. If the passcode system echoes the passcode, this echo should be destroyed before or immediately after turning the passcode into human readable form. In other words, the passcode you just entered should not be visible to the world.

A password system should not enable snoopers or crackers to try as many passwords as they want. The system should effectively prevent anyone from guessing a passcode through trial and error. Most systems prevent you from entering passcodes ad infinitum (in a brute-force attack).

Secrecy

Ownership is the authorized possession of a passcode. Individual accountability is essential to any secure passcode system and is tied to ownership. The reason a password is associated with an access code is to provide accountability. If your access code is used with your password, you are accountable for anything done by using your account. Normally, you shouldn't share your passcodes. If you do, you must change the password as soon as you can so that the other person doesn't know your password anymore. Sharing passcodes makes accountability difficult to prove. In other words, don't tell anyone your passcode. You may be tempted to provide your passcode to your significant other, but overcome the temptation.

You should select your passcode randomly from the acceptable passcode space. If the passcode originates from someone or somewhere else, such as America Online, you should change the passcode immediately. To ensure accountability, only you should know the passcode.

Storing Passwords

Maintain passcodes within your computer system so that they are protected from disclosure or change. The passcode system should control passwords securely. Specifically, the system must store and maintain the authentication list in a manner that prevents unauthorized access. This level of security may involve the encryption of the passcodes while residing on your system or during transmission. Chapter 14 covers encryption.

Transmitting Passwords

Transmission is the communication of a passcode from its point of origin for comparison with a valid stored passcode. The transmission may be just from your keyboard to your memory space; typically, you use passcodes to authenticate yourself when accessing the network. To authenticate the passcode, you send it to the file server over the network. Unless the system physically protects the line or encrypts the passcode, the passcode is vulnerable to discovery during transmission.

Password Do's and Don'ts

Table 8-3 offers some passcode guidelines that you should use, regardless of the access control system.

Table 8-3	Password Do's and Don'ts
Don't	*Do*
Select easily guessed passcodes.	Use unpronounceable words or phrases.
Write down your passcode.	Use an easy-to-remember passcode.
Share your passcode.	Keep your passcode secret.
Include your passcode in any file.	Hide your passcode.
Use your passcode forever.	Change your passcode frequently.

Don't	Do
Trust anyone else with your passcode.	Change your passcode if it's compromised.
Use the same passcode on multiple systems.	Use different passcodes for different systems.

Now review the list of *don'ts*. As we mentioned earlier, words from a dictionary are easy to guess; avoid them. Comparing your password file to a standard dictionary probably would result in guessing at least one in four passwords. This method is the way most crackers obtain passcodes. Fortunately, software exists that can help users derive strong passcodes — for example, Password Coach from Baseline Software. This software helps you to select strong passcodes, while learning what makes a good code.

Bank campaigns stress to customers the need to avoid writing their personal identification numbers on their cards. Yet bank investigators can tell you that this practice accounts for most automated banking machine "fraud." Because you know that this is human nature, you should never write down your passcodes.

Most communications software packages for microcomputers enable you to develop scripts to access remote systems. These scripts automate repetitive commands, but they can — and frequently do — include access codes and their corresponding passcodes. The major online service providers enable you to store your passcode so that you don't have to enter it every time. A periodic review of files on microcomputers can pinpoint these security lapses.

One last comment on passcodes. Some security practitioners feel that passcodes shouldn't be pronounceable. The advantage to this approach is that a dictionary attack would not work. However, you are more likely to write down an unpronounceable passcode. Personally, we don't agree with enforcing unpronounceable passcodes. Passcodes created by a transformation, for example, could be pronounceable but extremely difficult to guess.

Power-on Passwords: "More Power, Scotty! I Must Have More Power!"

Power-on password sounds like some '60s thing, doesn't it? "Power, brothers and sisters!" (For those who may be nostalgic for the '60s, get real! This is a computer book.)

The power-on password involves the power-on switch on your computer and a password. By now, you know all about passwords. The power switch, however, is another thing. Where is it? Would you believe us when we say that we don't know? When we walk up to a computer, we have to search for the switch, just like you. In truth, the power switch may not even be a switch, but a button or a keyboard key.

The point is that you can find these switches almost anywhere on a machine. Peter's Toshiba laptop has the power switch on the left side, near the front. Barry's Commodore laptop has the power switch on the inside, near the upper-right side of the keyboard. On Peter's Compaq laptop, the power button is above the keyboard, after you pop open the screen. Newer Macintosh desktops have a power-on key on an extended keyboard.

Now that you've found the switch, turn it on. Nothing happens? On most PCs, you have the option to set up a password that you must key in before the power-up sequence continues, rendering the machine useless to someone if the password is unknown. At least, that's what you may think.

How do power-on passwords work?

Most machines provide an option that you can turn on to prevent people from turning on your system. Toshiba and IBM are two vendors that provide power-on passwords for security.

The Toshiba 400 series enables you to set two passwords: a Supervisor password and a user password. Neat. This system is one step up from most machines, which offer only one password. You can use the Supervisor password to provide access for the owner of the system — system administrators or possibly technical support staff. In addition, this setup enables you to remove access to certain machine settings from someone. You can use the user password for the person who uses the machine on a day-to-day basis. In this manner, you can use power-on passwords, while minimizing some of the difficulties that can occur if an individual forgets his or her password, because the supervisor can reset it.

Additionally, you can create a password diskette for gaining access. Be careful with this option, however, as possession of the diskette dictates who has machine access. If you use a diskette, don't leave it lying on the desk next to the machine — lock it up! And we don't mean in a high-security device such as a diskette caddy. (It sometimes seems as if those plastic diskette storage devices [caddies] have only one key!)

IBM Thinkpad laptops also have power-on passwords. But IBM goes one step farther and adds a hard drive password. After you turn on the machine, you must enter two passwords before gaining access. You can override the power-on password by using the methods discussed later in this chapter, but the hard drive password is encrypted and pretty secure from attack. Of course, if you forget the password, you lose your data. The drive is useless; you have to low-level format it and start again. Not a pretty thought.

If you forget the password and have no password disk, contact your vendor and beg to regain access to your machine. Be sure that you have some method of identifying the machine as yours, such as the bill of sale.

Should you use power-on passwords?

Power-on passwords are bound to be controversial. If we say that you shouldn't use them, some security professionals scream that we're wrong. If we say that you should use them, other experts voice strong disagreement. So what are we to do?

We believe it was Shakespeare who wrote in *Henry V,* "Once more into the breach, dear friends . . ." or something like that.

We don't generally support the use of power-on passwords. There, we've said it. Why? Because they provide a false sense of security. Yes, using them forces anyone who wants to use the machine to know the password before gaining access. And you add a few minutes to the time someone takes to break into the machine, which may be sufficient for your needs. However, a bunch of fundamental issues with the power-on password approach exist.

First and foremost, on most machines, the password is easy to bypass. Without getting into a cracker's dream and promoting methods, we just mention that removing the CMOS chip or shorting out an internal battery eliminates the password. How do you think the companies that use power-on passwords overcome problems with users who forget the darn password? Using this method as a means of protection from any determined threat is out. On the other hand, such a password provides a small degree of protection against a casual attempt to access your machine. If your notebook or workstation is stolen, however, whatever is on it is available to the thief, regardless of your power-on password.

Problem number two is that many individuals and companies operate under the false assumption that their computers are safe. A false assumption of security can be worse than no security at all. Why? Because people are less careful if they believe that the computer is safe. If someone tells you that no security exists and that you must be careful, you are more likely to react positively. If you must enter a password each time you power-on the machine, you may believe that security is adequate, so you don't need to do anything more.

This protection against casual unauthorized access may be enough for your home or office computer. But think about it carefully. Determine what you are attempting to secure, how likely the threat is, and what the ramifications of unauthorized access are. Reread Chapter 5 if you forget about risk management. If the data on your machine is important, use a reasonably secure tool to protect it, such as those described in Chapters 7 and 10.

Finally, how do you manage these passwords? Many homes have two computers, and a few have even more. What do you do when you forget the password? Does each person set her own password, rendering the machine useless whenever she is unavailable, as no one else knows the password? Do you keep a central inventory of each machine, its user, and the associated password? Do you ever change the passwords? The longer passwords remain in use, the more likely they are to be compromised. How often have you given someone the password so that they could access the machine? Did you change the password afterward? Based on our experience, you probably haven't changed the password since day one, when you created it. So how many people know it now?

If you insist on using power-on passwords, change them on the same schedule as all your other passwords. Ideally, that's every 30, 60, or 90 days. The more often, the better (within reason).

Logging in when you forget your password

This chapter was difficult to write. How do we draw the line between informing valid users and giving information to those who may subvert that information? We chose to follow the safer path and provide some broad guidelines rather than specific nitty-gritty details.

In almost all the machines we reviewed, you can try to gain access until the cows come home. Some machines may take longer; after three attempts, you have to turn the machine off and back on again. But when you are alone in the room, time isn't as critical. Merely guessing the password is always a viable option. This scheme is the brute-force method — trying all possible passwords until you get a match. (Except for those of you who read this book and take our advice on creating passwords. You make it too difficult for someone to guess your password, don't you?)

Unfortunately, when someone steals your machine, gaining access is almost trivial. On most machines, you can disable the CMOS or drain the battery to gain access. On the Toshiba, with its neat two-party-passwords, just drain the main battery and let the rest of the special little batteries drain naturally. (This process takes some time.) The machine begs you to plug in the cord and power it up — without passwords. Of course, you also must set up the machine's hardware BIOS.

The Last (Pass)Word

Why are passwords, passnumbers, and passcodes so important? Because they are the first line of defense against interactive attacks on your system. Simply stated, if a cracker can't interact with your computer, and he has no access to read or write the information contained in the password file, he has almost no avenues of attack left open to break your system.

The only way to get a reasonable amount of variety in your passwords is to make them up. Work out some flexible method of your own that isn't based on any of the following systems:

- ✔ Modifying any part of your name or initials
- ✔ Modifying a dictionary word
- ✔ Acronyms
- ✔ Any systematic algorithm

Now you know how to create a strong passcode that withstands all but the most determined attacks. (We hope you aren't trying to keep the National Security Agency off your system.)

We believe so strongly in password-control systems that we identify some Windows and Macintosh password programs (freeware and shareware) in Chapters 17 and 18. Take one out for a test drive today.

Chapter 9
Securing Word Processors, Spreadsheets, and Databases

. . . .

In This Chapter

▶ Using application security features

▶ Securing word processors

▶ Securing those lovable spreadsheets

▶ Securing databases

▶ Securing other applications

▶ Forgetting those passwords

. . . .

*E*veryone who uses word processors, spreadsheets, and database products has probably thought about using the security that these products offer. Is the security inherent in these products any good?

In this chapter, we discuss which products offer security features and whether you can use that security to safeguard your files.

Using Built-In Security Features

Many software packages have some level of built-in security. For the most part, this security is limited to file access, typically through the use of a password on the file in question.

This type of control can be very useful for basic protection. For example, when you go on vacation and leave your house in the care of friends or family members, how do you ensure that they do not pry into your personal files? You can lock your filing cabinets, right? But you've probably lost the keys to your computer, haven't you?

Using application-based security, you can rest assured that your files are reasonably safe from prying eyes. However, if your brother or sister is a computer nerd, then lock up the room and secure your machine with chains and padlocks.

If you are unsure whether a software package has any type of built-in security, click on the application's Help icon or menu and search for the term *security* or *password.* In most cases, this action displays whether any built-in security features are available for that application.

Word Processing Security

In this section, we provide you with tons and tons of the really cool security stuff that word processors provide.

Microsoft Word Versions 5, 6, and 7

You can password-protect a Microsoft Word file in two ways:

- ✔ **File access:** Prevents other users from accessing or reading a file without the password.

- ✔ **Write access:** Allows people to open and see the file information but not to change it. Cool!

  (Remember, however, that restricting file access and write access does not prevent someone from deleting a file by using the Mac Finder or the Windows File Manager.)

Word accomplishes this file protection by *encrypting* (scrambling) the file and *decrypting* (unscrambling) the file after you enter the proper password.

Microsoft Word passwords contain any combination of letters, numbers, spaces, and symbols and are up to 15 characters long. The password is *case sensitive,* which means that, if you enter a password with capital letters, you must continue to use those capitals, or Word cannot recognize the password.

Adding a password to a Word document file

To password-protect a Word document file, follow these steps:

1. **Open the file that you want to password-protect.**

2. **Choose File⇨Save As.**

   Word gives you the password option when you save a file. You can save the file under a new filename or keep the original filename.

If you don't want anyone to see the file, save your file with the original filename. Saving the document with a new filename leaves the old, unsecured file out there for all to see.

3. **Click on the Options button, the Windows version of which is shown in Figure 9-1.**

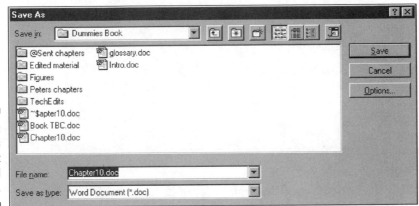

Figure 9-1: Word allows you to set special options.

4. **Select and enter a password in the Protection Password field. (See Figure 9-2.)**

   You can use this option to provide reasonable protection for a file. (You can't fully trust this protection because certain programs are available that can find your password. Look for a list of some of these programs in Chapters 17 and 18.) After you create the password, you must use the same password to access that file.

   If you enter a password in the Write Reservation Password field, other people can view the file but can't write data to it or change the file without the correct password. This option can be useful if you create form documents that you want people to copy but not modify. Word allows other people to create a new copy of the document by supplying a different filename when saving this Write Reservation-protected file.

5. **Click on the OK button.**

   Word asks you to verify the password by making you type it once more. When you click on the OK button again, if the two passwords match, your password is set and confirmed.

When typing a new password, some people mis-key, think that they typed something else, or press an extra key without noticing. Making you enter the password twice is a neat way of making sure that there are no mistakes.

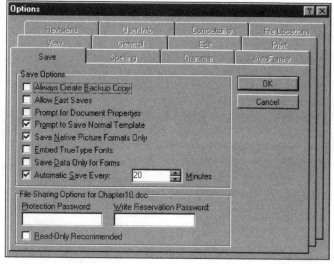

Removing a password from a Word document file

To remove a password from a Word document and make the file freely accessible, follow these steps:

1. **Open the file that contains the password you want to remove.**

2. **Choose File⇨Save As.**

3. **Click on the Options button.**

   You see the file's password displayed in the Protection Password field as a string of asterisks.

4. **Select the password and press Delete; then click on the OK button.**

   This step saves the file again without a password.

✔ If you give someone the password to a document, that person can change the password and prevent you from getting access to that file. Or that person can even remove the password. A password is really only useful if you are the only one who knows and uses it.

✔ Word provides a number of other opportunities for protecting your documents. For example, you can protect parts of a document by using the Tools⇨Protect Document command. Word 7 users can do a search on *security* and *passwords* in the Help Answer Wizard and follow the advice it gives. If you use Word 6, search for *password* by using the Help function.

✔ If you have earlier versions of Word and are unsure whether password security is present or how it works, use the Word Help command, search for the term *password,* and follow the advice you're given.

Adding a password to a document in Word 5 for the Mac

To password-protect a Mac Word file, follow these steps:

1. **Open the file that you want to password-protect.**

2. **Choose File⇨Save As.**

   Word gives you the password option when you save a file. You can save the file under a new filename or keep the original filename.

3. **Click on the Options button.**

4. **Select and enter a password in the Protection Password field.**

   You can enter a password in the Write Reservation Password field so that other people can view the file but can't write data to it or change the file without the correct password. This option is useful if you create form documents that you want people to copy but not modify. Word does allow you to create a new copy of the document by supplying a different filename when saving this Write Reservation-protected file.

5. **Click on the OK button.**

   Word asks you to verify the password by making you type it once more. Should you accept this mission, your password is set and confirmed if the two passwords match when you click on the OK button again.

When typing a new password, some people mis-key, think that they typed something else, or press an extra key without noticing. Making you enter the password twice is a neat way of making sure that you made no mistakes.

Removing a password from a Mac Word document

To remove a password from a Mac Word document and make the file as free as a bird, follow these steps:

1. **Open the file that contains the password you want to remove.**

2. **Choose File⇨Save As.**

3. **Click on the Options button.**

   You see the file's password displayed in the Password Protection field as a string of asterisks.

4. **Select the password and press Delete; then click on the OK button.**

   This step saves the file again without a password.

Users of Mac Word 5 can do a search on *security* and *passwords* in the Help Answer Wizard and follow the advice that it gives. If you use older versions of Word, search for *password*.

Corel WordPerfect 6.x

Although Corel bought WordPerfect from Novell, WordPerfect is still a tried-and-true word processing application. The security features shown in this section work with WordPerfect Versions 6.0, 6.0a, and 6.1. Password security is also available in 5.x versions. The WordPerfect Help command provides advice about earlier versions.

Like in Microsoft Word (mentioned earlier in this chapter), security in WordPerfect also consists of file password protection. WordPerfect also encrypts the file when you add a password and decrypts the file only if you supply the correct password.

Password protection is not available on older 4.2 versions. If you try to save a 6.1 password-protected file in 4.2 format, WordPerfect removes the password. WordPerfect also removes the password if you save the file in a non-WordPerfect format such as .TXT.

Adding a password to a WordPerfect document file

To password-protect a WordPerfect file, follow these steps:

1. **Open the file that you want to password-protect.**

2. **Choose File⇨Save As.**

   WordPerfect gives you the password option when you save a file. You can save the file under a new filename or keep the original filename.

   If you don't want anyone to see the file, save your file with the original filename. Saving the document with a new filename leaves the old, unsecured file out there for all to see.

3. **Click on the Password Protect field, as shown in Figure 9-3.**

4. **Click on the OK button. WordPerfect displays the Password Protection dialog box, as shown in Figure 9-4.**

5. **Type a password in the Type Password for Document field and click on the OK button.**

   WordPerfect asks you to verify the password by making you type it once more. When you click on the OK button again, if the two passwords match, your password is set and confirmed.

Removing a password from a WordPerfect document file

To remove a password from a WordPerfect document and make the file freely accessible, follow these steps:

1. **Open the file that contains the password you want to remove.**

2. **Choose File⇨Save As.**

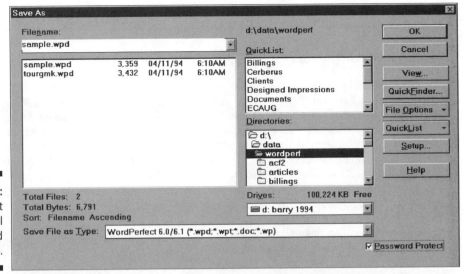

Figure 9-3:
WordPerfect
has a small
password
check field.

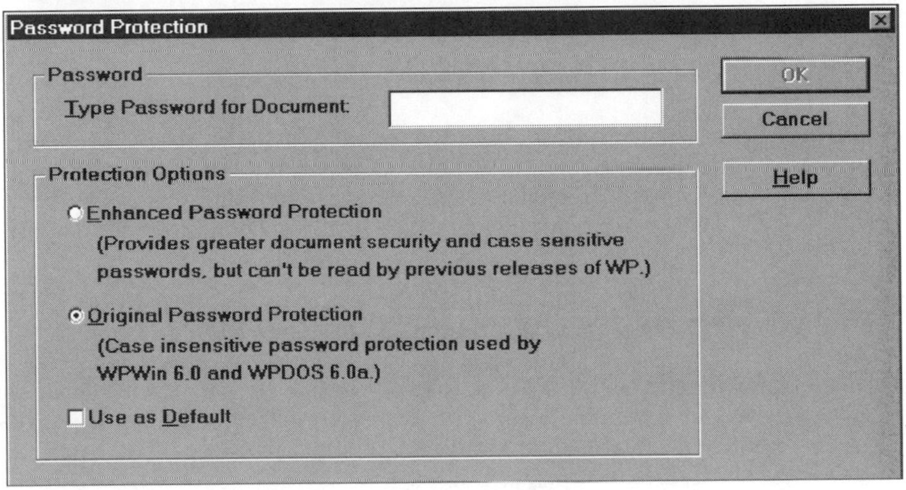

Figure 9-4:
WordPerfect
password
options
appear.

3. Click on the Password Protection field and make sure that it is deselected.

This step tells WordPerfect to save the file again without a password.

4. Click on the OK button and then click on the Yes button to replace the file.

WordPerfect removes password protection from the file.

File security can be useful for occasional file access or for protecting sensitive data from casual viewing. It does not prevent someone from deleting the file.

WordPerfect encryption

WordPerfect gives you a choice of using either Enhanced Password protection or Original Password protection. The Enhanced password option provides better security and improved password capability, such as the capability to use lowercase and uppercase letters. In both cases, WordPerfect encrypts your file so that no one can read it without using the password you assigned. However, Version 6.1 provides better encryption than the earlier versions and lets you decide whether to use this enhanced level of encryption. If you do, the file cannot be read on earlier versions of WordPerfect even with the correct password. For most purposes, Original Password Protection is sufficient. This enhanced level of encryption is implemented to counter claims by expert cryptographers (super technical people who use their mathematical genius to make and break encryption software) that the techniques used in the early versions of WordPerfect were too easy to break.

We guess that they were right, because we provide information about some of the programs that can discover your secret passwords in Chapters 17 and 18.

Spreadsheet Security

Spreadsheets like Microsoft Excel and Quattro Pro also have security options that you can use. These options are especially useful if you do financial work such as home or small business budgets. Typically, you don't want neighbors taking a peek at your financial files when they borrow your computer.

Microsoft Excel Versions 6 and 7

Microsoft Excel allows you to assign password protection to your spreadsheets. Like the word processors, Excel uses an encryption technique to guard the file and make it unreadable without the proper password.

As with the word processors mentioned earlier in this chapter, you can password-protect your Excel file in the following ways:

- **File access:** Prevents other users from accessing or reading a file without the proper password.
- **Write access:** Allows people to open and view the spreadsheet file information but not to change it.

For more-detailed guidance and for other options that are available, don't forget to select the Help Answer Wizard and look up the word *passwords* or *security*.

Adding a password to an Excel spreadsheet file

To password-protect an Excel spreadsheet file, follow these really neat steps:

1. **Open the file that you want to password-protect.**

2. **Choose File⇨Save As.**

   Excel gives you the password option when you save a file. You can save the file under a new filename or keep the original filename.

   If you don't want anyone to see the file, save your file with the original filename. Saving the document with a new filename leaves the old, unsecured file out there for all to see.

3. **Click on the Options button.**

4. **Select and enter a password in the Protection Password field. (See Figure 9-5.)**

   You can use this field to protect a file completely. After you create a password, you must use the same password each time to access that file.

   If you enter a password in the Write Reservation Password field, other people can view the file but cannot write data to it or change the file without the correct password. This option can be useful if you create form documents that you want people to copy but not modify. Excel allows other people to create a new workbook document by supplying a different filename when saving this Write Reservation-protected file.

5. **Click on the OK button.**

   Excel asks you to verify the password that you selected by making you type it once more. When you click on the OK button again, if the two passwords match, Excel confirms that you know the password that you originally typed.

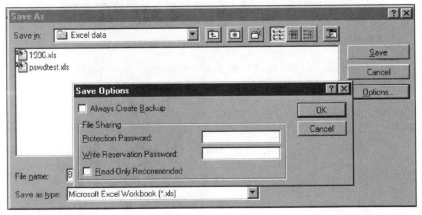

Figure 9-5:
Excel
password
options.

Removing a password from an Excel spreadsheet file

1. **Open the Excel spreadsheet file that contains the password you want to remove.**

2. **Choose File⇨Save As.**

3. **Click on the Options button.**

   You see the current password displayed as a string of asterisks in the Protection Password field.

4. **Select the password and press Delete; then click on the OK button.**

   This step saves the file again without a password.

Microsoft Excel 5 for the Mac

Excel 5 for the Mac allows you to assign password protection to your spreadsheets just like its Windows counterpart. Excel uses an encryption technique to guard the file and make it unreadable without the proper password.

As with the word processors mentioned earlier in the chapter, you can password-protect your Excel file in the following ways:

 ✔ **File access:** Prevents other users from accessing or reading a file without the proper password.

 ✔ **Write access:** Allows people to open and view the spreadsheet file information but not to change it.

For more-detailed guidance and for other options that are available, don't forget to select the Help option and look up the word *passwords* or *security*.

Adding a password to a spreadsheet file in Mac Excel 5

To password-protect a Mac Excel spreadsheet file, follow these really neat steps:

1. **Open the file that you want to password-protect.**

2. **Choose File⇨Save As.**

   Excel gives you the password option when you save a file. You can save the file under a new filename or keep the original filename.

   Remember, if you don't want anyone to see the file, save your file with the original filename, replacing your old file with this password protected file. Saving the document with a new filename leaves the old, unsecured file out there for all to see.

3. **Click on the Options button.**

4. **Select and enter a password in the Protection Password field.**

   After you create a password, use the same password each time to access that file.

   Just like Windows-based software, (Hmmm, who's copying whom here?) if you enter a password in the Write Reservation Password field, other people can view the file but cannot write data to it or change the file without the correct password. This option is useful if you create spreadsheets that you want people to copy but not modify. Excel still allows you to create a new workbook document by supplying a different filename when saving this Write Reservation-protected file.

5. **Click on the OK button.**

   Excel asks you to verify the password that you selected by making you type it once more. When you click on the OK button again, if the two passwords match, Excel confirms that you're a genius because you know the password that you originally typed.

Removing a password from a Mac Excel 5 spreadsheet file

1. **Open the Excel spreadsheet file that contains the password you want to remove.**

2. **Choose File⇨Save As.**

3. **Click on thc Options button.**

   You see the current password displayed as a string of asterisks in the Protection Password field.

4. **Select the password and press Delete; then click on the OK button.**

   This step saves the file again without a password.

Don't reinvent the wheel

Excel password protection works in the same manner as Microsoft Word password protection. This is Windows software at its best — no reinventing the wheel. Like Word, Excel passwords can contain any combination of letters, numbers, spaces, and symbols and can be up to 15 characters long. The password is considered case sensitive, which means that, if you enter a password with capital letters, you must continue to use those capitals or Excel cannot recognize the password.

Corel Quattro Pro 6.x

This popular spreadsheet also provides password protection through file encryption. As with the Microsoft software mentioned earlier in the chapter, Quattro Pro follows the WordPerfect format closely. This setup makes sense, because you can purchase both products as part of the PerfectOffice suite (just like Microsoft Office comes with both Word and Excel).

Adding a password to a Quattro Pro spreadsheet file

To password-protect a Quattro Pro spreadsheet file, follow these steps:

1. **Open the file that you want to password-protect.**

2. **Choose File⇨Save As.**

   Quattro Pro gives you the password option when you save a file. You can save the file under a new filename or keep the original filename.

   If you don't want anyone to see the file, save your file with the original filename. Saving the document with a new filename leaves the old, unsecured file out there for all to see.

3. **Click on the small Password Protect field.**

4. **Click on the OK button.**

   Quattro Pro displays a Password field. (See Figure 9-6.)

   The software gives you a field in which to type your selected password.

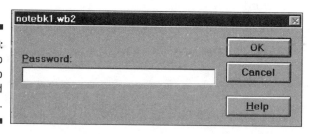

Figure 9-6: The Quattro Pro Password field.

5. **Type a password and click on the OK button.**

   Quattro Pro asks you to verify the password by making you type it once more. When you click on the OK button again, if the two passwords match, the program assumes that you know the password that you originally typed.

Removing a password from a Quattro Pro spreadsheet file

To remove a password from a Quattro Pro spreadsheet file and make the file freely accessible, you follow a slightly different path:

1. **Open the file that contains the password you want to remove.**

2. **Right-click on the notebook header bar.**

   This header bar typically contains the filename just above the cells A to Z. You see a small window with options.

3. **Select the Password Level option.**

   You see a series of Password level options with High selected. (See Figure 9-7.)

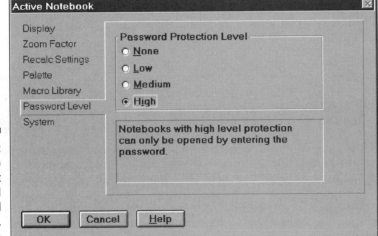

Figure 9-7:
The Quattro
Pro current
Password
Level
setting.

4. **Click on the None radio button.**

   This step turns off password protection for the file.

5. **Save the file.**

   You no longer need a password.

Quattro Pro provides a number of additional levels of security that you can apply to each worksheet. These range from None, Low, Medium, and High security and provide varying levels of protection. For example, the Low level lets anyone see the worksheet data but not any of the formulas being used. Use the Help command and look up *password* for more-detailed information about these options.

Other spreadsheets

Most modern spreadsheets offer some form of security. Both Lotus 1-2-3 and Lotus Symphony, for example, allow users to create passwords on their spread-sheets in a manner similar to those just shown.

Older versions usually offer password security, but you must implement it by using different techniques, especially in the DOS versions of these applications, because they do not provide the easier Windows look and feel. If you use a version that is too old, you are unlikely to find protection. As we consistently state throughout this chapter, if in doubt, check your product Help file by using the word *security* or *password.*

Database Security

Several popular database products are available, including Microsoft Access, dBASE, Paradox, and FoxPro.

Each product offers varying levels of password protection.

dBASE 5 for Windows

This popular Windows package from Borland does not appear to offer file-level password protection. You can lock individual records to prevent their inadvertent update, but the product does not supply any file-level encryption.

If you want to secure a dBASE5 file, consider using Pretty Good Privacy (PGP) or PKZIP. You can find both programs on the Internet in a number of places. Use one of the search programs mentioned in Appendix A.

Microsoft Access

Microsoft Access is another popular database product. It has a ton of security features embedded, mostly for use on a network of computers. Microsoft Access provides for many fundamental controls, such as user identification and authentication and authorization and audit. Way too much security for us! (Just kidding. However, there is too much information for this book.)

Access does let you encrypt the database so that only authorized users can use it. Follow these steps:

1. **Obtain the Security Wizard from Microsoft (or in the Excel forum on CompuServe).**

2. **Run the Security Wizard.**

   This program sets up a bunch of security stuff for you.

The mysteries of database encryption

Database encryption is used to prevent someone who is using a file or disk editor (such as PC Tools or Norton Utilities) from reading and writing data in your .MDB files. When you use database encryption, everything in the .MDB file is encrypted, including tables, queries, forms, indexes, and so on. Microsoft Access uses the RSA algorithm for database encryption. This algorithm is considered virtually unbreakable.

Our best advice for you is to visit the Microsoft Access Forum on CompuServe and look for the Security section. A wealth of information is available. In particular, we recommend that you download the file called SECFAQ20.ZIP and another one called WX0964.EXE. These files contain a wealth of detailed information for securing Microsoft Access.

3. **Encrypt the database by choosing File⇨Encrypt/Decrypt Database and selecting your database with the Encrypt option.**

   In order for this to appear on the File menu, choose the commands before opening any databases.

After you encrypt your Microsoft Access database, it is safe from casual access attempts. To protect yourself more completely, you need to take a number of other steps. See the following sidebar for additional information.

Other Applications with Built-In Security

One of the more common products that many home users employ is a money manager application such as Quicken or Simply Money. Both products offer file-level password protection using some type of encryption to scramble the file. To unscramble it, you must have the correct password.

Quicken for Windows Versions 4 and 5

This popular package contains security options that enable you to protect your financial files from snoopy neighbors and inquisitive in-laws.

In these packages, you may become quickly confused if you try to use the Help function and search for the word *security.* In finance, security takes on a whole new meaning! Search for *password* instead, and you find a whole bunch of password help files. Start with the one called File Password (Definition) and work from there to get more information.

Adding a password to a Quicken file

To set a file password in Quicken, follow these steps:

1. **Choose File⇨Passwords⇨File.**

   This command enables you to set a new file password. As you can see, you can also set passwords on transactions, but that task is for a later book.

2. **Type a password in the dialog field that appears.**

3. **Retype the password in the next dialog field when Quicken prompts you to do so.**

4. **Close Quicken.**

   When you next open the account, Quicken prompts you to enter your password, as shown in Figure 9-8.

Figure 9-8:
The Quicken Password field.

Removing a password from a Quicken file

To remove a password, perform the following steps:

1. **Open the file with the password you want to remove.**

2. **Choose File⇨Passwords⇨File.**

   Because the file already contains a password, you are presented with a slightly different dialog box this time. (See Figure 9-9.)

Figure 9-9:
The Quicken Change Password dialog box.

3. **Type the current password in the area specified for Old Password.**

   Leave the New Password field blank.

4. **Close Quicken.**

   The next time you open Quicken, you are not prompted for a password.

We wish that we had room for more product demonstrations; however, space is limited, and our editors are ruthless in keeping us from producing a 10,000-page book. (Thank goodness. Can you imagine 10,000 pages of security? All our readers would become paranoid.)

Mac Television

And now something a little different. Mac users likely know about the special card you can purchase and install in your Mac that lets you watch television all day instead of doing productive work. (The same type of card is available for all the IBM-compatible computers as well.) It works really well when you hook it up to your cable television company.

Peter has one of these cards on his Mac and uses it to watch shows that he otherwise might miss when he works late. The software that controls the television lets you put passwords on certain channels so that those channels cannot be received unless you enter the password. We bet you think that the V-Chip is the latest protection device for television, don't you?

Like any other password-protection scheme, what happens if you forget the channel password? Throw out the card and buy a new one? Watch all the other channels and ignore the one whose password you cannot remember? Or be one of the smartest people on your block and buy this book? We vote for the latter, of course.

You can recover your passwords if you forget them. Just follow these steps:

1. **Open the System Folder.**

   Make sure that you're not using the television.

2. **Locate and click on the Preferences folder.**

3. **Find the file called TV Preferences and drag it to the Trash folder.**

That's it! The password is gone. Toast. History.

When you next open the television, the program creates a new Preferences file without any channel passwords. Enter new passwords if you still want to, and this time, make sure that you remember them.

By the way, don't let your children see this section of the book, or they will realize how easy it is to bypass your Mac television password controls.

Retrieving Those Forgotten Passwords

What do you do when you forget a password? In many cases, you lose access to that file and have to re-create it. So don't forget your passwords!

This next sentence is heresy for true security persons, but what the heck, we know how to live dangerously. If you must, write your passwords down and lock up the paper you write them on. After all, going through the motions of setting up security is no good if you forget your passwords or leave them under the keyboard or in the desk drawer. That's where we look first during a security review! And we often find passwords in those places. Very naughty.

As a home and casual user, you should do the following things:

- **Write down the passwords.**

  You typically do not use them often enough to remember them as the months go by.

- **Safely file the paper on which you write your passwords.**

  If you write down the passwords on a scrap of paper, the paper might get thrown out, and then where would you be? Lock it up with your other important papers, like your will or your bank account numbers.

- **Remember where you file the list!**

  Maybe it's just us, but sometimes we know that we wrote down the information. And we know that we put it somewhere safe. But several months later, we're darned if we can remember *where* that safe place is.

If you didn't get this book in time and have lost some passwords, don't give up yet! In Chapters 17 and 18, we provide a number of tools designed to "crack" various word processor files and get them back for you.

In addition, several commercial vendors provide software that can recover these files. You can find some vendors on the Internet by searching for *passwords* and *crack*. Many vendors also advertise in the monthly personal computer magazines. One vendor of password-recovery software is a company called AccessData in Orem, Utah. You can reach AccessData at 800-658-5199.

Because software changes so regularly, be sure to know exactly which software version you are using, such as WordPerfect 5.2 or Word 6.0, before purchasing any recovery software.

Chapter 10

Backing Up and Restoring

• •

• •

A ccidents, try to change them — it's impossible. The accidental reveals man.

— Pablo Picasso (1881–1973), Spanish artist. Quoted in *Vogue,* 1 Nov. 1956.

We want you to remember to do three things on a regular basis after reading this chapter: back up, back up, and back up. Someone once said that two types of people exist: those who have already lost important data, and those who are about to lose it next.

Computers are extremely fallible machines. The people who own them are fallible. This fallibility usually results in something bad happening sooner or later. Have you ever deleted a file that you didn't want to delete? Duh! Everyone has at one time or other. Sometimes you can recover the file, and other times it is lost forever. After reading this chapter, you can join the growing crowd of people who can always recover lost files.

Why Back Up?

Most people have an "it won't happen to me" attitude toward data loss. And yet nearly everyone we know has accidentally deleted a file at some time or other. Barry once deleted the WINDOWS directory on his computer because he was talking on the telephone and not paying attention. He actually wanted to delete a temporary directory! If you are not backing up your files, it is only a matter of time before you lose some or even all of your data. Why? Because, like Barry, you may accidentally delete a file or a directory full of files. Your children may accidentally delete files. Or they may delete files deliberately to make room for additional games, thinking that the files they delete are not important.

Finally, all disk manufacturers use a term called *MTBF*. It means *mean time between failures,* or simply put, how long the manufacturer thinks the product should work before failing! This time frame is usually in thousands of hours for hard drives and sounds impressive, but do you know how many hours are in a month or a year? Roughly 720 and 8,640, respectively. So those thousands of hours quickly add up, and before you know it, your hard drive may fail. (Before vendors start harassing us, we realize that for most users, this time frame means that their drives are good for a few years. It does depend on the time the machine is in actual use, not just sitting around.) But sooner or later, your hard drive is going to fail and expose you to data loss.

So if everyone accidentally deletes a file at some point and hard drives eventually fail, why do people still not perform backups? We believe that it is partially because of cost and mostly due to lack of understanding of how and what to back up.

Figuring Out What to Back Up

Merely suggesting that you back up everything in your computer is easy. But that is not really helpful. Why? Because it depends on which methods you use to perform the backup and how long you want your backups to take. For example, using floppy disks to save your data is very time intensive — you need a lot of disks and you must manually insert and remove them until your backup is finished.

Follow a simple scenario: You decide to back up all the data on your computer by using floppies. You start a backup program (such as Windows 95 Backup) and select all files. Suppose that you have more than 9,000 files, and the amount of space you are using for all your files amounts to 354MB. (Barry has this many files on one of his hard drives!) You need about 270 disks and a lot of patience to finish.

In attempting to save *all* the data on your computer, you are backing up all the software that you have installed as well as all your personal data. You need not back up software such as Windows, WordPerfect, or Lotus because you should have the original disks for this software and can reinstall it at any time. What you do want to back up are all the files that you create and perhaps those programs that you retrieve from an online source such as CompuServe or the Internet. You want to back up your personal files because you do not want to retype all those letters or recipes that you have on the computer. You also may want to back up software from an online source so that you don't have to pay to download the files again. (All online services charge you for the amount of time you spend online, and downloading files can be time consuming.)

Creating a Single Directory for Your Data Files

How do you back up only your data files? Most people scatter their data all across the hard drive instead of putting it all in one place. Then you must search for all the places in which your data gets stored by all the programs you use and set up the backup program to remember each location. Or you can make life a little less complicated and create a directory on your computer (have a knowledgeable friend help you), call the directory DATA or MYFILES, and store all your day-to-day files there.

After you create this directory, you can tell each program, such as Word and WordPerfect, to use this directory when saving files. This way, you need to go to only one area of your hard drive to find all your files.

 ✔ In Microsoft Word 6.0 and 7.0, choose Tools⇨Options⇨File Locations from the menu bar and set the new location as desired. Then, each time you save a file, Word automatically places it in your new directory.

 ✔ In WordPerfect 6.x, use Edit⇨Preferences⇨File and specify your new directory in the space described as the Default Directory.

In addition to all your data files, you may want to back up several other system files on a regular basis. Chapter 20 lists these files and tells a little bit about what each one does.

Windows 95 automatically creates such a directory for you and calls it MY DOCUMENTS. Store all your personal files in there in subdirectories that make sense to you.

After you define a single directory (with subdirectories below it to separate individuals' data or to distinguish files from various products, such as Excel, Lotus 1-2-3, and WordPerfect), you can set up a backup strategy for saving your data.

As Figure 10-1 shows, Barry has a directory called MY DOCUMENTS with a number of subdirectories beneath it. The ones with funny names, such as WORDF~1, are Windows 95 long filenames. DOS doesn't like those names and shortens them to the old 8.3 format (eight characters for the filename, plus three characters for its file extension). You can still access the files with long names, however. As you can see, Barry has a data directory for this book (DUMMIE~1), his Web pages (HTML), and downloaded files (DOWNLOAD). Because all his data files are in the major directory called MY DOCUMENTS, backing them up without searching around the hard drive is simple.

For those people who have a few more dollars, we recommend purchasing a tape backup device. These devices can back up a lot of files very quickly and are relatively easy to use. We discuss tape backup devices in Chapter 23. These devices enable you to back up all the data on your hard drive, not just your personal files. This capability makes the process of recovering from a hard drive failure or a foolish deletion (such as the WINDOWS directory) much faster.

Tape Backups

Probably the oldest and most common backup products are tape backup devices, which are arguably the most cost-effective for now. Several new technologies are available that give tape a run for the money and therefore deserve consideration.

Tape backup devices are generally dependable, cost-effective, and easy to install. Don't forget that, as do VCR tapes, they wear out over time. Use more than one tape, and replace the tape every couple of years or so. These devices are sequential (you have to wind them to the spot where the file you want is stored and make sure that they are rewound when writing new data onto them), and therefore restoring a file takes longer than it does on the newer technologies, such as CD-ROMs and hard drives.

Figure 10-1:
Barry's file directory, MY DOCUMENTS, in which he saves all his data files.

```
C:\My Documents>dir

 Volume in drive C is S355962D001
 Volume Serial Number is 2A57-1300
 Directory of C:\My Documents

.                    <DIR>         01-16-96   1:10p .
..                   <DIR>         01-16-96   1:10p ..
WORDFI~1             <DIR>         01-16-96   4:31p word files
DUMMIE~1             <DIR>         01-16-96   4:21p Dummies Book
ISC2                 <DIR>         02-20-96  10:09a ISC2
DOWNLOAD             <DIR>         01-19-96   3:03p Download
SECURI~1             <DIR>         02-29-96  12:17p Security Info
HTML                 <DIR>         01-25-96   1:23p Html
CLIENTS              <DIR>         02-20-96   6:01p Clients
POWERP~1             <DIR>         02-06-96  12:47p Powerpoint files
EXCELD~1             <DIR>         02-07-96  11:52a Excel data
CERBERUS             <DIR>         02-06-96   4:00p Cerberus
BILLINGS             <DIR>         02-09-96  10:43a Billings
DEPAAK~1 RTF              3,257    02-12-96   9:40p depaak chpra.rtf
HACK                 <DIR>         02-29-96  12:15p Hack
          1 file(s)            3,257 bytes
         14 dir(s)       391,462,912 bytes free

C:\My Documents>_
```

There are more types of media (the stuff your data ends up on) than you can shake a stick at these days. Backup devices use everything from tape (very much like a VCR tape you record your movies onto) to CDs (like those with your music) to the really new PC Card technology. *PC Cards* are those tiny little credit card-type devices found in most laptop computers. Vendors have magically shrunken all kinds of devices such as modems and hard drives to fit into a little credit card that can plug into the laptop and provide those features with almost no weight. They are expensive, but for anyone who travels a lot, the weight and size savings are worth it!

A final note: By the time this book is printed and distributed, much is likely to have changed. This field is growing so fast that keeping up is impossible. For example, both SyQuest and Iomega have 1GB storage devices coming out to replace the 100MB to 130MB devices that they currently sell. These devices are expected to be priced around $600, which could easily mean that, by this time next year, they may be in the $200 to $300 range. Things change that fast.

Floppy Disk Backups

For some users, floppy disk backups are just fine. You may not need anything larger than the space available on a few disks. How can you tell? We suggest that anyone with less than around 10MB of data can get by with disk copying, because the compression techniques in most backup programs shrink the size of your files significantly. Therefore, you only need a few disks to hold this much data.

Using floppy disk backups does not make life easier if you lose the entire hard drive, however, as you must reload all the software that was on your computer, which is very time intensive. If you can afford the $150 to $200 for an inexpensive backup unit, you can significantly decrease the time needed to recover from a hard disk failure, because you can back up all your applications in addition to your data, and you can restore it all with little fuss.

Deciding How Often to Back Up

This question is difficult to answer, because how often you back up really depends on how often you create or change your data files. For the average home user, performing some type of backup at least once per month is probably sufficient. Back up more often if you use the computer each day. For example, if you have school children who do their homework on the computer each day, you may want to back up the data once a week. And you may want to back up an important school assignment right after your child creates it.

Most programs such as Excel, Word, and WordPerfect enable you to save what you're working on to disk every few minutes by using a feature called Autosave. If the power fails or someone unplugs your machine while you're typing a long document, the data is safely stored with your other files (except for the last few minutes' worth). Read about this feature in your program documentation, and use the feature. We recommend that the average person have the program perform a disk save at least every ten minutes or so. Fast typists may want to save more often.

Backup Techniques

No, we're not suggesting that backing up your data requires extensive knowledge and skill. But we do want to make sure that you protect these files, and merely backing up a bunch of files once in a while is not sufficient.

The simplest method for saving files is to back up your data directory every week or every day, depending on how much work you do on the computer. Just select all the files, run a backup program, and number and label the disks so that you know in what order they were created. This is important for the backup program to know so that it can find the files at a later time. Use two or three sets of disks and rotate them, using the first set and then the second, followed by the third set.

For example:

- ✔ Label the first set "Week1," the next "Week2," and the last "Week3." Then label a fourth set "Monthly."

- ✔ Use the set called Week1 on the first weekend. Use Week2 the following week, and then use Week3. At the end of the fourth week, use the set labeled Monthly. You now have one month of files safely backed up. At the start of the next month, reuse Week1 and go through the cycle again.

- ✔ If you want, use several Monthly sets. You can call them "Monthly1," Monthly2," and "Monthly3." Using this method provides you with a set of backup files protecting over three months of data.

Doing so enables you to recover older files that you may delete between backups. (If you delete a file, the next backup does not contain that file. If you need the deleted file later, you need to find the backup disks that include an old version of that file.) Change the number of sets to suit your personal needs.

Other techniques include the incremental approach. Home users performing backups by using DOS Backup are probably familiar with this approach. You use this method to minimize the number of files that need to be backed up to disk:

✔ First, perform a backup of all your files.

✔ Then perform *incremental backups,* which back up a file again only if the file has changed since the first backup.

Most popular packages such as Central Point Backup and Norton Backup automatically use an incremental approach to backing up data. Most backup programs ask you to perform a full backup first and then begin to increment that backup set of files each time you run the backup program on any files that change.

This process works best if you do not create many new files and instead only change existing files, because new files are not backed up during the incremental process. You need to run a full backup occasionally to capture any new files you create.

Using DOS Backup and COPY

All DOS users should be familiar with the COPY command, which is probably one of the most used commands within DOS — everyone copies files from one place to another at some point. Each time you create or modify an important file, copy it onto a floppy in addition to storing it on the hard drive. You are performing a backup! Should you accidentally delete the file, you can recover it by inserting the floppy and copying the file back onto your hard drive. Use this technique to back up small numbers of files that fit onto one disk.

DOS and Windows users have a built-in program available to perform backups. Additional software is not necessary. The DOS program is called Backup. If you have a lot of files to back up, you should use this program instead of the COPY command because it enables you to back up a lot of files onto several disks. Backup works a lot like the COPY command. For example, to back up all the files in your DATA directory, type this text at the C:\ prompt:

```
backup c:\data a: /s
```

This command backs up all the files in the directory called DATA and puts them onto a disk that you place in the A drive. (The /s part tells Backup to also back up the files in all subdirectories within the DATA directory.)

After you back up all your data files, you can use the Backup program to add those files that you create or change after the backup. Perform the full backup at the start of a month and then add the files you create or change during the month, perhaps each week. This way, you have one set of backup disks for the month. The backup command to use each week is

```
backup c:\data a: /a /m
```

The /a and /m tell Backup to add only new or changed files to the current backup diskettes.

Do a full backup at the start of a month, and then back up the changed files for that month each week. If you follow this scenario for three months, using a different set of disks each month, you can recover files from three months earlier by using only three sets of disks. Modify the frequency and number of backup sets to suit your particular needs.

Using Windows 95 Backup

Windows 95 also comes with a free backup program in addition to the capability to perform the DOS backup that we described earlier. The advantage of using the utility is that it guides you through a step-by-step process with no need to use DOS. It is also one step better than the DOS version because it enables you to use disks or tape devices. The program is also intuitive to use — you just follow the prompts:

1. **In Windows 95, choose Start⇨Accessories⇨System Tools⇨Backup.**

   You see the screen shown in Figure 10-2.

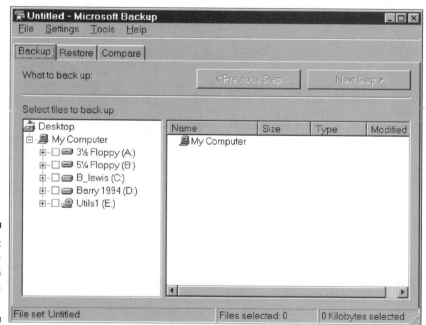

Figure 10-2:
The Windows 95 Backup program.

2. **Click on the drive containing the files you want to back up, and then select the directories from the list that appears by clicking on each directory that you want to back up.**

3. **After you select all the directories you want, click on Next Step and select the destination drive by clicking on the chosen icon.**

4. **Click on Start Backup and enter the name of your backup set, such as** Week1 **or** Monthly2.

You have the choice of protecting this file with a password. If you choose to do so, make sure that you remember the password! Store the finished disks or tape in a safe place.

Doing Mac backups

Backing up a few files on the Macintosh is relatively straightforward. You insert a diskette into your floppy drive, click to highlight the files you want to back up, and drag them to the diskette icon. To recover these files, you insert the floppy containing your backed up files, click on the diskette icon, select the files you want, and drag them back onto the desktop.

If you have a lot of files to back up, this process can be quite tedious. Freeware products, such as HDBackup from PBI Software, format the diskettes and back up a volume or directory that you select. In addition, you can purchase commercial backup programs that make backups a breeze and support all types of backup hardware, such as the devices listed in Chapter 23.

Because most backup hardware products can attach to your computer with a special interface called SCSI (Small Computer Systems Interface, developed by Apple) that enables you to use them with either Macintosh or IBM-compatible machines, you can follow our advice and purchase a tape backup. One of the more popular commercial software programs is Retrospect from Dantz Development Corporation.

Restoring backed-up files

To get backed-up files back onto your hard drive, you use a command called RESTORE. This command enables you to recover your files from previous DOS backups. For example, this command

```
restore a: c:\data\*.* /s
```

restores all the files that you previously backed up. By replacing the *.* with a filename, you can restore a particular file rather than the entire directory. Backup software such as Central Point and Norton Backup provide helpful menus to show you the recovery process.

Using commercial backup programs

You can purchase a number of good backup programs that provide easier and automated methods for performing backups. In general, we recommend using these programs only if you have a lot of data to back up and are using a tape or CD backup device. Why? Because the DOS and Windows 95 backup programs are free and do an adequate job for no additional cost.

One good reason to purchase a commercial program is that it can help you to automate the process. Automated backups help ensure that the backup gets done. Face it: You get busy and forget to back up, and before you know it, the file you need to recover isn't backed up. You really do need a tape device — backing up files onto disks is difficult if you are not there to put the disk into the drive when the program requests. Because a tape can hold much more data, you can insert the tape and go to bed, letting a backup program start up at midnight and copy all the new or changed files without any intervention on your part.

Most computer stores carry the more popular programs. The advantages of purchasing a commercial product include vendor support, automated services, and support for a wider range of backup devices. Some of these packages even include support for the newer writeable CD devices.

Some of the popular products include

- ✔ Norton Backup
- ✔ Central Point Backup
- ✔ Retrospect

You can find company names and telephone numbers in Appendix B.

The cost of a tape device and backup software (which is often included free with the tape device) runs about $200 to $300 — and might save your assets!

Storing Backups

Backing up your data is a good thing. (Apologies to Martha Stewart.) However, backing up is only one part of the equation. Making sure that the backups are available when you need them is just as important.

If you're like most users who actually back up their data, you probably just throw the disks or tapes in your desk drawer or leave them lying around the room. But these disks are your last recourse if something goes wrong and you need to recover those files. Treat them nicely!

Consider purchasing a storage container for your diskettes, CDs, and tapes. You can buy these containers at any computer store for less than $30, and they help keep dust, smoke, and other pollutants off your sensitive backups. Place them where they are less likely to be near food or drinks, perhaps on a shelf in the closet or on a bookshelf. Barry has converted one of his bedrooms into an office, and the closet is shelved for storing all his books, software packaging, and floppy disks.

In addition to storage, you need to consider fire and smoke damage. A small kitchen fire in your home can destroy your computer and all your files. For those people who believe that their computer is far enough from the kitchen, remember that it is the smoke that kills, and smoke in all likelihood fills the house before the fire is put out. How important are your computer files? If you really need them, consider giving a backup to your parents, brother, or sister once a month. This way, you at least are able to recover most of your files.

Barry manages his bank accounts with a commercial finance program and could not re-create his past spending history without the program's database. His wife has most of her favorite recipes and her home business records on the computer. Losing any of this data would be a disaster. Barry and his wife share backup responsibility with a friend who lives across town. Each holds backup files for the other.

We talk about storing backups with others, but you may be concerned that they can then pry into your personal data. Depending upon how sensitive you consider the information, you can do several things: First, make sure that you can trust the other party. Parents are usually a good bet for at least two reasons: One, they love and trust you and are unlikely to pry; and two, they may not own a computer, making your concern a moot point.

You can always obtain an inexpensive lock-box and use it to store your files. Tell the other party that the lock-box helps to keep the data safe from little fingers (if they have children) and also from dust, dirt, and smoke.

Testing Backups

Do not mistake *taking* a backup for *having* backup files. Too often, the backup program does not work, as you forget to change tapes or disks, or the program *glitches* (a technical term for messes up). Sometimes the backup program stops running because some other program is using a file, and you may not notice. Once in a while, you must test that the files are safely backed up as expected.

Test the backups at least once every other cycle. For example, if you back up files each day on an incremental basis and perform a full backup once per week, you should test the backup every second week.

How do you test your backups? Is the process a long and drawn-out affair? No. Simply attempt to recover a file or two from the backup disk, tape, or CD.

When Barry worked in a major financial institution, his department performed a daily backup of some critical security database files. Each day, administrative staff verified that the backup program had run the night before. The company relied on this process for months. One day, however, they discovered that the program had been failing and not performing the backups! The backup program did run each day, so the administrative staff were correct in their work. The program, however, developed a glitch and did not actually back anything up. The company was fortunate because it did not need to use that data to recover from some catastrophe, but the ramifications could have been very serious. They should have been regularly testing to be sure that they could actually use the data being backed up. You should also.

Restoring Lost Files

We discuss how to perform a backup at great length with little indication of how you can restore a lost file. Before you resort to your backups, you may want to see whether you can recover the file some other way. On DOS-based and Mac machines, you never actually delete a file when you issue the Delete command. The operating system removes the pointer to the file, so the system thinks that the file is gone. But guess what? If you act quickly, you can usually recover a file or directory that you accidentally delete.

How do you restore a deleted file? On DOS systems, use the command called UNERASE. Run this program immediately after deleting a file, and you can usually recover the file. As you run the program, it lists all the deleted files that it can find and provides an option to recover them. Beside each file is an indication of whether the program can recover the file. You see words such as *poor, good,* and *excellent.* As long as the prognosis is not poor, you can usually recover the file. Select the file that you accidentally deleted and click on the Unerase option. DOS asks you to supply the first character of the file (it removes this character as part of the deletion). After you supply the first character, your file should magically reappear.

Similar programs exist within Windows 95. Go to the Recycle Bin, select the file, and choose Restore. The file is placed exactly where you deleted it from. If the file isn't in the bin, you're out of luck — it's gone.

On the Mac, double-click on the Trash icon to see a list of deleted files. Drag the one you want back onto the desktop. If it isn't there, you're probably out of luck.

You can also purchase many commercial tools that provide file recovery. (See Chapter 23 for information about some useful backup devices.)

Finally, should you ever experience a problem with your hard drive and really need the data on it (because you only just read our book and realized that you should have been backing up all those files), a number of companies provide data recovery services. These companies do wonders with a damaged hard drive. They are so confident that most do not charge you if they cannot recover the data. A former partner of Barry had his laptop hard drive go bad and had no backup. (For shame, eh?) Fortunately, a data recovery outfit in Toronto saved the day and managed to retrieve all his data. This service costs around $500, however, and is probably not an acceptable alternative for recovering your recipes or old letters.

Some data recovery firms include the following:

- **ECO Electronics Inc.**
  Palm Beach Gardens, Florida
  Telephone: 800-339-3412

- **Total Recall**
  Colorado Springs, Colorado
  Telephone: 800-743-0594

- **Lazarus**
  San Francisco, California
  Telephone: 800-341-3282

TIP

Ten backup tips

We know that we are providing you with many reasons and means for performing backups. But we need to promote several tips:

Back up. Back up. Back up. Back up. Back up. Back up. Back up. Back up. Back up. Back up.

As the Nike commercial says, "Just do it!"

Chapter 11

Eliminating Viruses, Worms, and Other Pestilence

- -

In This Chapter

▶ Defining computer pestilence

▶ Understanding viruses, worms, Trojan horses, tribbles, bacteria, chain letters, and bombs

▶ Preventing a virus

▶ Recovering from a virus

▶ Finding virus sources and resources

- -

*A*fter crackers, viruses get the most press. Crackers like to break into computer systems for love or money. The popular press whips up horror stories about viruses and cracking out of proportion to the number of actual incidents. Reporters like to sensationalize the havoc that viruses cause because they can understand the idea. This sensationalism has led to a public perception that viruses and cracking are rife — contrary to the evidence. So far, the publicity has not shaken the public's faith in information technology. This is not to suggest that viruses are not a serious problem — you are likely to face this problem at home or at the office. How much damage the virus causes depends on the precautions you take.

Not only do reporters grab onto viruses and run with them, but so do many authors of security books. We would be remiss should we not contribute to the lore. Our contribution, however, is short.

Just as the Egyptians were plagued by pestilence in the Bible, computer systems are suffering as well. They are faced with many strains of computer pestilence: viruses, worms, and Trojan horses.

Malicious software taxonomy

Armored virus: A program that uses special tricks to make the tracing, disassembling, and understanding of its code more difficult.

Bacteria: Electronic mail that spreads itself to all users when read or otherwise executed.

Chain letter: Electronic mail that spreads the same way that chain letters do. Someone might send it to three people, who also send it to three people. Some chain letters use your address book to automatically send a message to everyone you know.

Companion virus: A program that, instead of modifying an existing file, creates a new program that (unknown to the user) gets executed by the command-line interpreter instead of the intended program.

Cuckoo's egg: A program that you maintain and nurture on your system, which you believe is yours, but is in fact someone else's. The program really is a malicious program waiting to do its evil.

Polymorphic virus: A program that produces varied (yet fully operational) copies of itself in the hope that virus scanners can't detect all instances of the virus.

Rabbit: A program that replicates exceedingly fast, referring to the celebrated reproductive capabilities of the rodent.

Time bomb: A program triggered on a specified date and time or an occurrence of a specific event or events (for example, Friday the 13th).

Tribble: Another program that replicates exceedingly fast; comes from those furry, pleasant animals on the original *Star Trek.*

Trojan horse: A program that appears to be one thing when, in reality, it is something entirely different (for example, a virus). Trojan horses insert damaging instructions in programs, which cause viruses or worms to spread to other programs when you execute them.

Virus: A program that infects other programs by modifying them to include code that instructs other computers to replicate the virus to still more computers. Viruses also can mutate or change during the process of replication, reproduction, or propagation. However, a virus's main goal is to make copies of itself.

Worm: A program that simply replicates itself repeatedly. A worm eventually uses all the memory in a computer or network, so nothing can be retrieved or entered.

Viruses Uncovered

A threat to your PC is the so-called *computer virus.* So what is a virus? To a biologist, a virus is a piece of genetic material that must infect a host organism to survive and reproduce. To be contagious, a virus usually carries instructions that cause the host to engage in certain pathological activities, such as sneezing and coughing, that spread the infection to other organisms.

To a computer programmer, a virus is computer code that must infect a host program to spread. To be contagious, a computer virus usually causes the host program to engage in certain pathological activities that spread the infection to other programs. For example, viruses modify programs by adding evil instructions for other computers to replicate the virus to still more computers.

Commonly, a computer virus is a program that can infect other programs by modifying them to include a copy of itself. A virus is designed to change its form or its target over time. Furthermore, it replicates itself and attaches itself to either a program or a file so that it can hide and travel from one computer to another. Viruses are programmed to erase hard disks, delete certain critical files, or prevent logon by authorized individuals, and they characterize themselves by replicating and attaching themselves to other parts of your system. A destructive virus can spread rapidly through your system and communication networks, infecting unprotected programs and data.

Giving an exact count of viruses is impossible, because people are creating new ones daily. Furthermore, different antivirus researchers use different criteria to decide whether two viruses are different or one and the same. Some researchers consider viruses to be different if they differ by at least one bit in their nonvariable code. Others group the viruses in families and do not count the closely related variants in one family as different viruses. So depending on the way you count them, anywhere from 50 to 6,500 different viruses exist.

The threat from viruses increases as microcomputer use grows, users become more sophisticated, and publicity about viruses inspires people to create new viruses. Any computer literate person who knows a few techniques, network addresses, and user codes and has a virus-writing kit (such as those for sale in West Germany or for free on the Internet) can wreak havoc.

The first computer viruses

In 1949, John von Neumann (a father of computer theory) presented a model of a virus program — a computer program that could multiply. The first recorded computer virus was the Core War game invented by M. Douglas McIlroy at Bell Laboratories in the 1960s. The point of the game was to write a program that erased the opponent or blocked its movement. EGABTR, the first pest for the IBM PC, surfaced in July 1985. Although the military establishment has known about computer viruses for dozens of years, viruses really came into their own only in late 1987, when the popular press drew attention to them. In 1987, the Lehigh, Brain, and Jerusalem viruses exploded onto the scene. In the same year, Dr. Fred Cohen published his article "Computer Viruses — Theory and Experiments" in *Computer & Security* (Elsevier Science Publishers), which outlined his theories and provided demonstrations of viruses.

By far, the greatest risk in the personal computer environment is from the user's ability to load a new program onto the system from a floppy disk. Unwittingly, you may install software that you think is useful only to find that it is a computer pest.

One day, Peter was reading the `alt.2600` USENET newsgroup to find out which cracker tools were hot. Someone posted a message to that newsgroup asking whether anyone knew where to get a virus-creation program. Immediately, someone directed the inquirer to a particular site, directory, and program. Had the person downloaded the suggested program, he or she would have downloaded an exceptionally nasty virus. No honor among thieves.

Can I pass a Macintosh virus to a DOS-based PC?

Conventional viruses such as nVIR are computer specific. Macintosh viruses don't affect DOS-based PC computers and vice versa, which greatly limits the destructive power of viruses. Currently, only one type of virus can spread from one type of computer to another: Macro viruses, which are application specific, can affect your copy of Word for Windows as well as your copy of Word for the Mac. Although the disk formats may be the same (for example, Atari ST and DOS), different machines interpret code differently. For example, the Stoned virus cannot infect an Atari ST because the ST cannot execute the virus code in the boot sector.

Cross-platform conventional viruses are possible but unlikely. Such a virus would be quite a bit larger than current viruses and may well be easier to find on your computer because of its size. Additionally, the low incidence of cross-machine sharing of software means that any such virus would be unlikely to spread — the environment would be poor for virus growth.

Can I pass a DOS virus to my Mac?

Generally, DOS viruses cannot run on non-DOS machines (for example, Macintosh or Amiga). However, on machines running DOS emulators (either hardware or software based), DOS viruses — just like any DOS program — can function. These viruses are subject to the file access controls of the host operating system.

Transmitting viruses

A virus, by definition, cannot exist by itself. It must infect an executable program. To transmit a virus by e-mail, someone would have to infect a file and attach the file to the e-mail message. To activate the virus, you would have to download and decode the attachment and then run the infected program. In that situation, the e-mail message is just a carrier for an infected file, just like a floppy disk carrying an infected file.

Some e-mail programs can be set to automatically download a file attachment, decode it, and execute the file attachment. If you use such a program, you would be well-advised to disable the option to automatically execute file attachments.

You should, of course, be wary of any file attachments that a stranger sends you. At the least, you should check such file attachments for viruses before running them. Don't open any files from strangers!

Some bad habits, such as using shareware, free software, and games, increase the chance of your getting a virus. However, in many documented instances, even reputable vendors inadvertently distributed commercial, shrink-wrapped software containing viruses. Avoiding shareware, freeware, and games only isolates you from a vast collection of potentially bad software.

You may have heard of the Winword Concept virus. This virus attaches itself to Microsoft Word for Windows documents and can infect every document that you save with the Save As command, including those that you open in Word for the Mac. Chapter 22 provides information about where to get a program to remove this virus.

The important thing is not to avoid a certain type of software, but to be cautious of any and all newly acquired software. Simply scanning all new software media for known viruses would be rather effective at preventing virus infections, especially when combined with some other prevention and detection strategy such as integrity management of programs.

Classes and types of viruses

Viruses are either *benign* — causing disruption but no serious damage — or *malignant* — destroying data or the integrity of the system.

Generally, two main classes of viruses exist. The first class consists of the *file infectors* that attach themselves to ordinary program files. These viruses usually infect .COM or .EXE programs, although some can infect .SYS, .OVL, .PRG, and .MNU files.

File infectors are either *direct-action* or *resident.* A direct-action virus selects one or more programs to infect whenever you execute the program containing it. A resident virus hides itself somewhere in memory the first time you execute an infected program, and, thereafter, infects other programs when they are executed or when certain other conditions are fulfilled. Most documented viruses are resident.

The second category is *system* or *boot-record infectors* that infect executable code found in certain system areas on a disk that are not ordinary files. DOS systems may become infected by ordinary boot-sector viruses, which infect only the DOS boot sector, and viruses that infect the Master Boot Record on fixed disks and the DOS boot sector on floppies. These viruses are always resident viruses.

Finally, a few viruses can infect both files and boot sectors. These are often called *multipartite* or *boot-and-file* viruses.

File system or *cluster viruses* modify directory table entries so that the virus is loaded and executed before the desired program. The program itself is not physically altered, only the directory entry. Some virus experts consider these infectors to be a third category of viruses, while others consider them to be a subcategory of the file infectors.

A typical file infector copies itself to memory when a program infected by it is executed and then infects other programs as they are executed.

A *fast infector* is a virus that, if it is active in memory, infects not only programs that are executed but even those that are merely open. The result is that if such a virus is active in memory, running a scanner or integrity checker can result in all (or at least many) programs becoming infected.

The term *slow infector* sometimes refers to a virus that, while active in memory, infects files only as you create or modify them. The purpose is to fool people who use integrity checkers into thinking that the modification reported by the integrity checker is due solely to legitimate reasons.

The new breeds of viruses

Virus authors are getting crafty and particularly nasty. They are developing viruses that are more difficult to detect. For example, a *stealth* virus hides the modifications it has made in the file or boot record, usually by monitoring the system functions used by programs to read files or physical blocks from storage media and forging the results of such system functions so that programs trying to read these areas see the original uninfected form of the file instead of the actual infected form. In this manner, the viral modifications go undetected by antivirus programs. To do this, however, the virus must be resident in memory when you run your antivirus software.

Virus authors are also writing *polymorphic* viruses that produce varied, yet fully operational, copies to prevent a virus scanner from detecting all instances of the virus. One method for making a polymorphic virus is to choose among a variety of different encryption schemes requiring different decryption routines — though only one routine would be plainly visible in any instance of the virus. A signature-driven virus scanner would have to exploit several signatures (one for each possible encryption method) to reliably identify a virus of this kind. A more sophisticated polymorphic virus varies the sequence of instructions in its copies by interspersing it with noise instructions (for example, a No Operation instruction or an instruction to load a currently unused register with an arbitrary value), by interchanging mutually independent instructions, or even by using various instruction sequences with identical net effects (for example, Subtract A from A, and Move 0 to A). A signature-based virus scanner cannot reliably identify this sort of virus.

Recently, someone discovered that some 32-bit virus-scanning programs for Windows 95 systems can't detect viruses with a special character (ASCII 229) in the first position of the file's name. DOS-based scanners, however, can detect these viruses. So use your old DOS scanner on Windows 95 to pick off these clever viruses. Look for the fix for the 32-bit scanners if you are going to rely on them entirely.

The most sophisticated form of polymorphism discovered so far is the MtE "Mutation Engine," written by the Bulgarian virus writer who calls himself the Dark Avenger. It comes in the form of an object module.

Any virus can be made polymorphic by adding certain calls to the assembler source code and linking to the mutation-engine and random-number-generator modules.

The advent of polymorphic viruses has rendered virus-scanning an ever more arduous and expensive endeavor; adding more and more search strings to simple scanners does not adequately deal with these viruses.

Nonexecutable viruses

Making a sharp distinction between executable and nonexecutable files is not always possible. Some files that are not directly executable contain code or data that can, under some conditions, be executed or interpreted. Some examples from the IBM-PC world are OBJ files, libraries, device drivers, source files for any compiler or interpreter, and macro files for packages such as Microsoft Word and Lotus 1-2-3.

Currently, viruses can infect boot sectors, master boot records, COM files, EXE files, BAT files, and device drivers, although any of the objects mentioned can theoretically be a carrier. PostScript files can also carry a virus, although no currently known virus does that.

Other computer viruses are spread by human actions. These viruses are a sort of thought virus. To be contagious, a thought virus causes the host to engage in certain pathological activities that spread the infection.

A good example of a thought virus is the Good Times virus. America Online, government computer security agencies, and makers of antivirus software have declared Good Times a hoax. Since the hoax began in November 1994, no copy of the alleged virus has ever been found nor has a single verified case of a viral attack occurred. The story is that a virus called Good Times is being carried by e-mail. Just reading a message with "Good Times" in the subject line erases your hard drive or even destroys your computer's processor. Needless to say, it's a hoax, but a lot of people believed it.

Warnings about Good Times have been widely distributed on mailing lists, USENET newsgroups, and message boards. System managers needlessly worry their clients by posting dire warnings. Supposedly, the Good Times virus is an opportunistic self-replicating e-mail virus that tricks its host into replicating it, sometimes adding as many as 200,000 copies at a go. It works by finding hosts with defective parsers that prevent them from understanding that a piece of e-mail that says there is an e-mail virus and then asks them to remail the message to all their friends is the virus itself. The original message was supposed to end with instructions to "Forward this to all your friends," and many people did just that.

The other major viral strain (infinite loop) encourages people to "Please be careful and forward this mail to anyone you care about," and "Warn your friends and local system users of this newest threat to the InterNet (sic)!"

Likewise, stories of a FCC modem tax encourage people to tell their friends and post a warning on other bulletin board systems. Every so often, someone posts a dire warning that the FCC is considering a tax on modems and online services. The warning encourages you to tell your friends so they can take political action. Obviously, this results in the creation of thousands of messages.

The Make Money Fast scam instructs people to repost the message to as many as ten bulletin boards. Devised by David Rhodes in 1987 or 1988, Make Money Fast (sometimes distributed on a BBS as a file called FASTCASH.TXT) is an electronic version of a chain-letter pyramid scheme. You're supposed to send money to the ten people on the list and then add your name to the list and re-post the chain letter (committing federal wire fraud in the process). Posting a Make Money Fast message is one sure way to lose your Internet or online account.

Craig Shergold is a youth from the United Kingdom who was dying of cancer. When he thought he was dying, he wanted to get in the Guinness Book of World Records for having received the most get-well cards. When people heard of the poor boy's dying wish, they began sending him postcards. And they kept sending him postcards and never stopped. Shergold is now in full remission. The Guinness Book of World Records officially recognized Craig in 1991. He really does not want your postcards anymore, and neither does his hometown post office.

These are just some of the urban legends that you're likely to encounter on the Internet. You'll find many more, such as those involving peanut butter, Neiman Marcus, Mrs. Fields, Rod Stewart, and the Newlywed Game, to name a few.

Worms

Worms are similar to viruses, except their aim is simply to replicate themselves repeatedly and eventually use all the memory in a computer or network so that nothing can be retrieved or entered. The first use of the term described a program that copied itself benignly around the network, using otherwise unused resources.

Reading science fiction provides insight into worms. In *Shockwave Rider* (Harper & Row: 1975), John Brunner describes a tapeworm program running loose in the network. He writes, "It's definitely self-perpetuating so long as the net exists. Even if one segment of it is inactivated, a counterpart of the missing portion will remain in store at some other station and the worm will automatically subdivide and send a duplicate head to collect the spare groups and restore them to their proper place." Other authors talk of the same theme. Thomas J. Ryan's *The Adolescence of P-1* chronicles a fictional account of the development of a worm. In the book, P-1, a software program, wanders from machine to machine, storing parts of itself and eventually taking control of 7,000 computers.

Some software vendors use worm technology to install and upgrade network software. The most notorious worm was unleashed by Robert Morris, Jr. and coined the *Internet Worm*. Morris launched a virus that invaded hundreds of computers on the Internet by exploiting known serious weaknesses. Perhaps Morris got the idea from reading science fiction.

Trojan Horses

A *Trojan horse* is a program that does something undocumented that the programmer intended but that users would not approve of if they knew about it. Some people consider viruses to be a particular variety of Trojan horse, namely one that can spread to other programs (that is, they turn the other programs into Trojans, too). Others believe that a virus that does not do any deliberate damage (other than merely replicating) is not a Trojan. Despite the definitions, many people use the term *Trojan* to refer only to a nonreplicating, malicious program, so the set of Trojans and the set of viruses are distinct.

A Trojan horse may be a simple back door to an application that you don't know about. A benign example of a Trojan horse is those Easter eggs that programmers put in commercial software. *Easter eggs* are neat little routines activated by some arcane combination of keystrokes. The routines may display the name of the author, run a clip showing the development team, or play the *1812 Overture.*

Some of the programs that people have dreamed up involve Trojan horses rather than viruses. A virus can exist only inside another program, which then automatically infects other programs. A Trojan horse is a program that pretends to do something useful, but instead does something nefarious. Trojans aren't infectious; they don't travel from computer to computer, so they're much less common than viruses. Trojan horses usually are installed on your system as seemingly legitimate programs. If you borrow a "copy" of Microsoft Word, the Word program could be Word, but it may do something else, such as store a hidden copy of every document you create. Trojan horses are difficult to detect. To prevent loading a Trojan horse, install software only from trusted sources.

Other Malicious Programs

IBM systems analysts coined the term *bacteria* — electronic mail that spreads itself to all users when read or otherwise executed. The most famous bacteria was the Christmas Tree, which spread itself until IBM shut down its worldwide mail system. Others prefer to call this pestilence a *tribble* (from *Star Trek*), *rabbit,* or *chain letter.*

A *time* or *logic bomb* is a virus triggered on a specified date and time or an occurrence of a specific event or events. For example, when someone leaves a company and that person's name is removed from the payroll file, the nefarious program (bomb) that the person left behind is triggered, destroying or deleting the payroll file.

Regardless of their names, these pests can cause untold damage if not handled correctly.

Viral Symptoms

In a favorable environment, a virus can spread rapidly and do great damage. New PCs and their operating systems and networks are usually more, rather than less, favorable to the rapid spread of viruses, because they are more open and have larger user populations and more contact among users. For example, you generally face more viruses if you're connected to the Internet or a commercial information provider, such as America Online, than if you are working on a stand-alone PC.

An infected system exhibits a number of noticeable symptoms that you should look for. The first noticeable symptom of a computer virus may be decreased system performance. One reported virus had so filled the network with copies of itself that getting warnings to potential victims was impossible.

Viruses try to spread as much as possible before they do their deed, but symptoms of virus infection usually arise before they do their damage. Use this opportunity to spot and eradicate the virus before any destruction occurs.

Some virus authors write various symptoms into their programs, such as messages, music, and graphical displays. However, the main indications of a virus are the following:

- ✔ Changes in file sizes and contents
- ✔ Changes to interrupt vectors
- ✔ The reassignment of other system resources, such as the boot sector

A virus may change the interrupt vector to have its routines do either of the following:

- ✔ Return a fictitious value for memory when the Memory Size interrupt is called
- ✔ Erase all memory when that interrupt is called

The interrupt vector is a table of possible routines stored in memory that your program can execute. This table is key to DOS, because all a programmer needs to know are the various interrupts to access memory or devices attached to the PC.

The unaccounted use of memory or a reduction in the amount of known memory is an important indicator of a virus. Chapter 19 talks about the CHKDSK DOS command that you can use to check available memory. If your system has 16MB of RAM and CHKDSK tells you that you have less, you should be suspicious. Examining the boot sector is valuable to the trained eye. However, these symptoms, along with unexplained disk activity when the disk starts up unexpectedly and strange behavior from hardware, can result from genuine software activity, harmless prank programs, or hardware problems.

The only foolproof way to determine that a virus is present is to analyze the code in programs and system areas, which is usually impracticable. Virus scanners go some way toward that end by looking in program and system code for known viruses; some even try to use analytical means to spot viral code, but this is not always reliable. Some analytical virus programs look for changes in the length of a program, so a clever virus writer ensures that the infected program retains its original length.

Arm yourself with the latest antivirus software, but also pay close attention to your system. Look particularly for changes in the memory map or configuration as soon as you start the computer. For example, your system reports to you when it starts — it tells you available memory and which programs it loads.

Practical Solutions

You probably wonder: How can I protect myself from viruses in general? The simple answer is to use a virus checker regularly.

A virus checker program can help you diagnose and identify viruses. To help identify problems early, run a scanner on new programs and diskettes. Because new viruses are created every day, you must keep scanning programs up to date. Get your vendor's updates at least every three months.

Freeware, shareware, and commercial antivirus programs are widely available. Which program you use isn't as important as how you use it. Most people get into trouble because they never bother to check their computers for viruses.

Most viruses spread through floppy disks, so isolating yourself from online services and the Internet does not protect you from viruses. In fact, you're probably safer online, simply because you have access to antivirus software and information.

Using the write-protect tab on a floppy disk helps stop viruses. The write-protection on IBM-PC (and compatible) and Macintosh floppy disk drives is implemented in hardware, not software, so viruses cannot infect a disk when the write-protection mechanism is functioning properly. But remember the following points:

- A computer may have a faulty write-protect system. You can test it by trying to copy a file to a disk that is presumably write-protected.

- Someone may have removed the write-protection tab for a while, enabling a virus to enter.

- The files may have been infected before the disk was protected. Even some disks "straight from the factory" have been known to become infected during production.

So scanning even write-protected disks for viruses is worthwhile.

Practice safe hex (or text)! You must be aware that viruses represent a real and potentially catastrophic threat, but you can safeguard your system to deter viral infection. Table 11-1 gives you some guidelines for limiting viruses on your system.

Table 11-1	Virus Do's and Don'ts
Don't...	*Do...*
Download executable programs from bulletin boards.	Use only reputable bulletin boards and networks.
Accept or use unlicensed software.	Use "shrink-wrapped" software.
Share software disks with other users.	Test all disks from strangers.
Allow access to microcomputers by people you don't trust.	Use access control to prevent unauthorized access to hard disks.
Leave disks unattended.	Use write-protect tabs on disks.
Ignore virus symptoms.	Install prophylactic and vaccine software.

Fortunately, should you not have success in preventing viruses, all is not lost, for corrective controls exist. Industrious entrepreneurs developed flu shot programs to combat computer viruses by scanning programs and looking for any potentially harmful instructions. Unfortunately, these corrective programs work only on known viruses. A prophylactic program, however, may take control and raise an alarm when any attempt is made to put data on media, such as on a floppy disk. These programs are loaded into memory and intercept any suspicious activity. They also take a snapshot of your system and report when the picture changes.

There is no "best" antivirus policy, and no program can magically protect you against all viruses. But you can design an antivirus protection strategy based on multiple layers of defense. Three main kinds of antivirus software exist:

✔ **Generic monitoring programs:** These programs try to prevent virus activity, such as attempts to change other programs or to reformat the disk, before it happens. Some generic monitoring programs are SECURE and FluShot+ for the DOS-based PC and GateKeeper for the Macintosh.

✔ **Scanners:** Most scanners look for known virus signatures (that is, byte sequences occurring in known viruses but not in legitimate software) or patterns, but a few use heuristic techniques to recognize virus code. A scanner may examine specified disks or files, or it may be resident, examining each program about to be executed. Most scanners also include virus removers. Some scanners are FindVirus in Dr. Solomon's Anti-Virus ToolKit, FRISK's Analyse and F-Prot, McAfee's VIRUSCAN, V-Shield, and VIRSTOP for the DOS-based PC and Disinfectant for the Macintosh.

✓ **Integrity checkers or modification detectors:** These detectors pass a program you want to protect through an algorithm to compute a small checksum or hash value (such as a CRC or cryptographic sum) when they are presumably clean or uninfected. A *checksum,* or calculated value from the algorithm, is maintained for each program. Later, the detector recalculates the value and compares the newly calculated value to see whether your program was changed. Any change to the program creates an entirely different checksum or hash value. This technique catches unknown viruses as well as known ones and thus provides generic detection. Some integrity checkers or modification detectors are Fred Cohen's ASP Integrity Toolkit, Integrity Master, and VDS for the DOS-based PC.

Of course, we give only a few examples of each type. All have their place in the protection against computer viruses, but you should appreciate the limitations of each method, along with system-supplied security measures that may or may not be helpful in defeating viruses. Ideally, you arrange a combination of methods that cover the holes between them.

Your protection may include programs stored in the boot sector on the hard disk to protect against viruses. (Ideally, this would be hardware or in read-only memory [BIOS], but software methods such as DiskSecure and PanSoft's Immunise are pretty good.) This would be followed by resident virus detectors loaded as part of the machine's startup (CONFIG.SYS or AUTOEXEC.BAT), such as FluShot+ and/or VirStop together with ScanBoot. You can put a scanner such as F-Prot or McAfee's SCAN into your computer's startup program (AUTOEXEC.BAT) to look for viruses as you start up, but this setup may be a problem if you have a large disk to check (or don't restart often enough). With a large disk, the scanner adds as much as a minute to your startup time. Most important, you should scan new files as you install them on the system.

Is it possible to protect a computer system by using only software defenses? Not perfectly; however, software defenses can significantly reduce your risk of being affected by viruses if they are applied appropriately.

All virus defense systems are tools — each with its own capabilities and limitations. Learn how your system works, and make sure that you work within its limits.

Recovering from a virus

Most people know what to do when they have a cold: Drink plenty of fluids and get plenty of rest. However, many people do not know how to recover from a computer virus. Following are some steps to take if you discover that your computer is infected:

- **Don't panic.** Because many of these pests are malicious, one false move can wipe out your hard disk. Thoughtful analysis at this point can save you months of work.

- **Terminate all connections to the outside world.** Disconnect your mail connection, log off from AOL or CompuServe, and so on. You don't want to risk reinfection while trying to eradicate the virus.

- **Try to recall your activities and previous symptoms.** Maybe you remember that you borrowed a disk from a neighbor. If you did, you can test that disk. These recollections may help you recover your system.

- **Determine the nature and extent of the infection.** You should be aware of what happened to your system. For example, was the hard disk affected and has the damage stopped? Or has your hard disk stopped spinning?

- **Power down the infected system.**

- **Power up by using the write-protected, uninfected, original system disks.**

- **Back up all documents and data files to tape or disk.**

- **Do a low-level reformat of the infected hard disk.** If you don't know how to reformat your hard disk, seek expert advice. You may want to start at the store where you bought your system. If they don't know how to fix it, the chances are great that they know someone who does.

- **Restore the operating system software from the original disks.**

- **Reload all files that were backed up.**

   Where backups of the infected files are available and appropriate care was taken when making the backups, this solution is the safest, even though it requires a lot of work if you have many files.

- **Scan all floppy disks that you use for infections and reformat those that are infected.**

More commonly, a disinfecting program is used. If the virus is a boot sector infector, you can continue using the computer with relative safety after you boot it from a clean system disk, but going through all your disks to remove infection is wise, because sooner or later, you may be careless and leave a disk in the machine as it reboots.

Only fool around with virus eradication if you know what you're doing; otherwise, get some help, or you could end up being really sorry. Most computer stores have people who can help or can point you to someone who can. Newspapers usually have a technology section, where computer and virus consultants place ads. These ads are a good source if you're trying to find a professional to help you recover.

For legal beagles

You may think that there aren't any laws against viruses, but the exact opposite is true. Dealing briefly with all the relevant legislation in one country, let alone all of them, is impossible. In many countries, writing viruses is not an offense in itself. In others, distribution of viruses, and even the sharing of virus code between antivirus researchers, is, at least technically, an offense.

Laws that governments use to prosecute virus writers or distributors include the following:

- **Unauthorized access:** You may be guilty of gaining unauthorized access to a computer you've never seen if you distribute a virus.

- **Unauthorized modification:** You may be held accountable for unauthorized modification if you infect a file, boot sector, or partition sector.

- **Loss of data:** You may be liable for loss of data or accidental or intentional damage.

- **Public endangerment:** You may be prosecuted if your virus affects public safety.

- **Incitement:** You can be charged for incitement if you make available viruses, virus code, information about writing viruses, or virus engines.

- **Denial of service:** You may be liable for lost resources if your virus denies legitimate users access to their computer systems.

- **Government interest:** Any of the preceding laws may apply if you infect a computer system or data in which the government has an interest.

Because the law varies widely from country to country (and even within countries), it is entirely possible for you to break the law of another country, state, or province without ever leaving home.

Damaging data within a computer system used or operated by the government is illegal in both the U.S. and Canada. If you write a virus and it eventually infects a government system (which is highly probable), you are violating the law. Included in this category are damages incurred due to computer stoppages (that is, writing a virus that causes a computer to crash or become unusable) and viruses that destroy data.

To keep downtime short and losses low, do the minimum that you must to restore the system to a normal state, starting with booting the system from a clean disk. It is very unlikely that you need to low-level reformat the hard disk!

Software licensing

Some software vendors install time bombs in their products to combat the theft problem. Also known as *keys, traps,* or *access codes,* these devices are set to bring down the software at a predetermined time, usually upon expiration of the contract. These keys or traps are illegal. In cases where the vendor caused the software to stop, the courts have held the vendors liable for any damage that occurred. Because vendors often hide these devices, you should ask for a warranty against time bombs or deal only with reputable companies.

Sometimes vendors distribute time bombs accidentally. In early 1995, Microsoft, the world's leading software developer, gave its software partners infected disks at a seminar in London. Fortunately, a developer spotted the virus after the seminar, and everyone who attended was immediately warned. It is believed that only a few disks contained the virus.

Virus Self-Help Groups

You can find antiviral information in several places on the Internet. For example, VIRUS-L is an electronic mailing list for discussions of viruses and antivirus products. To subscribe, send e-mail to `listserv@lehigh.edu`, and put this in the body of the message: **subscribe virus-l** *your-name*. `comp.virus` is a USENET newsgroup that provides a discussion forum focusing on computer virus issues. VIRUS-L is distributed in digest form (with multiple e-mail postings in one large digest), and `comp.virus` is distributed as individual news postings. However, the content of the two groups is identical. Both groups are moderated, with all submissions sent to a moderator.

VALERT-L is a moderated sister group to VIRUS-L, but it is for virus alerts and warnings only, not discussions. VALERT-L has no direct USENET counterpart; it is strictly a mailing list. All VALERT-L postings are redistributed to VIRUS-L and `comp.virus` eventually.

VIRUS-L and `comp.virus` include a series of archive sites that carry all the back issues of VIRUS-L, as well as antivirus software (for various computers) and documents. The back issues date back to the group's inception on April 21, 1988. The list of archive sites is updated monthly and distributed to the group; it includes a complete listing of the sites, what they carry, and how to access them, as well as information on how to access FTP sites by e-mail. The anonymous FTP archive at `cert.org` in `pub/virus-l/docs/` contains information about viruses and antivirus products, with pointers to other FTP sites.

Good Virus Resources

Several major sources of information about specific viruses exist. Patricia Hoffman's Hypertext VSUM is probably the biggest one; however, it describes only DOS viruses. You can download it from most major archive sites. Appendix B provides a list of these sites, as does Chapter 17.

The Computer Virus Catalog (CVC), published by the Virus Test Center in Hamburg, contains a highly technical description of computer viruses for DOS, Mac, Amiga, Atari ST, and UNIX. The CVC is available for anonymous FTP from `ftp.informatik.uni-hamburg.de` in `pub/virus/texts/catalog`. You also can get a copy of the CVC by anonymous FTP from `cert.org` in the `pub/virus-l/docs/vtc` directory.

Another source of information is the documentation that comes with Dr. Solomon's Anti-Virus ToolKit. This documentation is more complete than the CVC list and is just as accurate, but it lists only DOS viruses. However, the documentation is not available electronically; you must buy the software package.

The best source of information for the Macintosh is the online documentation provided with the freeware Disinfectant program, available at most Macintosh archive sites. Appendix B and Chapter 18 provide a list of these sites.

Your antivirus program itself can be infected, so obtain your software from good sources and trust results only after you run scanners from a clean system.

The Last Word on Viruses

Access control systems should form part of your virus-control strategy. They are designed to protect your data from other users and their programs. However, an access control system protects your files from viruses no better than it protects your files from you.

Of course, having some access control is better than not having it at all. Just don't develop a false sense of security and rely entirely on an access control system to protect you.

Viruses are a very important issue for personal computer owners and users. You must know how to protect yourself against the malicious pestilence lurking out there. If you don't follow the advice in this chapter, you may become one of the unlucky who suffers a virus firsthand. Good luck.

Part III
The Places

"C'MON BRICKMAN, YOU KNOW AS WELL AS I DO THAT 'NOSE-SCANNING' IS OUR BEST DEFENSE AGAINST UNAUTHORIZED ACCESS TO PERSONAL FILES."

In this part...

This part describes the different places where the need for security arises: on the Internet and when using online services such as America Online, CompuServe, and Prodigy; when sending electronic mail either through your office network, over the Internet, or through an online service; and when composing, storing, and sending files. You'll find information about a wide range of hot topics that have cropped up along with the ever-expanding popularity of the Internet, such as keeping snoopers from reading your files, maintaining the privacy of your e-mail by using encryption, and keeping your kids safe on the Net.

Chapter 12

Accessing the Internet and Other Online Services

• •

In This Chapter

▶ Understanding Internet security

▶ Avoiding password sniffers, viruses, and other online threats

▶ Using commercial services securely

▶ Obeying copyright laws

▶ Understanding the dangers of electronic commerce

▶ Filtering offensive material

• •

Currently, the most popular stretch of the Information Superhighway is the Internet. You probably remember the Information Superhighway (or National Information Infrastructure), a term attributed to U.S. Vice President Al Gore. The Information Superhighway refers to all networks, public and private, free and commercial, that connect people around the globe. The Internet is where everyone wants to be these days. It's a huge web of computer networks spread all over the planet.

During the last decade, the Internet grew from 50 to more than 30,000 interconnected networks. These networks connect perhaps as many as 4.8 million computers, linking over 25 million users by copper wire, fiber optics, microwave, satellite, and radio with an amazing level of goodwill and trust. To continue this growth, the Internet will need to go on a high-fiber diet.

In 1988, the National Science Foundation estimated that over half a million Internet users existed. Today, the NSF estimates that 20 million people around the world use the Internet. But that number is just the tip of the iceberg. Over 3 million new subscribers joined the commercial online services and the Internet between January and March 1995 — a record number for a three-month period. Twelve million new users are expected to go online in each coming year.

If you are not an Internet user, but you know someone who is, check out the list of Internet Service Providers at http://www.yahoo.com/Business/Corporations/Internet_Access_Providers/, or http://www.celestin.com/pocia/index.html.

The dramatic increase in the Information Superhighway population arises from high-performance multimedia personal computers, equipped with high-speed modems (14.4 and 28.8 bits per second) and CD-ROM drives, and the recent addition of Internet access to America Online, CompuServe, and Prodigy. In addition, Internet use is increasing due to the recent convergence of personal computer technology and telephones, video and audio recorders, answering machines and voice mail, pagers, fax machines, copiers, printers, TV, and even home security and process-control systems (for example, your thermostat). Just look at the new Compaq and IBM PCs for the home. They do everything but make the coffee in the morning, and you can program them to do that! The new high-performance multimedia computers, modems, and networks have created unprecedented opportunities to increase every personal computer user's personal and business productivity.

The Internet enables people to meet thousands of others with shared interests, communicating quickly and inexpensively. Unlike television, radio, conventional cable, talk radio, 900 numbers, or even CB radio, the Internet lets you meet and participate with thousands of people in an online event; talk to dozens of people at a time; exchange ideas, words, and experiences — without having to leave your home or office. New videoconferencing systems enable you to type, view documents and images, and hear the voices or see the faces of others by using the latest multimedia technology.

But with all this activity, some implicit trust exists. Users of the Internet trust that their data will be transmitted and stored properly, and that their communications will not be intercepted, rerouted, altered, modified, or read by the wrong set of eyes. The sheer open nature of the Internet, and the fact that it is connected to so many computers and people, has made it a snooper's and cracker's gold mine.

Internet Security

The Internet pioneers didn't give much thought to security, at least not until business decided to exploit the benefits of the Internet. Now, everyone is concerned about security, as evidenced by all the Internet security stories in *USA Today.* So far, though, a lot of talk and not much action has occurred.

In essence, no codes of Internet conduct exist beyond some vague notion of "Netiquette," *de facto* rules of the road. No policing of inappropriate behavior exists, and anyone who chooses to do so (in Canada, the U.S., Europe, and Asia) can drive onto the Internet without first getting a license.

The rapid increase in commercial traffic is also making tracking and stopping breaches more difficult. Although nothing yet exists but anecdotal evidence of companies with Internet links suffering significant losses as a result of security breaches, you have to figure that more breaches will occur in a matter of time. Most attacks have been aimed at universities, research centers, the military, and other noncommercial sites. Obviously, such attacks have financial implications associated with them, but they are difficult to quantify. Authorities tried to compute the damage caused by the Internet Worm, but various amounts were given, and finally the court decided to compromise on a total of more than $6,000. (See Chapter 11 for more information about Robert Morris, Jr. and his Worm.)

Despite all the benefits of the Internet, some grave issues are associated with its use. Some problems of late on the Internet involve password sniffing and compromise, viruses, e-mail interception, and offensive behavior.

Password sniffing

A cracker breaks into a computer, gets privilege, and installs a *packet sniffer* — a program designed to monitor network traffic passing through the machine. Essentially, a sniffer captures the userids and passwords that the computer's clients enter before connecting to another machine. The sniffer grabs the first dozen or so characters entered during these sessions — containing the userids and passwords — and stores them in a hidden file. Later, the cracker retrieves the secret file and uses the userids and passwords to break into other computers. This attack is by far the most common type of reported Internet security incident, according to the Computer Emergency Response Team, or CERT.

These attacks are successful because they are difficult to spot. In one reported episode, a system's administrators were unaware that a sniffer had been installed until it had captured so many userids and passwords that the computer's hard drive became full and the machine crashed. CERT reported that as many as 600,000 passwords were compromised by sniffer episodes.

E-mail

One of the most compelling reasons for people to connect to the Internet is to send and receive e-mail. You can send messages to people in different time zones on your own schedule. Your correspondent doesn't have to be waiting to receive your message. However, your message is at risk at various points along its journey.

The message travels from your computer through other computers and arrives at your friend's machine. The administrators of those computers, or anyone along the way who wants to do so, can intercept your messages and can read your e-mail.

CERT

CERT is the Computer Emergency Response Team, located at Carnegie Mellon University in Pittsburgh, Pennsylvania. Originally, it was funded by the U.S. government in response to the Robert T. Morris Jr. Internet Worm of November 2, 1988 (as Chapter 11 discusses). CERT disseminates advisories on potential security weaknesses on the Internet. If you think you are being compromised when using the Internet, contact CERT. They would like to hear from you. The U.S. CERT is a member of FIRST, which is a consortium of country emergency response teams. Jump to Appendix A if you want to subscribe right now to their invaluable advisory service. (You don't have to be American.)

One thing is certain: Some messages are okay to send as e-mail, and others aren't. You know which of your messages you don't want other people to read. As a rule, never e-mail your credit card numbers or nasty notes about anyone. If you don't want anyone else to read your e-mail, encrypt it before you send it. Chapter 13 gives you a look at an encryption program called Pretty Good Privacy. It's free, it's easy, and it works.

Those nasty viruses

When you download files, nothing keeps you from downloading viruses as well. When connecting to the Internet, ensuring that your PC is running antivirus software is critical.

One time, Peter was lurking in the `alt.2600` USENET newsgroup (a cracker group — see Appendix A for more information), looking for new tools. A rather naive individual asked whether anyone knew where to get a copy of a virus-writing program. Now, before you laugh, such a program exists: the Virus Creation Laboratory (VCL). It has a really nice graphical user interface (just like Microsoft Word for Windows) that enables you to pull down menus to decide what damage you want to do and to what device you want to do it. Then you create a run-time version of the virus and give it to your friends (just kidding). Back to the story at hand, a nasty person answered the naive individual and said to go to a particular site, a particular directory, and download Goldbug. Besides being the title of an Edgar Allan Poe story, Goldbug is a particularly vile virus. When the naive individual clicked on the self-extracting file — oops, you said you wanted to *create* a virus.

A virus needs to latch onto a program before it can execute. Because e-mail messages aren't files or programs, nothing exists for the virus to use as a launching pad. However, a virus (or any kind of computer code, for that matter) can be attached to an e-mail message and sent to you. If you open the e-mail message and then open the code attached to it, you might get hit by a virus — for example, the Word Concept virus. To be safe, you should scan all programs that you download for viruses. In addition, use WordPad (if you have Windows 95) to open Word documents from strangers (or even careless friends). WordPad won't execute Word macros and won't spread the Word Concept virus.

You should be aware of both naive and nasty individuals. The Internet, like any other society, is filled with people who enjoy the electronic equivalent of tagging other people's walls with spray paint, knocking over mailboxes, sitting in the street honking car horns, or breaking into homes. The Internet is a lightning rod to the world's troublemakers. These truths can be disturbing because some people try to get real work done over the Internet, and others have sensitive or proprietary data that they must protect.

Cracking scripts available online

Security is compromised in other ways besides viruses and password sniffing, of course. Some crackers have resorted to using *attack scanners,* which is software designed to probe a machine for known security weaknesses. These attack scanners, such as the Security Analysis Tool for Auditing Networks (SATAN) in particular, were designed as security tools. Theoretically, you try the scanner against your own site — before others do — and then close whatever loopholes you find.

The disturbing fact is that these "White Hat" programs are available to the "Black Hats" as well. Hacker BBSs are home to lots of attack software for the downloading. This causes problems for you, because crackers make attack scripts available quickly after discovering a security weakness or flaw. Shortly after someone pointed out the password flaw in Windows 95, a clever individual made available a program that exploited the flaw. This cycle of events is typical, which means that you have to keep informed to stay one step ahead of people attacking your system. Subscribe to a full-disclosure mailing list, such as Bugtraq or 8lgm. (See Appendix A for information about these mailing lists.) In addition, you should keep abreast of update information from your vendor. For example, Microsoft's World Wide Web site (`http:www.microsoft.com`) provides a fix for the password flaw in Windows 95.

Here's looking at you, kid

When you're looking at a World Wide Web page, how do you know that the page isn't looking at you? That question is not as far-fetched as you may think. When you access America Online, CompuServe, Prodigy, and other online services, all sorts of fancy graphics are sent to your machine, whether you ask for them or not. For example, when you log on to these services, they send a message to your desktop telling you how many e-mail messages are waiting for you. If an online service can write to your machine, what prevents it from reading what you store there?

Internet communications are *full-duplex.* What does that mean? Well, think of the difference between a walkie-talkie and a telephone. Walkie-talkies are half-duplex, which means that only one person can send (that is, speak) at a time. With a telephone, which is full-duplex, two people can talk at the same time. So someone could be looking at your hard drive as you look at that person's Web page! If your hard drive spins up unexpectedly, someone may be browsing your system.

Several programs take a look at your system's configuration, perhaps during installation and setup, or as part of warranty information-gathering. You may have heard all the criticism of The Microsoft Network (MSN) product; sources alleged that MSN checked out your system when you enrolled. Central Point got into trouble by including an electronic registration form for its PC Tools for Windows software. The software scanned the owner's machine to determine the configuration before sending that information along with the registration to Central Point. Reportedly, Central Point says that the scanning was unintentional, but they put a halt to it after owners complained.

Using Commercial Networks Securely

Generally, commercial services do the best that they can to provide a secure environment. But some risks are associated with use of commercial online services. The following sections look at what to do when you sign up with an online service provider — your on-ramp to the Information Superhighway.

Nosy online providers

When you sign up with an online provider, the service asks you to provide information about yourself. Find out what information is required by the provider and ask what information it shares with other subscribers. Also, ask whether credit card records are stored online (Netcom used to do this). Ask whether the provider will give out reference customers who are happy with the service.

If you want some degree of privacy and anonymity, don't provide any more information than you must. Following is some information that you might consider not giving out:

✔ Middle name (where possible)

✔ Street address (Provide your mailing address instead, where possible.)

✔ Phone number (Why would an online provider call you anyway?)

✔ Social Security (or Insurance) number (Large providers don't ask for this number; don't give it to anyone. SSNs and SINs are reserved for government use.)

✔ Long-distance telephone company calling card or credit card number (The service doesn't need this unless they intend to charge something to you.)

✔ Family member names

✔ Household income (This information is between you and the tax collectors; don't give it out.)

✔ Race, political party, and religion

✔ Age

✔ Sexual orientation

✔ Occupation

✔ Employer's name and work phone number

✔ University, college, or school

✔ Make and license plate number of your car

✔ Other questions unrelated to online service and usage

Who do you want to be?

Prodigy enables you to search by a fellow member's name. CompuServe enables you to search by name, address, city, and state. America Online's search facility is the most powerful. It's extremely fast and easy, enabling you to search by using multiple simultaneous keywords. When you know someone's screen name, real name, city, interests, and place of work, finding someone is easy and takes about five minutes. Obviously, knowing about this facility should cause you to think about what goes in your profile. But most AOL members aren't even aware that their profiles can be searched by keyword.

America Online and many other services permit subscribers to create profiles or mini-autobiographies about themselves. If you don't supply a profile, people can't search for it, but they can find your screen name when you are online.

America Online's subscribers can actually scan thousands of users by real or screen name, sexual preference, race, occupation, interest, company, and even religious beliefs — when that information is in a profile. And many people put the most revealing information about themselves in their profiles. But many users are unaware that their interests may attract unwanted individuals.

When you don't want e-mail from strangers interested in your profession or interests, you probably shouldn't supply a profile. If you are conducting business on the Internet, provide only what information is necessary, not what could compromise your security. For example, when you supply the *type* of computer you use, anyone can design a virus just for your system and send it to you as an e-mail attachment. Table 12-1 shows the items on the AOL profile input screen and suggests information that you should consider not supplying.

Table 12-1	America Online Secure Profile Recommendation
Profile Item	*Recommendation*
Screen Name	Screen name only
Member Name	Full name when doing business
City, State, Country	Post office only; never give street address
Birthday	Do not supply; could be used to find you
Sex	Consider omitting when doing only business
Marital Status	Omit unless you are interested in meeting friends
Hobbies	Omit unless you are interested in meeting friends
Computers Used	Do not provide under any circumstances
Occupation	Provide when not doing business on the network
Personal Quote	Avoid if you need anonymity

Be careful about giving out too much information, regardless of which online service you use.

Online services and encryption

AOL, Delphi, and Prodigy don't transmit encrypted messages. Still, if you want to have Internet access, using a commercial service is a secure way to go about it. Just don't use e-mail to send sensitive information. (Or simply subscribe to CompuServe, which enables you to send encrypted files and e-mail.)

Free speech and online services

Online service providers make their own rules about the types of speech permitted on their services. America Online is regarded as the most stringent enforcer of online speech restrictions. The restrictions don't apply just to chat room conduct and language.

On America Online, and possibly a few other services, e-mail content is subject to review and evaluation by an unseen group called Terms of Service Staff. When subscribers break the Terms of Services provisions, their service can be cut off immediately with no prior warning. The Terms of Service Staff typically don't respond to e-mail from those who have been kicked offline, they don't take phone calls, and they don't respond to faxes unless they choose to do so. In short, if you want to indulge your sexual fantasies and spew forth obscenities, America Online is not the place for you — try the World Wide Web instead.

Note, for example, these points from AOL's general rules:

- AOL provides parental control features that can prohibit minors from accessing various areas of the service.

- AOL makes information about members available to third parties such as advertisers, unless members know how to prevent it.

- Members aren't allowed to use screen names that are vulgar or offensive or that serve to impersonate living persons.

- Members are encouraged to report any violations to the Terms of Service Staff.

- Chain letters and pyramid schemes are prohibited.

- Vulgar, abusive, or hateful language is forbidden and may lead to an on-screen-warning or immediate termination.

- "Unsolicited advertising, promotional material, or other forms of solicitation to other Members" are prohibited in most areas.

- "Room disruption," which is defined as "purposefully interfering with the normal flow of dialogue in a chat room" by, for example, "repeatedly interrupting conversation between Members, or by acting in such a way as to antagonize, harass, or create hostility in a chat room" is forbidden.

- Scrolling, or causing other members' screens to scroll faster than the Member can type by, for example, holding down a Return key, is forbidden.

- Harassing another member by targeting that person for "distress, embarrassment, unwanted attention, or other discomfort" or by attacking that person's "race, national origin, ethnicity, religion, gender, sexual orientation, or other such affiliation" is forbidden.

Of course, most people agree that these actions should be forbidden! AOL positions itself as a family-oriented service and chooses to control the actions of its membership to promote a family atmosphere.

Prodigy isn't quite as restrictive as America Online, but it does have a policy that explicitly forbids profanity. CompuServe is far less restrictive in its online censorship. Basically, CompuServe members agree not to post anything that "violates or infringes upon the rights of any others, or which would be abusive, profane, or offensive to an average person." They also prohibit "advertising, promotion, or solicitation of goods or services for commercial purposes." And whether or not you understood the CompuServe Information Service Operating Rules, they reserve the right to "suspend or terminate Service to any member at any time."

Chat rooms

Chat rooms are virtual conferences. Customers with a variety of interests can chat in groups of up to 50 people. Public rooms on America Online are always monitored, but private rooms created by individual subscribers are not. U.S. courts have ruled that private rooms are protected by the First Amendment, because consent is implied when a person enters a private room. Rules govern chat areas, and the online providers have a right to establish their own standards. The rules generally discourage the following behaviors:

- ✔ Name calling, beratement, or personal attacks
- ✔ Threats
- ✔ Shouting (typing in ALL CAPITAL LETTERS)
- ✔ Scrolling (see below)
- ✔ Chat room disruption

The term *scroll* came into use after people out of boredom used to type a word followed by the Enter key, causing the word to be printed and scrolled up on everybody's screen in the chat room. This action made chatting difficult, of course, as it interrupted the conversation. Some scrollers are very creative and transmit character art during chat sessions. Even though the art might be pleasing, this transmission is also against the rules and can get you kicked offline when your service's Chat Cops are lurking. Read Chapter 13 to find more information about this practice.

No precise definition of this behavior exists, and the online provider has the discretion to determine when a violation has actually taken place. Sometimes enforcement of online rules is dependent upon the censor and sometimes upon the person lodging the complaint. America Online seems to be the harshest enforcer of chat control, with Prodigy being less strict, and CompuServe hardly monitoring its rooms. AOL has been accused of throwing people off simply because they disagreed with other users and made them angry.

Chat spoofing and replicating

AOHell (a widely available program) enables a user to replicate another America Online subscriber's screen name while in a chat room. Impersonators who want to hurt another person's online reputation go into rooms and insult subscribers or behave in an unfriendly way. The results can be quite harmful emotionally, with possible legal consequences and account termination for those caught doing it.

The same program also is used to harass a member. Imagine going into your favorite room and finding a member you don't like, and then going to another area and finding that same person there. You then leave all rooms and decide to write a letter, when you are bombarded with three messages from the same screen name. Before you can respond to one, you are bombarded again — this time by more angry messages than one person can possibly type. (Normally, more than one person can't sign on with the same userid and password — or even on the same account — at the same time. If you log on and someone is already logged on to your account, contact the Internet or online service provider immediately!)

This harassment is what it is like to be a victim of AOHell, or online replicating. If you think that someone is targeting you for harassment, tell the AOL staff.

Online service integrity

Just like your local and long-distance telephone companies, online services can give their employees access to your name, phone number, credit card number, employer, and Social Security (or Insurance) number. The largest online service, America Online, once allowed employees to access password files, supposedly to help change passwords. Now, America Online employees can only change subscriber's passwords or view the last four digits of credit card numbers. An audit trail is supposed to exist for every transaction, together with a reason why the record was viewed. But to be safe, don't keep information that is important to you on AOL.

America Online, CompuServe, and Prodigy all advise customers to download only from trusted, sanitized sources. Otherwise, the only way to remain virus-free on the Information Superhighway is not to download any files — not from e-mail, FTP, Web sites, newsgroups, or any Internet resource. The services are about 98 percent virus-free because of their continuous scans of software. But about 2 percent of the time, viruses get through. Because new viruses are introduced all the time, following strict antivirus procedures is important, whether or not you think you are infected. Also remember that before you upload anything to the Internet or an online service, you should scan it as a courtesy to others.

Sending e-mail to the right place

Your e-mail is at risk when you mis-address it and send it to the wrong place. If you are like us, you have received misdirected mail. Some simple rules exist for sending mail from the Internet to the major commercial online services, as the following sections describe.

Internet to America Online

Creating the Internet version of an America Online address requires you to ignore the case, remove the spaces, and add @aol.com to the name. Thus, an America Online name of *Jane Doe* becomes janedoe@aol.com. To find addresses, send e-mail to NameSearch@aol.com and provide the person's real name, state, and city; you also can try its World Wide Web service at http://home.aol.com/.

Internet to CompuServe

If someone's CompuServe ID is *77777,7777,* you can send Internet mail to 77777.7777@compuserve.com (change the comma to a period and append the site name). You also can check out CompuServe's Web site (http://www.compuserve.com) to see whether your friend has an alias, such as Jane Doe, in which case send it to janedoe@compuserve.com.

Internet to Delphi

Delphi users can receive Internet e-mail at username@delphi.com — for example, JDOE@delphi.com. Usernames are subscriber-defined and vary from "handles" to real names. Only Delphi customers can gain information on other Delphi users from within Delphi — no Internet-wide facility to look up Delphi subscribers is available.

Internet to GEnie

Creating the Internet version of a GEnie address requires that you add @genie.geis.com to the end of the address. Thus, GEnie address *J.DOE3* becomes J.DOE3@genie.geis.com. GEnie addresses aren't case-sensitive, but you should preserve periods.

Internet to Prodigy

Prodigy users can receive Internet mail via the address format kzll68a@prodigy.com, where *kzll68a* is the recipient's Prodigy user ID.

Copyright Law Online

Many people wonder whether copyright law as we know it can be enforced on computer networks. Copyright laws protect all original copyrighted work, whether in printed or electronic form. But some exceptions exist to the copyright protection on the Internet. A major exception in copyright law is the *fair use principle,* which permits quotation from copyrighted material when you meet certain conditions. But fair use implies that you must avoid abusing this right by following these rules:

- ✔ Minimize the amount of text you quote (usually less than five lines)
- ✔ Make the quotation a small percentage of your overall work
- ✔ Ensure that your work doesn't compete with the sales of the original work
- ✔ Don't depend on the quoted material as a way to sell your work
- ✔ Quote material for reasons of educational or societal benefit

Examples of the fair use law are TV stations airing short film clips of as-yet-unreleased movies, short excerpts from books in the news, screenshots in computer books, and limited photocopying for one-time educational use. All these forms of fair use can be extended to online systems.

Copyright and e-mail

E-mail and the law have had a little bit of exposure in the courts, but the decisions came out against privacy and for property and propriety of the owners of the e-mail facility. E-mail is private when it's sent from one individual to another person or organization. When the e-mail is sent at work, through an employer's computer, it isn't private and is in fact the property of the employer. (Employers aren't liable even when they lie, saying that they aren't monitoring when they actually are monitoring.)

Knowing that your mail is not private, you should use your organization's e-mail system to send only work-related messages. In addition, say in your e-mail only the things that you would want everybody to know, or at least wouldn't mind them reading.

Copyright and data files

Online systems store computer files in mass quantities. The basic rules of online ownership of data files are simple: The creator of the file is the owner of the file, under copyright law. For a file to warrant this kind of protection, the work must contain original, new, copyrightable material such as text, photographs, drawings, music, or video material.

Downloading commercial programs

Because commercial programs are copyrightable, all provisions of copyright law are enforceable against copying programs. In addition, routines or segments of a program can be copyrighted. The downloading rules apply to e-mail, file transfer, and all other types of network downloads.

When you send a commercial program to a friend, technically you commit a copyright violation unless you get special permission. But you probably won't be prosecuted unless your friend rats you out.

When someone posts a copy of a commercial program on a message board, that action is illegal — and may get the person into trouble.

When a software program contains a patented process or formula, such a program is protected under federal patent law. Patents cannot protect numbers, but in cases where formulas protect unique processes that are specifically related to the area of application of the program, those patents can be protected so that anyone using the formulas must pay license fees to the owners of the patent. This fact is the case with RSA, which purchased many of the patents that provide for private and public key encryption. Every software product sold in the U.S. that uses RSA-owned patents must pay patent fees to RSA.

Shareware

Many people think that shareware is free, but it isn't. Shareware is regular software, and it is commercial, not free. The term *share* is misleading because the software isn't actually shared like multiuser software; it's just distributed freely.

Shareware is passed from one user to another on floppy disks, or can be posted on BBSs, online services, and the Internet. Hundreds of thousands of shareware programs are available, and everyone is free to load them onto their systems. The authors simply ask that when you use the software, you pay the fee, which is usually displayed when you start the program. Nobody will ever break down your door to confiscate your computer because you use shareware without paying the fee. But every time you start the program and see the message reminding you the pay the fee, it works on your subconscious and sense of right, and you eventually pay just to get rid of the `Your evaluation period has expired. Please register now.` message.

Copyright, freeware, and public domain software

Freeware or public domain software is completely and totally free of charge, with no restrictions on the transfer and use of the program. Some people actually sell this software, usually in compilations. Although this practice isn't exactly ethical, no law rules against this practice.

Copyright and images

Online images are fully copyrightable upon creation by the photographer or artist. Copying images and using them in another image is a copyright infringement. Unfortunately, with electronic photo-retouching, where you can modify, cut, paste, distort, and combine images, identifying the original image often is difficult or impossible. The general rule says that when the original image is recognizable, the act of copying is possibly an infringement.

Copyright and music

Sounds also are protected under copyright laws. Musicians are attempting to extract both copyright and performance fees for copying music from the Internet (one fee for a copy of the music, plus another fee for the performance on TV-like media, such as a multimedia computer).

Digital Commerce

You want to know where the action is on the Internet these days? Get on the World Wide Web (WWW). In only a short time, it has become amazingly popular, partly because it's easy to get around.

Everyone who has set up shop on the WWW has a display window called a *home page,* with text, sound clips, video, photographic images, and other graphics. Click on a highlighted bit of text on one home page and you are linked to yet another page.

Thousands of companies are scrambling to set up shop on the WWW to show off their wares. They're gambling that Web cruisers like you and me will buy goods and services at the click of a mouse button. This won't happen, however, until someone finds a way to exchange money securely.

Cryptography (the process of encoding messages, as described in Chapter 13) is expected to grow with the growing use of digital cash, which is a way of passing real money — actually, the electronic equivalent — over the Internet. Digital cash combines the benefits of anonymous legal tender with the speed and convenience of online commerce. No risky exchange of credit card information occurs. The digital cash resides in a computer protected by a multitude of passwords, access restrictions, and encryption.

Electronic cash must prevent consumers' names and personal habits from being diverted to nosy databases that are designed to capture records deemed usable by commercial advertisers and solicitors.

Economists say that digital cash will be good for society, helping to reduce the cost and delays in commerce, thus providing cheaper goods and services to consumers. Criminals will love digital cash, because anybody can use it to transfer money for legal or illegal purposes.

Online banking

Some online services offer online banking, which permits subscribers to view account status, transfer accounts — even pay credit card bills, utilities, and mortgage payments.

VISA and MasterCard announced that they will be working together on a standard for providing secure encrypted credit card transactions. They also have reached agreement with the developers of Netscape and Mosaic to permit credit card purchases for Web shoppers. These agreements reinforce the positions of industry authorities, who predict that the Web will replace a significant portion of the mass commercial market; with the two leading credit card companies establishing a standard, that prediction now is closer to reality.

A lot of people talk about electronic commerce on the WWW. Not much is going to happen until consumers can be confident that when they order products and use their credit cards to pay for them, no one is going to grab their card number and rack up expensive purchases. Until using encryption and digital signatures is a standard way of doing business on the Web, don't provide anyone your credit card data, either on a Web page or in an e-mail message.

Although electronic commerce on the Internet is in its infancy, the trend toward providing a secure environment, where consumers can safely supply vendors with credit card information at the time of purchase, is seen by many as the preferable way to do business on the Internet. This method of payment is similar to a traditional credit card purchase, where the consumer presents the seller with a credit card, or just the card number when doing business over the phone. As the customer, you aren't limited to only a specific card that you have preregistered. The vendor has the opportunity to process the transaction with the bank at the time of purchase, just as merchants do now when they swipe the card in a reader.

In fact, a whole system of financial procedures that depend on encrypted signatures, secure message transmission, and a wide acceptance of secure protocols is fairly far along in the development process. One of the brighter stars in this market is Netscape.

Netscape Communications Corporation

In the early days of the Web, no thought was given to securing communications for financial transactions. Early users of the Web exploited the Internet for pure research or fun. When they wanted to communicate securely, they simply encrypted their messages using PGP, PEM, or some similar program. Chapter 13 discusses these encryption programs.

The explosion of the use of Web browsers as the vehicle for getting onto the Information Superhighway has changed every previously conceived notion of the role of Web browser software. Netscape's Navigator browser now accounts for approximately 75 percent of all traffic on the World Wide Web. Suffice to say that the vast majority of the estimated 25 million Web surfers use Netscape.

With encryption routines licensed from RSA and support for a number of protocols, Netscape Navigator provides a model for secure communications and commerce on the Internet.

Secure Sockets Layer protocol

The major contribution of Netscape to electronic commerce is the Secure Sockets Layer protocol (SSL). Based on encryption technology developed by RSA, SSL enables secure point-to-point communication over the Internet. If Netscape is successful in gaining widespread acceptance of the SSL protocol by users, Web software developers, vendors, and financial institutions, perhaps the company can overcome the mistrust people have of conducting financial transactions over the Internet.

The whole problem with passing payment information across the Internet is the openness of the Internet itself. The protocols specifying how e-mail and documents are transported from one computer to another across the Internet are based on plain text. The original assumption was that the application would worry about the security of the message or text. But that situation didn't happen, which begged for another solution. The SSL protocol is one solution that enables you to use several security mechanisms when required, without interfering with those messages or transactions that don't need security (such as surfing Web pages for research or entertainment). SSL is a layer that plugs in between your transport protocols and application-specific protocols.

When a consumer connects to a secure server doing electronic commerce, the browser — in this case, Netscape — and the server perform a handshaking routine that authenticates the identity of the server by its digital signature. The server and the client (Netscape's browser) then secretly agree on the security level needed for the transaction and the public encryption keys for use. After the connection is established, the data stream between the user and the merchant is encrypted.

Not only is credit card information encrypted, but the entire transaction is scrambled as well. Snoopers are prevented from discovering anything about the transaction, including what items are ordered, quantities, price, and so on. The transaction is completely private on both ends.

In addition, Netscape provides for users to obtain their own digital signatures so that merchants can authenticate the source of orders. Authentication is the equivalent of a customer providing identification in a normal transaction by presenting a driver's license or some other picture identification card.

In the secure environment provided by SSL and in complementary protocols like secure MIME and secure HTTP, you can provide payment information without fear that your credit card information will end up in the wrong hands.

HTTP is the abbreviation for HyperText Transfer Protocol, which is a connection protocol that automatically links WWW sites. Simply, the World Wide Web links documents marked up by HyperText Markup Language (HTML), using

HTTP. HTML is the native dialect of the WWW. MIME is the Multipurpose Internet Mail Extensions protocol for transferring non-textual data, such as audio or pictures, by using e-mail.

Digital signatures

Authentication services for Netscape's security implementation are provided by a trusted third-party arrangement with VeriSign, a spin-off company from RSA Data Security.

VISA, the world's largest issuer of credit cards, is aggressively supporting the development of viable payment mechanisms using public networks like the Internet. To that end, VISA is involved in the funding of experimental projects ranging from the issuance of smart cards, to VeriSign, to developing standards in partnership with Microsoft. Understandably, their mission is to facilitate the use of the millions of credit cards already in circulation.

Under this arrangement, companies setting up a Netscape Commerce Server can register with VeriSign for a small fee to receive a digital identifier that browser software can use to authenticate the server. In addition, users can establish their own digital signatures to identify themselves to merchants.

The *digital signature,* or Digital ID as VeriSign calls it, consists of a public encryption key, the user's name, an expiration date, and the digital signature of the certifying authority issuing the Digital ID. Thus, a merchant's system can identify the user and authenticate that the user's digital signature is genuine by using the issuer's digital signature.

By combining encryption of the transaction with authentication procedures, the Internet becomes a viable vehicle for electronic commerce. Consumers are protected from losing credit card information to snoopers and crackers, and merchants can handle purchases in real time, including authenticating customer information and processing credit card authorizations. If the system performs as designed, soon the 95 percent of computer users who don't trust sending credit card information via the Internet will change their minds. When that happens, electronic commerce will explode.

The Bogeyman and Parental Control

Just as your neighborhood isn't truly safe, the Information Superhighway's fastest lane — the Internet — is not a safe place for unsupervised children or teens. Online perverts are everywhere, and lewd photos (in GIF and JPEG format) are available for downloading. Kids should be taught the two cardinal rules of the road on the Information Superhighway:

✔ Never give out personal or family data such as phone numbers or
  addresses.

✔ Never respond to suggestive messages.

All kids should be told to report such instances to parents. It seems simple, but
you would be amazed at how little parental control is exercised. Parents must
study what's happening on the Internet and keep tabs on what their children
are downloading and viewing and with whom they're chatting.

GIF, or *graphic interchange file,* is a format developed by CompuServe for
transmission of pictures, drawings, and graphics to all computers. JPEG (which
stands for *Joint Photographic Experts Group*) is another popular graphic file
format, which reduces the size of image files by up to 20 times at the cost of
slightly reduced image quality.

The Internet thrives on consensual anarchy, and it has no official cops, top
dogs, ombudsmen, arbitrators, or negotiators. It has become the *de facto*
electronic town hall to discuss and disseminate information related to just
about every area of human thought and endeavor. But it also is a place where
sick people reside, using the voiceless, faceless medium of plain text to deceive,
manipulate, and seduce minors (and a surprising number of adults) into doing
things they might not otherwise do, and in some cases harm those whom they
snare. The process usually starts with chat, because that's where the stalkers
hunt for naive youths. In 1995, there were a rash of cases in which minors ran
away from home after conversations with adults in chat rooms. Although
federal and state legislators are passing laws to lock up online stalkers, no law
can protect your child better than your supervision.

America Online, CompuServe, Prodigy, Delphi, GEnie, and other online services
give parental advisories and provide controls to restrict access to certain areas
of the network.

AOL's Parental Control can be used only by the *master account,* or the permanent screen name that you create during your first sign-on to America Online.
AOL allows you to have more than one screen name, so you can give a separate
screen name to your spouse or children. Parental Control enables the master
account holder to restrict access to certain areas and features. You can set
Parental Control for one or more screen names for the account. After you set
Parental Control for a particular screen name, the control is active each time
that screen name signs on. The master account holder can make changes to
Parental Control at any time.

Using the master account, you can set any or all of the four Parental Control
features to block access for any screen name associated with the account. Table
12-2 describes AOL's Parental Control features.

Table 12-2	Parental Control in America Online
Option	**Description**
BLOCK INSTANT MESSAGES	Turns off Instant Messages — immediate, person-to-person conversations that only the sender and receiver can view.
BLOCK ALL ROOMS	Blocks access to the People Connection — the live, interactive chat area of America Online.
BLOCK MEMBER ROOMS	Blocks access only to the member-created rooms within the People Connection.
BLOCK CONFERENCE ROOMS	Blocks access to the special-interest rooms found throughout America Online, such as the NeverWinter Nights role-playing games in Games and Entertainment.

Prodigy allows the Membership Holder (the member whose ID ends in *A*) to control household access to areas of the service. The *A* member can control access to Chat, the Lifestyles bulletin board, and the USENET newsgroups.

In order for members B to F to enter these rooms, they must be enrolled by the A member. CompuServe allows you to set parental controls as well. The owner of the account can set Permanent or Session Only restrictions for the Internet and CompuServe services. Use of Parental Controls is password-protected.

See the following section for information about additional products you can use to block offensive material.

Blocking Offensive Web Content

You may not have children, but you may still find some material on the Net offensive. Regardless of any laws passed and regardless of any sort of shift in the judicial winds, the Web will always contain smut, hate speech, radical political ideas, and the like — what you may consider "offensive" Web content. Whether you are easily offended, simply don't want to come into contact with offensive materials, or have a self-imposed duty to protect your child, a number of products are available that you can easily pick up and install on your computer to limit access to whatever material you deem inappropriate.

Cyber Patrol

Effective self-regulation is the best way to avoid government-imposed restrictions. One available self-regulation approach is to screen Web addresses against a master list of known sites with potentially offensive materials and to analyze page content for profanities and other catchwords and phrases. In this way, parents can help protect their children from adult themes and topics. This methodology is called *filtering*.

Cyber Patrol is one of the best applications providing Internet filtering. By installing Cyber Patrol on your system, you can effectively block out a broad range of unwanted material. A free Home Edition (which you can download from `http://www.microsys.com/CYBER/` or from CompuServe or Prodigy) is available to demonstrate the program's features. Cyber Patrol blocks not only Web sites, but also USENET newsgroups, chats, and other Internet protocols. The program allows parents to restrict Internet access to certain times of day and to limit the total time spent online in a day. Cyber Patrol even can control access to local applications, such as games and personal financial managers. If you like what you see, you can order a more versatile and customizable version of Cyber Patrol from the same home page. Cyber Patrol is available for both Macintosh and Windows computers.

According to its creators, the object of Cyber Patrol is not to promote censorship on the Internet. Rather, it is an attempt to avoid the imposition of censorship.

During the installation process, you are prompted to enter a master password; in Cyber Patrol's cop-like jargon, this is called the *Headquarters Password.* This password controls the actions of Cyber Patrol. As well, you can create a Deputy password that enables someone to gain unfettered access to the Internet. You might make your spouse the Deputy.

After you install the software, you can use the Options menu to customize the program. In Figure 12-1, you see the control panel for Cyber Patrol. Using this panel, you can control access to Internet Relay Chat (IRC, which computer crackers use a lot), WWW and FTP sites, newsgroups, games, and applications. Select one of these categories, and you see the window shown in Figure 12-2. To add a text string to the wildcard list, follow these steps:

1. **Type the text string in the Reject Wildcards field (for example,** sex).
2. **Press the Enter key.**
3. **Click the <Save> button.**

By editing a time line for each day of the week, you can establish times of day, maximum daily hours, and maximum weekly hours for accessing the Internet. By restricting access to those times when you are most likely to be available for supervision, you can increase the effectiveness of Cyber Patrol filtering.

When you or your kids find a site that should be blocked, you can use the Headquarters Password to add that site to your CyberNOT Block List, which already has more than 6,000 researched Internet resources containing dubious material. You also can unblock blocked sites, making them available to you. The CyberNOT list is similar to the databases of viruses used by most antivirus software. Because of the way Web sites spring up and disappear, however, such a list quickly becomes obsolete. The basic CyberNOT list is updated weekly, and the Cyber Patrol program can download it automatically.

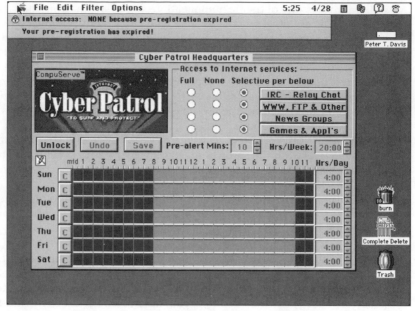

Figure 12-1:
The Cyber Patrol control panel, which enables you to block access to areas that have offensive content.

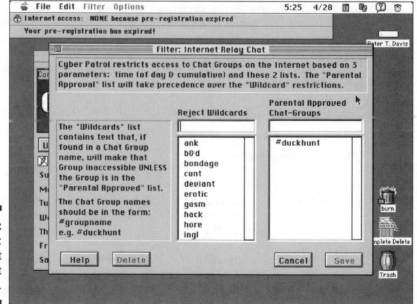

Figure 12-2:
The Filter: Internet Realy Chat window.

After you install Cyber Patrol, Internet connections work exactly as before, except that when Cyber Patrol locates an Internet resource that it thinks should be blocked, it notifies you that a block is being enforced.

If no objectionable content is detected, your attempts to access Internet resources occur normally. You may detect a slight slowdown when Cyber Patrol scans the resource to see whether it should be blocked on the basis of the CyberNOT list or the blocking criteria, but other operations continue as usual.

Remember the password you use in installing Cyber Patrol; you need it to remove the program or to control the features of the program. Should you forget the password, you may end up having to reformat the hard disk to get unrestricted access to the Internet.

As a result of a German investigation into Internet content in December 1995, CompuServe temporarily suspended access to more than 200 newsgroups. The German authorities deemed that those newsgroups were sexually explicit. (You can see a list of the banned sites at `http://www.epic.org/free_speech/censorship/CIS_banned.txt`.) Shortly thereafter, in February 1996, CompuServe introduced parental controls (GO CONTROLS) and Cyber Patrol (available free). At the same time, CompuServe made available online the *Child Safety Online* publication jointly produced by the National Center for Missing and Exploited Children and the Interactive Services Association.

Other filtering sources

Spyglass, Inc. offers a product that specifically blocks all adult areas on the Internet and the World Wide Web. *Surf Watch,* software distributed by a California company, includes a program that automatically blocks children's access to adult locations on the Internet. It still doesn't enable adults to leave their children unsupervised with the computer (any more than with the TV), but parents don't have to worry as much about their kids winding up in adult-oriented chat rooms, alternative newsgroups, and other locations where the words and images may not be acceptable for young minds. SurfWatch's developer is constantly surfing the Internet, updating the growing database of locations that parents dread their kids visiting.

Three similar programs are worth noting. They use techniques similar to Cyber Patrol to provide a barrier between you and whatever you want to block. The first is Net Nanny, which you can view and download at `http://www.netnanny.com/netnanny/home.html`. Check out CYBERsitter at `http://www.solidoak.com`. This program enables you to block Web sites, newsgroups, pictures, files, and mail. Another popular site blocker is SurfWatch, which you can find at `http://www.interserf.net/surfwatch.html`.

Each commercial online service has individual policies concerning adult materials and parental lockouts. Ways are also available to track the activity on your online service account to see what the kids are doing. For specific information, contact your online service provider or check its member services information online.

On the other side of the fence from the filtering approach is SafeSurf. Instead of identifying objectionable resources, the SafeSurf ratings system proposal encourages authors of Web sites to place a tag in their documents, certifying that the page has no adult themes or objectionable content, and to register their sites so that they can be inspected and certified as kid-friendly.

Both Netscape Communications and Microsoft are looking into supporting the SafeSurf rating system in future versions of their software. Cyber Patrol includes built-in support for SafeSurf (as well as the Platform for Internet Content Selection, another rating system).

Taking the positive approach to identifying kid-friendly Web sites may provide a secondary benefit. Sites that sport the SafeSurf identification may make it easier for parents to find Web sites specifically designed for and in line with the tastes of their children. You can find out more about the SafeSurf program at `http://www.safesurf.com/`.

The Last Mile on the Information Superhighway

Here are some important but simple steps to keep out of trouble on the Information Superhighway:

- Create strong passwords.
- Change your password frequently to foil packet sniffing.
- Don't store your passwords for online services with the program. Encrypting them doesn't necessarily help, either.
- Learn Internet etiquette (or "Netiquette").
- Refrain from sending offensive messages to anyone.
- Use parental controls to block offensive sites from your children.
- Never send credit card information in clear text. Encrypt all important information.
- Use encryption to scramble messages so that snoops can't read them.
- Scan any software that you download from the Net for viruses.
- Don't provide your password or credit card number to anyone who asks for it. Crackers have broken into AOL sessions and asked for both pieces of information.
- Limit the amount of information that you provide to strangers online.
- Obey all copyright laws.
- Obey all privacy laws.

If you follow the advice in this chapter, you won't end up as roadkill on the Information Superhighway. Watch those who come careening your way, and don't get blinded by the lights.

Chapter 13

Using E-Mail Securely

· ·

In This Chapter

▶ Defining e-mail

▶ Avoiding common e-mail problems

▶ Tracing an e-mail message

▶ Tracing a posted message

▶ Spamming

▶ Public-key and private-key encryption

▶ E-mail tips

· ·

O ver 100 years ago, when you wanted to get a message to a friend in another town, you sent a telegram. You've seen the old Westerns; you know that the person working in the telegraph office had to read every note in order to wire it. Security was not an issue. Society may have come a long way, but today's electronic mail (e-mail) has some of the very same pitfalls.

If you are connected to a commercial network, such as America Online, CompuServe, Prodigy, or the Internet, chances are great that you are using electronic mail. You probably signed up to a commercial network for this very reason. E-mail is a wonderful tool that allows you to communicate with people all over the globe. You can exchange ideas, keep in touch with your children at college, talk to experts about your favorite hobby or passion, or collaborate on projects — all without leaving your house!

This chapter talks about some of the risks associated with sending and receiving e-mail and gives you some strategies for keeping your messages safe from prying eyes.

What Is E-Mail?

When you use your modem to send messages to another person using a local bulletin board (BBS), a commercial online service, a company network mail system, or the Internet, the messages you send are generally referred to as *e-mail*. Just as every telephone in the world has a unique number that identifies that phone line, every e-mail address is different and serves a single, particular In box.

In the case of a local bulletin board, you can make your message publicly readable (just as if your message was pinned to the cork on the hallway bulletin board), or it may be stored as a private message until the recipient reads it. Some networks convey messages posted to the board to other computer systems in a relay hand-off situation, where computer A calls computer B to deliver all its new messages. Computer B is, in turn, called by another computer, and so on down the line. In this way, people subscribing to different local bulletin boards can send messages back and forth, even though no permanent link between their BBSs exists.

Major commercial online services, such as CompuServe, America Online, and Prodigy, offer e-mail services. With these services, you can send messages to other users of your service, to other commercial services like MCI Mail, or to any Internet address in the world. Most large companies have internal e-mail systems that also connect to the outside world. Other companies have ways of routing messages to places outside their internal networks.

Whether you're on a *local area network* (LAN) like NetWare or a *wide area network* (WAN) like the Internet, anyone with authority, such as the system administrator who runs the network or an intruder who has usurped authority, can access everything on the network, or at least the traffic that passes through the system.

Electronic Mail versus Paper Mail

When you send a snail-mail letter to your friend by using the postal service, known risks exist. First, you may put that letter in your mailbox in the morning before you leave to go to work. You pull up the little metal flag that tells the mail carrier that you have outgoing mail. That little flag also tells everyone else that a letter is waiting. Your letter may sit in the mailbox, vulnerable, for several hours before the mail carrier picks it up. Anyone who wants to can also pick it up!

At the post office, employees handle your letter and transport it in many different mail vehicles until it is placed in your friend's mailbox, where it lies unguarded until your friend checks the mail.

We can name numerous examples of ways in which physical letters can be lost or tampered with. The post office might misplace the letter, or someone looking for money might steal it. Someone looking for information about you may even steam open the letter and read it.

Is your Internet e-mail any more or less secure than a paper letter? Probably not. Although there are numerous possible pitfalls to a letter arriving at its destination intact and unread, postal services around the world deliver the vast majority of letters without incident, and they do it millions of times a day.

The same is true of Internet e-mail; millions of messages arrive safely at their destination addresses intact and unread every day. The sheer volume of messages dictates that it is impossible to try and intercept all but a few. However, someone may try to target your mail.

E-mail, whether sent across a company network or the Internet, differs radically from a letter in several respects. Although some e-mail routing programs like Lotus cc:Mail and Microsoft Mail can encrypt messages as they pass from one "post office" to another, most e-mail currently travels from origination to destination as plain text. Most Internet Service Providers use POP (Post Office Protocol) or SMTP (Simple Mail Transfer Protocol) to send messages from sender to recipient. By default, both protocols use plain text, which anyone with access can read.

Sending e-mail messages can be compared to sending postcards.

✔ While most letters are tucked safely inside an envelope, a postcard (like your e-mail) can be read by anyone who gets their hands on it.

✔ If somebody peeks at one of your personal letters, the envelope almost always shows evidence of tampering. A snoop, on the other hand, can read your postcard (or your e-mail), and leave few clues that would aid detection.

✔ Just as a snoop can make a photocopy of your postcard (without altering the original in any way), an e-mail message can be duplicated before it is sent on — and the receiver may never know it.

One thing that a letter and an electronic message have in common is that people handle them; e-mail resides on computer systems maintained by people. Just like your average postal worker, system administrators usually have much too much work to do to worry about reading your mail, but an unethical or unscrupulous administrator can monitor your mail.

However, a major difference between paper and electronic mail exists. One of the tasks of a system administrator may be to make archive copies of all e-mail that passes into and out of the system so that the system can be restored in the event of a crash. That way, you won't miss an important message if the system goes down. However, this also means that the system administrator has full access to read any and all e-mail on the system — often for good reason. For example, the system administrator may read an undelivered message in order to reroute it to the proper person.

E-Mail Crackers and Snoops

Besides the system administrator, who else may be interested in reading your e-mail? Two threat agents come to mind immediately: crackers and snoops. It's hard to say which are the more dangerous.

- ✔ **A cracker** is someone who breaks into computer systems for fun or profit, usually with malicious intent.
- ✔ **A snoop** is a busybody who wants to read your e-mail to find out where you are going, what you are doing, when you are doing it, or who you are doing it with.

A cracker may be an ambitious college student who wants to change that midterm research paper grade from a *D* to a *B,* a white-collar hoodlum stealing credit card numbers, or a business competitor spying on your latest sales figures.

Snoops, on the other hand, can pop up anywhere; a snoop may be a family member, a coworker, the traveler beside you on the airplane, or the technician who repairs your computer. All these people may have an opportunity to read your confidential files. For example, a family member may read your files if you don't secure your home computer. A coworker can peek at your work if you walk away from your computer without logging out from the network. A potential spy on an airplane can look over your shoulder as you madly type a report. Even the technicians at the computer store can read your data when they repair your hard disk or install new memory.

Sniffers

No, a sniffer has nothing to do with a nose. Although a Macintosh program called Sniffer does sniffle when installed.

A *sniffer* is a system administrator's tool that enables him or her to monitor traffic patterns so that network connections can be inspected.

An administrator can use a sniffer to intercept all traffic and to generate reports on the messages that fit some criterion, such as specific words or phrases, or messages to and from a specific address or group of addresses.

Easy pickings

The two most dangerous places for e-mail are your Out box and the recipient's In box. Almost every e-mail software package enables you to *archive* (keep a copy of) your incoming and outgoing messages. Some, like Netscape's mail reader, have an option that lets you send a copy of every outgoing message to the address of your choice. This option lets you use a second account as a repository of your outgoing correspondence. A stack of e-mail messages stored on the server system is easy prey to inquisitive eyes.

Similarly, the length of time an e-mail message sits on the recipient's server waiting to be downloaded to the recipient's computer is a problem. In some cases, gaining access to these messages is a simple matter.

A message in storage, or one waiting for delivery, is a more likely target for crackers because of the trouble and expense of setting up a *sniffer* (a traffic monitoring utility). Setting up a sniffer is expensive, takes a fairly high degree of technical proficiency, and is easy to detect because the sniffer has to be plugged into the network. A cracker who goes to all the trouble of setting up a sniffer is usually targeting a specific account or is looking for specific types of information, such as unencrypted credit card numbers. It is a lot easier to read a plain text (or an unencrypted) message stored on a system somewhere.

On the other hand, for an experienced cracker, logging into some systems and gaining privilege is a snap, especially on systems not rigorously managed by security-conscious administrators. After gaining privilege (for example, by guessing or finding a password), a cracker can look at anything on the system, including e-mail stored or waiting to be delivered.

Some users prefer not to delete messages until they are sure that they no longer need them, so they choose to store old incoming messages in their In boxes. The In box simply stores your messages in a file in a directory of the server's hard disk. In effect, selecting to remove the mail from the server deletes it from your mailbox. That doesn't necessarily mean that the message is removed from the server entirely. Most service providers *mirror* (write twice) all incoming traffic to a separate hard disk or a second server so that, in the event of a system crash, your e-mail messages can be recovered.

A cracker who gains privilege on a system that mirrors can read several days' worth of messages at will, even though the user thinks that the messages have been deleted. Other systems may make tape backups that are stored for weeks or months until the tape comes up in rotation to be reused. Lots of people get caught on this one. You may remember Ollie North, whose links to the Iran Contra affair were confirmed by old e-mail messages on backup tapes, even though Ollie thought that his e-mail messages had been erased.

Unless you are a potential target of industrial espionage, your biggest risk probably is from a plain snooper or eavesdropper. Snoops come in all sizes and shapes, each with his or her own reason for being interested in reading other people's mail. Snoops range from unscrupulous system administrators to curious kids who find your e-mail and decide to read your messages to employees who want to know what the boss is doing.

Generally, system administrators are pretty good about not reading people's e-mail, but there always are exceptions. For example, the administrator may have to put a sniffer on the network to resolve a problem. Or, he or she may use an "over-the-shoulder" utility such as Norton's Administrator for Networks (NAN) to see what you have stored on your hard drive or what you are entering at your keyboard. The sniffer and over-the-shoulder utilities both have legitimate uses for the administrator, but it is easy for an overly curious administrator to use these devices for inappropriate snooping purposes.

Copies, copies everywhere

Another weak link in the e-mail security chain (which is what crackers and snoops look for) is the fact that your message may pass through several other computers on its way to its destination.

The design of the Internet (and most large networks) lets messages move between computers by using the shortest possible path — wherever that path may be at the given moment. You may send five e-mail messages to a friend and every message travels to its destination by a different route.

When you do send a message to a friend, you probably think that your message exists in, at most, two places: on your computer (if you keep copies of outgoing mail) and on your friend's computer. That may not be the case. Consider how many copies of your e-mail message are actually created in the following scenario:

- ✔ First, you type your mail and save it in your Out box of the mail software on your hard drive (copy #1).

- ✔ You are attentive to backups, so you likely make a copy of the message on tape (copy #2).

- ✔ You mail the message to your friend through your provider, where it may get onto the service provider's daily backup (copy #3).

- ✔ Along the way, the message passes through any number of computers before it arrives at your friend's service provider, where it is placed in your friend's In box (copy #4). Snoopers can read your message as it travels through those various computers.

- ✔ The service provider also does a backup of its system and copies your messages onto tape (copy #5).

- ✔ When your friend retrieves the message, the message is written to the hard disk (copy #6).

- ✔ If your friend archives the mail and backs up, the message eventually makes it onto one or more tapes (copy #7).

The sheer number of opportunities to copy a message in a system like this makes it more likely that the security of a document may be compromised by a cracker or a snooper.

Snooping is insidious because the perpetrator doesn't alter the original message in any way. Unlike our snail-mail example, no envelope shows that the snooper opened and read your message. The original message simply shows up at its destination.

The bottom line is that a savvy snooper or determined cracker can read your plain text e-mail message. Because most e-mail programs don't hide or scramble your message, you should consider using encryption software, or at least make sure that you don't say anything in your message that you wouldn't want repeated in church or at your next board meeting.

The use of electronic mail is fraught with other dangers. You can get yourself into trouble if you use e-mail in illegal or unethical ways: harassment, forgery, spamming, and fakemail, to name a few.

E-Mail Harassment

People sometimes use e-mail systems to harass other people by sending them sexually charged, crude, racist, or vulgar messages. In the past, some of these low-lifes protected their identities by signing on using someone else's userid and password and then sent a "nasty-gram."

Sharing your userid and password with other users makes it easier for a cracker to send nasty-grams using *your* name and e-mail return address — one more good reason to keep your password to yourself. Check out Chapter 8 for more information about protecting your password.

The problem of e-mail harassment has become so acute that many states have enacted or are preparing to enact laws to restrict this kind of antisocial behavior. Many states have broadened existing laws to prohibit people from sending harassing or threatening e-mail.

If you suspect someone is harassing you, send an e-mail complaint to the system administrator of the site where the offending message originates. If you don't get a satisfactory response from the administrator and the harassment continues, contact your local law enforcement agency.

Keeping Your Private Mail Private

Maybe you use an e-mail system for running your side business. You send messages to prospective clients and information about your services or products to outsiders. Or you may use e-mail to communicate with your stock broker. Chances are that you don't want everybody knowing about your trades. You may even be communicating with your paramour by using your PC. In a recent case, a wife sued her husband for allegedly reading her steamy love letters that she stored on the household computer.

Many people mistakenly believe that their e-mail is private correspondence. They actually think that sending e-mail is the same as sending a letter in a sealed envelope, and that tearing open that electronic envelope is unethical. Well, they're wrong and they're right. Reading someone else's mail is extremely unethical. We don't need to tell you that, because your mother must have mentioned it to you once or twice. However, we can guarantee that no matter what you say and whom you say it to, somebody can read your mail. Snoopers are always a problem, no matter what data is stored and how you store the data.

Several reasons to protect your e-mail spring to mind. Your private message could be compromised by any of the following situations. Your message could:

- ✔ Go to the wrong person
- ✔ Be intercepted
- ✔ Be read by an e-mail supervisor

Using e-mail for anything other than everyday, routine communication is asking for trouble. If you wouldn't say it in a crowded restaurant, you probably should think twice about saying it on a public network.

Tracing an e-mail message

You may receive a message from someone you think is your mother, but someone may have forged her address. The easiest trick in the book is to forge an e-mail return address. Most personal computer e-mail software lets you type in just about any e-mail address you want to. Also, most machines seem to accept e-mail from any other machine.

This risk is not new. Think of your current snail-mail system (that is, your post office). Nothing stops you from putting a return address of 1600 Pennsylvania Avenue, 10 Downing Street, or 36 Sussex Drive on an envelope. The big question is whether the recipient believes that your letter came from one of those places. If the recipient routinely gets mail from those places, you may have a problem. Perhaps you shouldn't trust mail from those addresses.

And that is the key: trust. How much trust should you put into the address? Not much, unless you have some other way of authenticating the contents of the message. Maybe you have a special word that you share to show your correspondent that it's really you. Alternatively, you may use encryption to hide the contents of the message. (I discuss encryption later in this chapter.)

You can run, but you can't hide

Sending harassing e-mail or otherwise misusing electronic communications can result in jail time, depending on where the culprit lives. So, if you're thinking of sending nasty-grams, you'd better think again — it's not always easy to cover your tracks.

For example, over a two year period, infamous *cyberthief* Kevin Mitnick stole thousands of data files and over 20,000 credit card numbers from computer systems around the U.S. Although Mitnick thought he could electronically hide his identity, he was eventually arrested by the FBI in Raleigh, North Carolina, with the help of Tsutomu Shimomura, a researcher at the San Diego Supercomputer Center.

To determine where a message came from, you need to look at the headers on the message. Sometimes the header tells you who really sent the message. Check to ensure that the originator in the header matches the sender in the message.

Fakemail

How about a message from `GOD@heaven.org`? Sending such a message really isn't hard at all. All you have to do is *telnet* (this is a virtual terminal connection, really a remote login) into port 25 (the sendmail port) of a UNIX system that is part of the Internet and enter a few commands. Following is an example of a message that is sure to stir some action:

```
HELO yoursystem.com
MAIL FROM: purchasing@yoursystem.com
RCPT TO: orders@idgbooks.com
DATA
Please send me one thousand (1,000) copies of "Computer
          Security For Dummies" by next Monday.
          Standard terms apply.
QUIT
```

Just put the return address from which you want the message to appear to originate in the MAIL FROM line. This is spoofing the return address, which works because of the e-mail transport protocols. Current e-mail protocols make use of the metaphor of an envelope and letter. Each message is surrounded by a digital envelope in the form of a header and a terminator. The header is separate and distinct from the message itself and contains several pieces of information, including the return address for the message. All you need to do is change the header before sending the message.

Ryan Scott's fakemail Web page

For a time, Ryan Scott's Web page (try `http://www.netcreations.com/fakemail/`) allowed visitors to send fakemail messages. You can go to this page and get the story of how he created one of the most controversial sites on the Web by inviting people to send fakemail. Unfortunately, some people don't have a sense of humor, and other people abused the service to send nasty messages.

In other words, should the recipient look carefully at the header information printed in the message, it is obvious that the message was faked. Thus, the morons who used the service to send threats and other nasty e-mails to public officials were easily identified. Still, the service caused more problems for Ryan than it was worth. All that remains is a testimonial to what was once a fun Web site.

The lesson to be learned in all of this is simple: "Things are not always what they seem." When you get an e-mail that just doesn't quite ring true, check it out very closely. Anyone with a rudimentary knowledge of e-mail protocols can cover their identity very easily, making the possibilities of fraud very tempting.

Pass the Spam, please

Every once in a while, someone on a public network "spams" the users of a mailing list or chat group. The term *spam* is from a Monty Python skit (yes, those British chaps, and yes, it is very silly), where a couple go into a restaurant and try to get something other than Spam (a packaged meat by-product). In the background, a bunch of Vikings are singing the praises of Spam.

The Vikings get louder and louder, and pretty soon the only thing you can hear is the word Spam. Spam. Spam. SPAM. SPAM. The same thing could happen on the Internet if individuals were to flood it with large-scale inappropriate postings. You couldn't distinguish the real postings from the Spam.

Spammers send messages that are commercial in nature to mailing lists or USENET newsgroups. The subject line in the message appears to be *on topic* (pertaining to the subject matter of the list or newsgroup), so people open the message — only to find an unsolicited advertisement. Spamming is generally against Internet "netiquette" and usually results in suspension of the spammer's account.

Therefore, spammers like to transmit their potted-meat messages using *throw-away accounts* (those ten-hour free trials offered by on-line service providers). The spammer knows that the service provider will cancel the trial account as soon as other users begin to complain about receiving unwanted solicitations. Spammers usually provide a second e-mail address or perhaps a name, phone number, or a postal address so that prospective customers can contact them.

If you get spammed, be sure to send a complaint to the postmaster of the provider from which the spam originates. Most postmasters are quick to give the heave-ho to these processed-meat-mailing pirates. And besides being annoying, receiving loads of spam can tie up your e-mail program and make your system unavailable for your use. (Refer to Chapter 11 for a discussion of the potential problems caused by spamming.)

Anonymous re-mailers

An *anonymous re-mailer* is a mail server designed to take a message sent to it, strip off all the identifying information in the header, replace it with anonymous information, and then pass the message along its way. When the e-mail message arrives, the recipient has no way of telling the actual origin of the message. The truly cautious (some would say paranoid) even use multiple re-mailers, sending their messages through several re-mailers. Any number of reasons exist, legitimate and not so legitimate, for wanting to remain anonymous. These range from secret business negotiations and intimately personal communications to covering up illegal activities. Often, people use anonymous re-mailers as a way of participating in controversial or objectionable USENET newsgroup discussions without revealing their true identity.

USENET is a loose aggregation of more than 14,000 Internet special interest groups. USENET works similar to a bulletin board: No matter what interests you may have, a USENET group specializing in the topic is sure to exist. (See Appendix A to find out about some of the computer security newsgroups present on USENET.)

Many newsgroups deal in controversial political, social, and sexual topics. It is not uncommon for people who participate in these groups to hide their identity by using an anonymous re-mailer. Perhaps the best known and most used anonymous re-mailer is `anon.penet.fi`, run by the Finnish computer scientist Johan Helsingius.

According to a March 6, 1995, *Time* magazine article, "Helsingius has become the keeper of the Who's Who of the computer underground. Stored in his 200-megabyte database is a master list of the names and e-mail addresses of everybody who has ever sought the shelter of his service: pornographers and political exiles; software pirates and corporate whistle blowers; the sexually abused and their abusers." The fact that these "fringe-dwellers" use re-mailers to conduct their business shows you that *they* think re-mailers keep their identities secure.

Sending E-Mail Securely

E-mail security is at best difficult. Nothing about electronic mail is secure. All your messages go through countless other machines before they finally end up at the right destination. The only thing working for you is the relative insignificance of your letter, relative to someone else's e-mail. Still, almost any transmission has the potential to be intercepted. How do you stop it? Just as locking your car, using the Club, and installing an alarm system can help to discourage car thieves, you must discourage crackers and snoopers from reading your e-mail. The most effective way to prevent e-mail tampering is to encode your messages.

Encoding your messages

Encoding messages to keep secrets from spies goes back to at least the time of Julius Caesar. Today, encoding is perhaps the single most important security tool that you can use to protect your personal and private information from snoops.

Recently, Peter's mother was in Florida and sent her granddaughter one of those "Wish you were here" postcards. If someone at the post office read her postcard, who would really care? However, suppose Grandma wanted to send the combination to the safe in her basement — the one in which she keeps the family jewels. That's pretty personal stuff! When sending personal or confidential information, Grandma should seal the letter in an envelope before mailing it. You can think of encryption as writing that letter in a language (such as "Davis-ese,") intelligible to only Grandma and the granddaughter.

You should apply the same sort of caution to your electronic mail. Sending an e-mail message is like writing on the back of a postcard. (It's really more like writing a letter and putting it in a see-through envelope.) You cannot trust the information superhighway; it just isn't safe. Messages traveling that highway can be hijacked.

Encryption revealed

Encryption is any procedure that converts an original message (or *plain text*) to encoded text. Encryption works by passing your plain text through an *algorithm* (a series of mathematical procedures), along with another variable called a *key*. The disguised, scrambled message is called *cipher text*. The process can be reversed by passing the cipher text through the algorithm along with the key in order to *decrypt* the text, or convert cipher text back into plain, readable text.

Government and encryption

The U.S. government, and others, it seems, are not thrilled that people have strong encryption software available to them. Several law enforcement and intelligence agencies, chiefly the FBI and NSA, worry that strong military encryption may help criminals and terrorists. The executive branch of the U.S. government has made several proposals that will have the effect of regulating or else banning the use of strong encryption software by average citizens.

Despite the worry of the U.S. government, the concerns of individuals and businesses about the privacy of their messages demand the availability of viable and usable encryption. We feel that average citizens should start using strong encryption, thereby legitimizing it at the user level, making it more difficult for the government to outlaw strong encryption.

A short history of encryption

Evidence shows that Julius Caesar, Chaucer, and Thomas Jefferson all used some form of cryptography to conceal important information from their adversaries.

When Caesar sent messages (via untrustworthy messengers) to his trusted acquaintances, he used a cipher system that replaced every *A* with a *D,* every *B* with an *E,* and so on, for the entire alphabet. Only someone who knew his *shift by three* rule could decipher Caesar's messages. (This early example of a cryptosystem is still in use today in some rudimentary algorithms that protect e-mail from would-be intruders.)

Through the Middle Ages, little need existed for encryption — only the nobility and their trusted servants could read or write. Then, thanks primarily to Johannes Gutenberg who invented the printing press in the 15th century, more and more people learned to read — and write. The need arose to protect one's written words should a secret document be intercepted by a hostile (and literate!) enemy.

So began a long history of one group trying to protect their messages and another group trying to figure out what their adversaries' messages said. As this war of ciphers became intertwined with modern, military warfare, the encryption business got inventive — and interesting! For example, in World War II, the U.S. military employed Native Americans as radio operators: Even the most sensitive military secret was secure being spoken in an ancient and virtually unknown language.

With the advent of the personal computer and new telecommunications technologies such as local area networks and the Internet, society is generating, transmitting, and storing more information than ever before. While the information protection business has existed for a long time, never before in history has so much information been in need of encryption.

Some terms specific to the cloak-and-dagger world of encryption are as follows:

- **Cryptosystem or cipher system:** A method of disguising messages
- **Cryptography:** The art of creating and using cryptosystems
- **Cryptoanalysis:** The art of breaking cryptosystems — seeing through the disguise
- **Cryptology:** The study of both cryptography and cryptoanalysis

Very private keys: Single-key ciphers

The first cryptosystems used *single-key* or conventional ciphers. With single-key ciphers, the same key must be used by both the sender to encrypt and by the recipient to decrypt a message. Anyone possessing this key can decrypt the message, which means that single-key ciphers must be rigorously protected.

With a single-key cipher, both the sender and the recipient must possess and use the same key at the same time in order to decrypt a message. The use of single-key ciphers requires some type of secure channel to transmit the key to the recipient. For example, sending a single-key cipher to your recipient via snail-mail would be considered secure, because the encrypted message and the key are not sent together. Keep in mind, though, that secure channels are difficult to establish and are also open to compromise.

Most commercially available encryption equipment uses this conventional, single-key encryption, which is also referred to as *symmetrical* encryption — you must have the same key for *both* encryption and decryption.

The principal challenge with conventional, single-key encryption is to effectively control the distribution and use of cipher keys.

The most rigorously tested cryptographic algorithm available commercially is called the *Data Encryption Algorithm* (or DES). DES has been in use for over 10 years, and can generate about 10^{17} possible, unique cipher keys. (That's like 10 quadrillion, one-of-a kind cipher keys! Most calculators go into error mode if you try to multiply it out.) The dramatic increase in computing power found in today's computers allows for more sophisticated encryption, and more challenging code-busting. Originally developed at IBM, the DES algorithm is publicly available.

Very public keys: Two-key ciphers

The alternative to private key encryption is a *public key* encryption process, which is also called *asymmetrical* encryption because it involves *two* keys: One for encryption and another for decryption. In a public key cryptosystem, you freely distribute the encryption key — it's only the *decryption* key that must be kept secret. Therefore, anyone can encrypt and send a message to you, but only *you* can decrypt their message with your own unique decryption key. This system solves the problem of having to protect encryption keys by sending them through a secure channel.

Three scientists named Rivest, Shamir, and Aldeman invented public key cryptography, which represents a breakthrough that makes routine message encryption both practical and widespread. Bearing its inventors' initials, the RSA algorithm is based on the mathematics of exponentiation. Later in this chapter, we discuss a popular algorithm that uses RSA: Pretty Good Privacy (or PGP).

Digital signatures

Sometimes, verifying who is actually sending you a message is more important than the confidentiality of the message itself. Message authentication codes, or *digital signatures,* are one way to confirm the identity of the sender and the integrity of the data in an e-mail message. Message authentication codes validate the identity of the sender, are transmitted along with the e-mail message, and are decoded by the message recipient.

In the paperless electronic office of the future, digital signatures will be used to sign purchase orders, job applications, business contracts, and other important e-mail messages. Use these hints when creating a digital signature to use with your important e-mail messages:

- ✓ Use a digital signature for e-mail messages that need *write protection* instead of just *read protection.*

- ✓ Vary your digital signature slightly for each individual message. If your digital signature is always the same — for example, a string of symbols — then the signature can be easily counterfeited by simply copying the string of symbols.

- ✓ Use a commercial encryption program like PGP to digitally sign documents and to verify signatures.

PGP: Pretty good software

As a result of software author Philip Zimmermann's six months of unpaid labor, you can use the widely available freeware program Pretty Good Privacy (PGP) to send electronic mail messages to anyone in the world in complete privacy. In addition, you can sign your messages so that the recipient can verify that the message really came from you. You can encrypt sensitive files on your computer so that the files remain private even if your computer and disks are stolen. PGP truly is Pretty Good Software.

From a user's point of view, PGP behaves like a public key encryption program. In public key cryptography, two keys are needed for the encryption process: a *public key* that can be freely distributed and a *private key* that you must protect from everyone else. Anything encrypted with your public key can be decrypted only with the corresponding private key. You can also use your private key to sign documents digitally, and people can use your public key to prove the authenticity of your signature.

In practice, you create a secret and public key pair and publish the public key. When PGP encrypts a file, it creates a random conventional encryption key and then sends that key to the recipient using a header block that is encrypted with RSA public key encryption. Thus RSA serves as the secure channel used to transmit a conventional key, solving the key distribution problem. The bulk of the message, however, is encrypted by using a conventional or private key cipher called IDEA, which is much faster and more secure than RSA.

When you're using PGP, your secret key is stored on a file on your disk. Thus you must carefully back up your disk. The secret key is encrypted, so you must specify a pass phrase anytime you want to perform an action that uses your secret key. Thus you are asked for your pass phrase when you want to decrypt a message or sign a message. You should choose your pass phrase so that you can remember it but no one else can guess it.

Because PGP is a UNIX-style command line program, PGP is not very user-friendly.

Unfortunately, PGP has

- ✔ No menus
- ✔ No mouse buttons to click
- ✔ No fancy graphics for you to look at
- ✔ No curious sounds to waft from your computer

The only way to use PGP is to enter a UNIX-like PGP command, which typically consists of filenames, key identifiers, and other encryption options.

You *can* get a user-friendly Macintosh version of PGP. If you want a GUI front-end (an easy, Windows-based interface) for Windows, consider Viacrypt PGP, the commercial version of PGP.

Zimmermann's PGP has emerged as a practical standard for encrypting e-mail and other documents. Many current e-mail programs support PGP, and you can expect future versions of e-mail application to also support PGP.

A number of Web pages are devoted to PGP and cryptography. The primary PGP distribution site for North America is `http://web.mit.edu/network/pgp-form.html`. You can find links to other sites from there.

PGP can authenticate messages

PGP can also authenticate or sign messages using a *digital signature,* which verifies that a given document really came from a given person. PGP can check digital signatures to determine whether someone tampered with the document.

Authentication can be combined with encryption, creating an encrypted, signed file. The encryption takes place after the signature is added so that a casual viewer cannot tell who signed the file.

A PGP digital signature shows that the person who signed the document had access to the PGP secret key and the passphrase. A PGP signature also indicates that the document has not been modified since it was signed.

Using the Windows version of PGP, ViaCrypt, click on the Sign button and select the file you want to digitally sign. Viacrypt PGP uses your private key to create a unique signature — anyone with access to your public key can verify that this message came from you.

PGP and mail readers

If you want to get started with encrypting your most sensitive messages, you can use PGP-Eudora (try downloading the software from `http://www.xs4all.nl/~comerwel/`), which integrates PGP with Eudora Lite, from Qualicomm (download Eudora Lite from `http://www.qualcomm.com/ProdTech/quest/`). Eudora Lite is a free version of Eudora Pro for 32-bit Windows (which includes Windows 95 and Windows NT). After you download these programs, you can use PGP-Eudora to easily encrypt mail messages.

Eudora is not the only mail reader into which you can link PGP. Plug-ins exist for just about every popular mail program, including Elm and Pine on the UNIX platform.

May I see your license, please

Because of U. S. government export regulations, PGP and other strong encryption tools are classified as munitions of war. Under these regulations, the North American version of PGP is treated just the same as the Stealth bomber. You need a license to export both, and you aren't going to get the PGP license. Exporting this version of PGP outside the United States and Canada can get you several years in jail. Adding links to direct downloads of PGP to your Web page or putting copies of PGP on your bulletin board for others to download is not a good idea. Phil Zimmermann, the author of PGP, was under federal grand jury investigation for over a year because he was suspected of exporting PGP.

TIPEM, RIPEM, and Tyler, too

TIPEM (or Toolkit for Interoperable Privacy-Enhanced Messaging) is an encryption program that allows a programmer to integrate encryption techniques into other computer applications. You can find out more about TIPEM at `http://www.rsa.com/rsa/prodspec/tipem/rsa_tipm.htm`.

RIPEM (RSAREF-based Internet Privacy Enhanced Mail) is the second most popular freeware e-mail encryption package. PGP is more widely used, but if for some reason you want to check or generate a PEM (that is, Privacy Enhanced Mail, a competitor to PGP) signature, you must use RIPEM. The RIPEM software is available at `ftp://ripem.msu.edu`. An exportable RIPEM version is also available.

Other popular commercial encryption programs include the following:

- Scrambler for Windows (available from Scrambler Technologies, 800-834-4005)
- Encrypt-It (from MaeDae Enterprises, 719-683-3860)
- SafE Mail (try SafE Mail Corporation, 800-252-9938)

E-Mail Rights

Who has the right to read your e-mail? Obviously the intended, addressed recipient, but the intention of the e-mail sender is not always reality in cyberspace. For example, the system administrators of your service provider are governed by the Electronic Privacy Act. Under this law, system administrators can read your mail only when doing so is necessary to perform their duties. Unfortunately, the language in the law is a bit vague about which duties require reading your personal mail. The intent of the law, it seems, is to protect system administrators from liability when they have to read a misdirected message to figure out where it should be sent, need to make sure that the system is delivering messages to the proper mailboxes, or perform other similar duties.

Some system administrators have taken the vague language in the Electronic Privacy Act to mean that they should scan messages to protect their organization, Internet service provider, or bulletin board system, because they could be closed down by law enforcement officials if illegal user activity is occurring on their service.

Speaking of law enforcement, do police officials have a right to read your e-mail? To wiretap any communication, law enforcement officers must get a court order after supplying enough evidence to a judge showing probable cause.

You should keep in mind, however, that no employer can control all actions of every employee. Even though a company may have a policy of respecting privacy in the workplace, individuals do not always share that respect. Human nature being what it is, there will always be system administrators who will read your mail. Always be aware that such people are out there.

Tell your e-mail administrator if you suspect that someone is tampering with your mail (that is, assuming that you don't suspect the administrator). Because e-mail is copyrightable, someone who changes e-mail is violating your copyright. You may, therefore, have legal recourse against someone who tampers with your e-mail — assuming that you can prove who did it.

E-Mail Security Tips

In this chapter, we explain that the vast majority of e-mail is sent across the Internet and other online services as plain text, which anyone can read. But all is not doom and gloom. You can do some simple things to lessen the risks of using electronic mail:

✔ **Delete messages that you have read or don't need anymore; don't let them pile up.** When you receive messages that you want to keep, copy them to your hard drive or a floppy disk. Otherwise, they sit around on a computer where someone might see them. You should know that trusted personnel acting as network administrators have all the tools they need to read your e-mail as it passes through their system. Sometimes it is necessary for them to look at e-mail to make sure that the system is running smoothly.

✔ **Make sure that you regularly delete the mail in your Out box.** Often, your e-mail systems make backup copies of your messages (ones that you create as well as ones that you receive and think that you deleted). Just because you trash an e-mail message does not mean that it's actually gone for good. You may need to go into the "trash" and delete those messages by using a real delete program such as Symantec's Norton InfoWipe. See Chapters 17 and 18 for true erasure programs for DOS and the Mac.

✔ **Encrypt confidential or sensitive information that you are sending across networks.** When you have sensitive information that you want to protect, use PGP, PEM, or a similar program to encrypt your message before sending it. Otherwise, you should assume that someone, somewhere is reading your mail. Crackers and snoopers differ in the way they gain access to your mail, but both categories of individuals can read your mail unless you encrypt it.

✔ **Before replying to an e-mail message, check to see who the originator of the message is.** Lots of people use mailing lists or carbon copies, so the same message goes to a group of people. If you respond to a mailing list on most systems, your message goes to everybody on the list or everyone who was copied, not just to the person to whom you want to reply. If you're not careful, you might send your message to thousands of people!

Chapter 14

Securing Your Files

• •

• •

*E*veryone has files on their computers — typically thousands of them. Do you need to protect them? How much protection do you need? How should you provide that protection? This chapter answers these questions and more.

Do You Need to Secure Files on Your Computer?

Chapters 4 and 5 discuss some of the threats and risks that you need to consider when deciding whether to protect your files. Read those chapters, ingest the material, and then consider appropriate levels of control for your files. Here's a short list of reasons why you should consider securing your files from unauthorized access:

- ✔ Keeping your personal finance data on the computer

- ✔ Maintaining all your credit card and PIN numbers in a file in case you forget them

- ✔ Writing personal letters to close friends and storing them on the computer

- ✔ Maintaining all the information that's necessary for running your home-based business venture

- ✔ Bringing home files from the office to work on over the weekend

- ✔ Writing an unauthorized biography of Elvis to set the record straight — he is still alive!
- ✔ Keeping each child's homework assignments safe from the other children

Does protecting your files need to be an in-depth, labor-intensive task? No. You probably know whether losing any of your files will cause a loss that you don't want to suffer. Data such as your genealogy program input (collected over years of tracing your family tree), or thousands of really good recipes, can be irreplaceable — and therefore securing it is important.

Why secure the data? Because accidents happen. Whether something silly happens, like not paying attention and deleting the wrong directory, or letting the kids play with the computer and run the DOS FORMAT command, data loss is always just around the corner. In addition, you just may not want anyone seeing what you have in a particular file — it might be a personal letter, self-improvement material, or maybe even the start of your autobiography. Regardless, the information is yours, and you choose to control who can see or delete it.

One part of protecting yourself is to back up all your files, as Chapter 10 describes. This strategy protects your data from accidental deletion or modification. The other part is to follow some of the advice in this chapter and prevent the deletion or access from happening in the first place.

Security gurus use the following phrase to describe this information:

Security is implemented to prevent accidental or intentional disclosure, modification, destruction, and misuse.

Using DOS to Help Secure Files

A number of features available in DOS can help protect your files. Chapter 19 provides a list of DOS commands that you can use.

Basically, DOS enables you to set certain fields that prevent people from deleting a file. This method is a good, inexpensive way of protecting your files from an inexperienced user who may accidentally delete them. Typing the following command at the DOS prompt enables you to set a file attribute to *read-only:*

```
ATTRIB +R
```

When a file is read-only, you can't update, move, or delete the file. When you want to update the file, you need to reset this attribute by specifying the following command:

```
ATTRIB -R
```

Typing the following command at the DOS prompt sets the file called BARRY.FIL to read-only. Change the plus sign to a minus sign to clear the read-only setting.

```
ATTRIB +R BARRY.FIL
```

Another version of the ATTRIB command hides the file so that no one but you can tell that it exists. You can still use a hidden file, even though you can't see it. This version of the ATTRIB command hides the file:

```
ATTRIB +H BARRY.FIL
```

Changing the plus sign to a minus sign removes the hidden component, making the file visible again.

The ATTRIB command helps you to keep your files a little safer from accidental harm or deletion, but be aware that anyone with knowledge of DOS commands can easily bypass these safeguards.

Inexpensive and free password protection

What do we mean by *password protection?* After all, free stuff is of no value unless you understand what you're getting and can use it. You can use passwords to prevent people from accessing your computer at all, thus helping to keep your files safe. Chapter 17 discusses a number of login tools. These tools provide you with a deterrent against casual file access, because you need to know what the password is before you get access. Some of the tools we mention in Chapters 17 and 18 are shareware and therefore typically have a small cost attached to their use. (*Shareware* means that you run the program to try it out before paying some small amount. Shareware authors are renowned for giving you really neat programs for small sums around $15 or $30.) Please support your local shareware author by sending the required amount if you continue to use their software. After all, it's not only the law, it's a good thing.

Power-on passwords provide a similar deterrent. They are part of the software that comes with your computer and can be considered free (if you discount the fact that you just put out a couple grand for the actual computer) and can help keep the kids and visitors from using your computer. When using power-on passwords, you must enter your secret password each time you turn on the computer before you can use the machine.

A number of free password-protection tools are also available on the Internet. Try the following addresses and see whether the files you find can help you:

```
http://ciac.llnl.gov/ciac/ToolsDOSSystem.html#COPYNOT
```

```
http://www.jumbo.com/
```

Many, many programs provide various types of password controls. Try them out on unimportant files first, until you are sure that they work, that you understand them, and that you can remember the associated passwords.

One of the programs we downloaded, EPW, provides a way to put a password onto a program. After EPW controls a program, you can't run the program until you supply a password. Of course, after someone finds out the password, you need to change it to maintain control. You can find EPW on the Jumbo Web page at the address listed earlier in this section.

Finally, we talk about using the free password protection that comes with various word processors, spreadsheets, and databases in Chapter 9.

Encryption

To provide protection for a few files rather than for your entire system, you can use software that usually is reserved for electronic mail messages. *PGP (Pretty Good Privacy)* is encryption software that scrambles your data so that it can't be read until you provide a "key." Rather than use it in electronic mail, you can use PGP to scramble the contents of important files on your computer, ensuring that no one can read them without your approval.

We describe how to use PGP for electronic mail in Chapter 13. Here we use the same principles, but for a different purpose. First, we'll review some elementary encryption terms.

Suppose that we want to send you a message, but we don't want anyone but you to be able to read it. We can "encrypt" the message, which means that we scramble it up in a hopelessly complicated way, rendering it unreadable to anyone except you, the intended recipient of the message. We supply a crypto-graphic "key" to *encrypt* the message, and you have to use the same key to *decrypt,* rendering it readable.

By using that same analogy, you can encrypt any file you want to protect, making the file very safe from prying eyes. This scheme doesn't protect a file from deletion; it only stops people from seeing what the file contains.

Because PGP is virtually unbreakable, you must take care to keep your secret key very safe! If you lose this key, you will never be able to read the file. You create your special key when prompted by PGP the first time you use the program. To protect this key, PGP makes you enter a passphrase. (*Passphrase* is another term for password, except it is usually longer and consists of a series of words. For example, this sentence could become your passphrase.) PGP then uses both the secret key and your passphrase to provide protection. It uses the secret key to actually encrypt the file, and it uses your passphrase to ensure that only you can use the secret key. You must keep this password available, however. If you lose it, you lose access to the file. As we state in Chapter 8, make sure that you pick a good password — *and don't lose it.*

To use PGP, you must first download a freeware version from the Internet or buy a commercial version from Viacrypt. We provide you with contact information and Internet addresses in Appendix B. Purchasing the commercial version provides you with customer support for installing and using this software. The Internet version is free, but you're on your own.

Using PGP with DOS or Windows

To encrypt a file with PGP in DOS, type the following command:

```
pgp -c barry.fil
```

This example encrypts the file called BARRY.FIL, producing a *new* file called BARRY.PGP. The program then prompts you for a passphrase to use as a conventional key to encipher (scramble) the file. After you create this new file, delete the old one by using a true delete program (such as those found in Chapter 17) and keep the BARRY.PGP file. Each time you want to use the file, you need to decrypt it by running the PGP program and creating a new file.

To decrypt the file with PGP, type this command:

```
pgp barry.pgp
```

PGP asks for the passphrase that you used when creating the file. PGP then creates another file that anyone can read. This method is a bit of work, but, as we said before, it keeps that file very safe.

If you add **-m** to the command, you can view the file on-screen without altering it or creating a new readable file:

```
pgp -m barry.pgp
```

A number of Windows shell programs are now available that provide the Windows "look and feel" to DOS-based PGP. Make no mistake, however; the program still reverts to a DOS window to perform the encryption, and not all these products are easy to install. We attempted to use one Windows shell and found it difficult to set up.

To end on a positive note, PGP is gradually coming of age and joining (belatedly) the Windows world. You can purchase an actual Windows version from Viacrypt. If you have Internet access, go to the following Web site:

```
http://www2.csn.net/malls/rmcm/computer/ice/viacrypt
            index.html
```

Using PGP on a Mac

Whether you use PGP on a Mac or some other platform such as DOS or UNIX, the essential elements are the same. Only the method changes. On Mac machines, the program is far more drag-and-drop oriented, and it is not necessary to use the program on a command line basis, as we show in the section on PGP for DOS.

To use PGP for encrypting a Macintosh file, follow these steps:

1. **First, obtain a Mac version of the program from one of the Internet sites that we list in Appendix B or from AOL or CompuServe. Follow the directions for installing the program.**

2. **Use the Finder and select MACPGP.**

3. **Double-click on the program name that you highlighted in step 2. (Or choose File⇨Open.)**

    You see a window with the copyright notice displayed.

4. **Double-click on the copyright notice.**

    The PGP Messages Window appears. The four menu options are File, Edit, Key, and Options.

5. **Choose File⇨Encrypt/Sign.**

    You see a document window, where you can select the name of the file you want to encrypt. Select the name of the document by highlighting it.

6. **Choose Open.**

    A window with a list of public keys and an option appears.

7. **Double-click on Key to (un)select recipient(s).**

8. **Double-click on your public key (or choose a friend's key if you want to send him or her an encrypted document that only he or she can open) to select it.**

    A check mark appears next to the key.

9. **Click on the OK button.**

   A new window appears with a number of options. On the left are three options for managing the file:

   - Encrypt
   - Encrypt and Sign
   - Sign only

10. **Click on the Encrypt option.**

    A number of other options are in the window. Each one provides additional features, but using any of them is not necessary in this scenario (encrypting a file on your hard drive). You may want to select the option to wipe out the source, however, especially if your intent is that no one except you can read the file.

    Remember that PGP uses a file-in and file-out approach. The file PGP creates after encryption is finished has an extension of .PGP. Your original file remains the same unless you choose the Wipe option.

11. **Click on the Do It button.**

    This step finishes the process and creates the new encrypted file with the last three characters *PGP.* Your file can now be read only by someone who knows your secret password.

You sign a file to let the recipient know that whatever you send actually comes from you and was not changed by anyone. Only the person to whom you send a file can read an encrypted file. Anyone can read a signed file, but the person cannot change that file without people knowing. Use the signature option when you aren't concerned with anyone seeing the information but want to make sure that it isn't changed by anyone before the person to whom you are sending the file receives it.

To use PGP to sign a Macintosh file, follow these steps:

1. **First, obtain a Mac version of PGP from one of the Internet sites that we list in Appendix B or from AOL or CompuServe. Follow the directions for installing the program.**

2. **Use the Finder and select MACPGP.**

3. **Double-click on MACPGP. (Or choose File⇨Open.)**

   You see a window with the copyright notice displayed.

4. **Double-click on the copyright notice.**

   The PGP Messages Window appears. The four menu options are File, Edit, Key, and Options.

5. **Choose File⇨Encrypt/Sign.**

   You see a document window, where you can select the name of the file you want to sign by highlighting it.

6. **Choose Open.**

   A window with a list of public keys and an option appears.

7. **Double-click on your public key to select it.**

   A check mark appears next to the key.

8. **Click on the OK button.**

   A new window appears with a number of options. On the left are three options for managing the file:

   - Encrypt

   - Encrypt and Sign

   - Sign only

9. **Click on the Sign only option.**

   A number of other options are in the window. Each option provides additional features, but none is absolutely necessary.

10. **Click on the Do It button.**

    This step finishes the process and appends your public key to the document.

11. **Mail the file to your friend.**

This is a simple overview of a complex program. PGP is a powerful program, and you must take care when using it. Read the documentation that accompanies it very carefully, and be sure you understand it well before getting yourself too involved. Above all, *don't forget any passwords.*

Other software

Other software programs that perform a similar function to PGP are available. One Windows-based package called Puffer provides simple, effective file encryption. This program also offers true file erasure and its own text editor that makes encrypting your electronic mail a little easier. Another program called RSA Secure is available from RSA Data Security.

Puffer

How does Puffer work? It uses the standard Windows interface instead of a command line like DOS programs do, which makes it easier to use. When installed, Puffer shows a menu with document-type tabs instead of the more familiar File, Edit interface. Figure 14-1 shows Puffer's main screen.

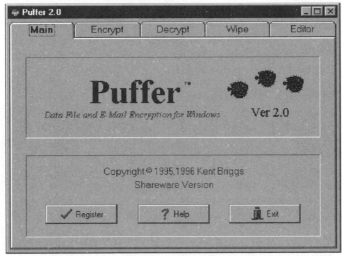

Figure 14-1:
The Puffer
File
Encryption
main
screen.

To encrypt a file, just follow these steps:

1. **Click on the Encrypt tab.**

2. **Click on the +Add button to select the file(s) you want to encrypt.**

   The file or group of files you select shows up in the Encrypt window.

3. **Click on the Encrypt icon.**

   You are presented with an option Window called Create PUF file that lets you rename your file. A PUF extension is standard, but you can use any name you choose. You may want to use the PUF extension to remind you that you encrypted the file.

4. **Type the filename you want to use and click on OK.**

   You need to enter a secret password in the Encryption Password dialog box, as shown in Figure 14-2.

This password allows you to recover the file. Don't lose or forget it, because you will never be able to use the encrypted files again if you do. As in most other programs, you must enter the password twice to verify what you first type. Puffer then encrypts the file, creating a new file. Delete the original file if you don't want anyone to see the data. Use the Puffer Wipe option to do so. As we discuss in the next section, this method allows for true erase, making the deleted file unrecoverable.

Puffer is a simple-to-use program that you should find useful if you need to keep your files safe. The author provides a 30-day free evaluation period, after which you need to register the program if you continue to use it.

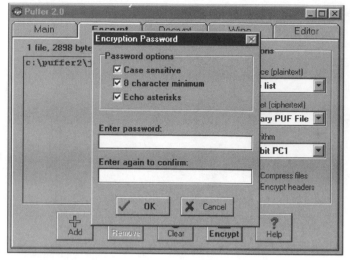

Figure 14-2:
The Puffer
Encryption
Password
dialog box.

You can get a copy of Puffer from http://execpc.com/~kbriggs or send the author a message on CompuServe at 72124,3234 or the Internet at kbriggs@execpc.com.

RSA Secure

Finally, you can get a program called RSA Secure from the RSA Data Security company to encrypt files. When you install RSA Secure on your Windows computer, it becomes a part of your Windows File Manager, where it makes itself available to you anytime you manipulate files. After installation, you see a new RSA menu item on your File Manager menu bar. On a Macintosh, RSA Secure becomes integrated with the Finder program.

This program also lets you define sets of files and directories that are automatically encrypted and decrypted every time you use Windows or start or shut down your Mac. RSA Secure lets you encrypt individual or groups of files quickly and easily.

The company provides evaluation copies that you can try out, but you need to purchase the program if you continue to use it. Contact the RSA on the Internet at www.rsa.com. If you don't have Internet access, you can reach the RSA at the following address:

RSA Data Secure
100 Marine Pkwy, Ste. 500
Redwood City, CA 94065
Phone: 415-595-8782

True File Erasure

When you delete a file, you can recover the file if you act fast enough. The DOS UNDELETE command and the Windows 95 Recycle Bin are there to help users with slippery fingers. On your Mac, the Trash works like the Recycle Bin.

In Windows 95 and on the Mac, file protection goes one step further. These systems place a deleted file in a special folder (the Recycle Bin or the Trash); you can recover the file from these folders by selecting and moving the file. The files get "deleted" only when you empty the folders.

To empty these folders on a Mac, click on Empty Trash, and in Windows 95, choose File⇨Empty Recycle Bin. Emptying these folders every month or so is a good idea (even more often if you are using proper backup techniques such as those discussed in Chapter 10, because you can recover a deleted file from your backups), especially if your usable hard drive space is low. These folders can become very large quite quickly as you delete files you no longer need, such as shareware and freeware programs you try and decide not to keep.

After you empty the folders or use the DOS DELETE command, the system no longer recognizes the files — they're gone. Or are they? On all these systems, you can often recover a deleted file if you act quickly enough.

Why? When you press the Delete key or empty the Recycle Bin or Trash, you may think that the file is gone. But neither DOS nor the Mac was designed to actually delete the file; it was designed to remove the file's "address," because that method is faster. So you recover a deleted file merely by replacing the deleted "pointer," which the DOS UNDELETE command does. In addition, many third-party utilities for Mac and IBM-compatible machines, such as PC Tools and Norton Utilities, help you recover files as well.

DOS works by using a File Allocation Table (FAT) to get the information it needs about where all the files are. All DOS does when you delete a file is remove the entry in this table. After the FAT entry is removed, DOS can reuse the space that the file occupies on your hard drive. If you act quickly enough, this space is untouched, and therefore your file is still there. By replacing the entry in the table, Undelete and other utilities can often recover your file. Macs work in a very similar way.

So what does this capability mean to you? It is definitely useful for recovering a deleted file — everyone makes the occasional mis-key and deletes the wrong file. But other people can recover files that you thought you had deleted. You need to take definitive action if you don't want anyone gaining access to a file after you delete it.

You get into the most trouble with deleted files when you share floppy disks with someone. For example, perhaps you save your files to floppy disk until you finally purchase a new tape drive for backups. Upon purchasing a tape drive, you decide that you can re-use all those floppy disks that once contained your backed-up files. So you delete all the files on each floppy disk and begin to re-use the floppy disks. Suppose that you send us one of those floppy disks with a small file on it that we requested from you. Using the UNDELETE command, we can recover most of the backed-up files that remained on the floppy disk, leaving you vulnerable to our sense of morals and fair play.

To protect yourself from this hazard, you need to do one of two things. If you intend to share a floppy disk with others, first copy a bunch of system files (select a bunch of files from a WINDOWS, DOS, or MAC System directory) onto the floppy disk until it is full. Then delete these files and copy the file you want to share onto the floppy disk. With this method, the recipient can recover only files that don't contain any of your personal data.

An easier method is to use a program designed to delete the actual file (not just the table entry). These programs typically delete files by writing zeros all over the spaces where your deleted files used to be. After you use one of these programs to delete a file, the file is effectively gone for good! You can find a number of programs that provide this capability on the Internet and on services such as CompuServe and AOL by doing a search for the term *wipe*. We provide you with the locations of two such programs in Chapters 17 (for DOS users) and 18 (for Mac users). The first program is called Exodel and is Windows based. The second example is a program for Macintosh computers called Burn. Finally, you can use an option provided with Puffer, which we described earlier, to provide true erasure in addition to file encryption.

Gone for good

Although we indicate that the file is gone for good, an expensive method that is available can recover even these files. It's so expensive, though, that you can rest assured that your deleted data is gone unless you are deleting secret government files or messages from James Bond, where paying hundreds of dollars might be worth it. We discuss recovery methods in more detail in Chapter 10.

To truly delete a file, you need to follow the steps outlined in the publication called "A Guide to Understanding Data Remanence in Automated Information Systems," NCSC-TG-025, September 1991. Be warned, however, that this document is technical in nature. The gist of it indicates that a file must be written over by 0s and 1s at least three times to ensure that even sophisticated recovery tools cannot recover the file. You can get a free copy by calling 410-766-8729, the National Security Agency INFOSEC Awareness Center.

File Access Control

What is *file access control?* Not file passwords. Although you can put passwords on every file you create and manage access to the files through such pass-words, that's the method of the '60s, and we are now in the '90s. File passwords are fine for one or two files, but they quickly become unmanageable when you're dealing with hundreds of files.

You can provide better protection for your files by using a software program designed to provide data protection. These programs typically utilize a form of access control list that enables you to create lists of users and assign each user certain "rights" to files.

This method of protection is fairly complex and isn't for the fainthearted. But it does provide a sound method for giving every person in the house or office access to only his or her own files and not to anyone else's. This section gives you a brief overview of file access control and lets you decide whether you want to find out more.

For file access control to be effective, it must first identify each user individually and then provide a way to give access to some files while refusing access to others. While doing this, the program needs to allow for simple administration of the necessary tasks. Windows-based programs are beginning to offer fast, effective ways for an administrator (or Mom and Dad) to set up and maintain these users (their children) and their file restrictions.

The first task is to create a logon account for each person who uses the com-puter. The idea is to give each member of the house his or her own account and password. This way, you can manage exactly who can do what, and even prevent someone from using the computer by changing the password. One person needs to be the boss, such as Mom and Dad (okay, so that's two people), and have access to everything, commonly called the *administrator account.* This account creates all the users, assigns passwords, and performs file access restrictions. Although we seldom let two people use one account, because this diminishes user accountability (see Chapter 2), there are always exceptions to every rule. In the home, this exception makes sense. A home doesn't usually need the levels of accountability that an organization does.

You can simplify this strategy by creating only two accounts. One is the admin-istrator, and the other is a general account for everyone to use. You can then restrict any sensitive files so that only the administrator can access them, letting the other account do anything else. After you set up accounts, you can set file access levels.

An effective program offers a detailed level of control over your files. For example, you may want someone to be able to see the contents of a file but not be able to change those contents or delete the file. This plan is referred to as *read-only access.* A good access control program should offer four levels of control. In most software packages, each control is exclusive of the others. In other words, you may be able to delete a file but not see what's in it, or see what's in a file but not change it. Table 14-1 describes the four typical controls.

Table 14-1	The Four Types of Control
Setting	*Description*
Read-only	You can read the contents but not change anything or delete the file.
Write	You can add data to an existing file.
Create	You can create new files.
Delete	You can delete files that already exist.

Good file access control programs enable you to set these "rights" in any combination. Most home users use these rights to restrict access to each other's files. The easiest way to do so is to set up a directory called DATA and give each person a subdirectory below the DATA directory in which to store personal files. Then restrict access to everyone else's personal files. You might get really creative and prevent younger children from access to anything except those programs you approve.

Most access control programs do strange things to your hard drive to prevent unauthorized access. If the access control program fails during installation, you may lose files. Play it safe and back up your hard drive before starting the installation process. (Do this anytime you mess around with your computer, such as when installing a new version of DOS or Windows 95.)

How do these programs perform this control? They take total control of your personal computer. Everything that happens after their installation is then managed by the access control software. Although this situation may sound scary, most shareware programs are designed to be fairly simple for any technically competent person to install. If you can install games and word processor software, for example, you should have little difficulty in installing these programs.

Commercially available security software

Even though a number of shareware security programs are available, you may decide that you want to use a commercial security program. A primary advantage of using one of these programs is the support you get from the vendor. Average home users may need someone to walk them through the installation process and help them if they don't understand something. In addition, these programs are generally more effective than shareware programs at securing your computer, because they are usually *vetted* (tested) far more heavily.

Finally, if you have very sensitive data on your computer, such as your home business files, that you really do not want family members, friends, or a thief who steals your computer to access, you probably need a stronger commercial program such as StopLight, PC/DACS, or Watchdog. Appendix B lists a number of firms that offer such software.

Part IV
The Part of Tens

The 5th Wave

By Rich Tennant

©RICHTENNANT

"I ALWAYS BACK UP EVERYTHING."

In this part...

This rather lengthy part includes several short chapters, each composed of ten (or so) tidbits that you can use to protect your personal computer and your precious data. You'll find information about popular Mac and PC security utilities, common viruses, useful backup devices, and more in Part IV.

Chapter 15

Ten Things All PC Users Should Do

*I*f you use a computer, you can do a number of things to ensure that you have a long and happy relationship with your machine. People often forget to manage the simple things in their zeal to create or discover on their personal computers. This chapter highlights ten important tasks that you must do to keep your computer available for use.

Turn Off the Monitor or Use a Screen Saver

If you use a laptop computer, you may want to skip this section, because screen savers for laptops are generally unnecessary. Most laptops use liquid crystal displays, which are not affected by continued operation. All other monitors, however, use the chemical phosphorus to display a picture on-screen. If you leave the display turned on for excessive amounts of time (days or weeks), the screen image "burns in," and whatever image is showing remains on-screen forever. After a screen image burns in, the only recourse is to purchase a new monitor.

If you use a desktop computer, turn off the monitor when you are not using the computer. Do not leave the screen turned on all the time. Powering off the monitor while the computer is still running is okay. Do not turn the monitor on and off all day long, however, as this practice wears it out, and you'll have to replace it anyway. Only turn it off if you are planning to run the machine for a few hours and do not need the display. For example, Barry uses his desktop machine to receive and send faxes, and therefore his machine is powered on almost all the time. However, because he doesn't actually use the machine, he turns off the screen and turns it on only once a day to check for incoming faxes.

If you prefer, turn down the monitor instead of turning it off. Most monitors have a control that lets you adjust the brightness. Turn this control until the screen is black, and leave it like that until you need to see the display. Then just turn up the brightness.

Finally, you can use a screen saver program. These programs put a picture on-screen and constantly change it so that one image never remains in one place, preventing burn in.

In Windows 3.1, turn on your screen saver by using the following steps:

1. **Double-click on the Main icon.**

2. **Double-click on the Control Panel icon.**

3. **Double-click on the Desktop icon.**

   You see an area called Screen Saver.

4. **Select an appropriate picture and time delay and click on OK.**

   You can modify the speed and add a password by using the Setup box.

In Windows 95, follow these steps to turn on a screen saver:

1. **Open the Control Panel.**

2. **Double-click on the Display icon, and then click on the Screen Saver tab.**

3. **In the section called Screen Saver, select a picture and then click on OK.**

   To control speed and colors, use the Settings parameter.

Buy a Surge Protector

A surge protector is a must for every person who uses a computer on a regular basis. Electricity is a tenuous thing, and too much or too little power can seriously damage delicate computer parts. These devices also help protect against nearby lightning strikes. Why nearby? Contrary to popular belief, lightning does not need to strike your home directly to damage your computer. A lightning strike anywhere nearby can travel through the underground cables and into your home, unknown to you but felt by your computer.

In addition, you can be affected on a clear, sunny day, so believing that you can turn off the machine only when it storms is a false sense of security. The home is subject to summer *brownouts* (drops in power) as millions of people turn on their air conditioning, which can damage your machine. Plugging a vacuum cleaner or large electrical appliance (like the fridge) into the same circuit breaker as your computer can also cause damage.

Surge protectors come in various sizes, costs, and degrees of effectiveness. Buy one relative to the cost of your computer. If you just plunked down $3,000 for a computer, consider a decent surge protector costing around $100. Midrange devices cost between $50 and $100. The really inexpensive $20 protectors probably provide a false sense of security, because their effectiveness is limited.

Back It Up!

In Chapter 10, we discuss this need to back up your files in detail, so we will not rehash every point here. However, backups are important enough, and forgotten often enough, that we want to highlight the main point once more: However you decide to do it, back up your data regularly!

Clean the Monitor

What does cleaning the monitor have to do with security? Not a heck of a lot unless you get overzealous and clean your monitor incorrectly, which can result in destruction or damage. Then you have an availability problem — no monitor. Funny how the lack of a monitor can impede the use of a computer, no matter how fast or big that computer is.

Be careful when cleaning! Treat the monitor like the electrical gadget that it is. Most screens are allergic to water being poured on them. Dampen a cloth and use it to clean the screen. If you have one of the specially coated screens, be especially careful of commercial antistatic and other cleaning agents. These screens have a chemical coating to reduce dust accumulation and are more susceptible to damage from the chemicals in some of these sprays.

Dust the Components

Dust and dirt are anathema to a computer. Keep the computer clean, and it will serve you longer. Turn off the computer and dust or vacuum it lightly at least once a month. If you live in a new home where heavy construction is still going on, buy a cover and keep it over the computer except when you are using the machine. If you want to clean the monitor case, carefully pour some cleaning fluid on a cloth and then use the cloth to clean the case. Never spray liquid directly onto any part of a computer.

We do not recommend that beginners take the cover off the machine and dust inside. Although it does get dirty there, the potential for damage from your dusting techniques are far greater than the potential for damage from the dust and dirt that find their way inside. Just leave this part alone.

You can purchase several neat dusting cloths, special vacuums, and sprays if you have money to spend. While they are not necessary, they can make life a bit easier. For example, we often see ads for compressed air that helps to clean really well between the keys of your keyboard. This is the same stuff that camera enthusiasts use to keep their cameras dust free.

Take the time once in a while to clean your machine. Even if it doesn't prolong the life of your personal computer, the machine sure does look nicer.

Protect the Computer from Static Electricity

Static electricity is the bane of all computers. Keep your house reasonably humid, and static electricity will never bother you. It's that simple. Using a humidifier during winter months prevents static from occurring.

You can purchase static mats, special metal plates, and even antistatic sprays, all designed to reduce the natural tendency of a dry climate. Use whatever you need for your particular environment. For the most part, the computer case transfers static harmlessly away from critical components because the case is electrically grounded. Although you can generally touch the outside of your computer without causing any damage from static (unless you have a really bad static level and shock yourself on everything you touch), it is best to not take any chance at all and eliminate the static in the first place.

Being aware of static is especially crucial when you are messing around inside the computer. If you are the type of hardy soul who opens up the case to add memory or components like a CD player or modem, take extra precautions against static.

Consider a Keyboard Cover

A keyboard cover is an essential item for anyone with small children — or anyone who likes to drink coffee or soda while working on the computer. Those sticky fingers can mess up the keys very easily. Ever tried to get jam off one or two keys? It isn't easy! And heaven forbid that you drop anything between the keys. The process of removing the item isn't always as simple as turning the keyboard upside down and shaking the item loose.

A keyboard cover costs around $15 to $25 and is a good investment. It not only protects your keyboard from sticky fingers, but it also helps to prevent damage from accidental liquid spills and keeps dust, dirt, and loose hair from messing up the keys.

Monitor the Modem

Most computer users eventually obtain a modem to connect to the Internet or an online service such as AOL or CompuServe. The *modem* is the device that translates what your computer says into something that other computers understand. The device is absolutely necessary for dialing up other computers, which is, after all, exactly what you do when you connect to those online services.

A lot of discussion is going on about the potential for crackers to get access to your machine while you are connected to these services. Let us help set the record straight — yes, someone can do the necessary things and perhaps get access to a personal computer attached to the Internet. However, it is so unlikely that it's not worth worrying about. In the business community, where people may be connected to the Internet all day, the risk does increase, but it still remains minimal. Although getting access to other computers is technically achievable, it takes a lot of effort, and quite frankly, enterprising crackers can find far better targets.

A far worse risk concerns the access to inappropriate material that is available to your children (or coworkers). Without us getting into the issue of censorship, many, many things are available that we do not want our children to see and are not appropriate in a business office. For example, parents may want to restrict their children from accessing the huge amount of sexually oriented information on the Net. On the plus side, of course, so much positive material is available that refusing access seems limiting. Better to control what your children see by using supervision and some of the tools that are becoming available. (See Chapter 12 for more information.)

If you are concerned that others are using your modem to access your machine, turn off the modem. Or set it up so that it does not answer incoming calls and can be used for outbound calls only. (Look in your manual for information about the autoanswer feature and turn that feature off.) Be aware that you should not turn off autoanswer if you use the modem for receiving faxes. Leaving a modem turned on and your computer set to receive faxes does not pose any risk to you, apart from the junk faxes you may get.

Repair the Hard Drive

No, we don't mean getting out the screwdriver and pliers and going at it. We mean paying some attention to the needs of the drive and running some of the utilities that help to keep your files and drives in good shape.

On all drives, occasional problems occur. These problems consist of *bad sectors,* which are pieces of the drive that don't properly accept data anymore, and *logical file errors,* which arise when a file does not close properly. We will not get into technical discussions here, as entire books are devoted to that level of detail. Suffice it to say that if you use some of the common utilities once in a while, your data is safer.

All PC users should run the DOS SCANDISK program that comes with DOS once every few months. This program (or CHKDSK that comes with DOS Versions 5.0 and back) checks for errors on the drive and, if prompted, corrects those errors. These errors are typically files that were messed up when you powered off in the middle of using a program. To run this program, close Windows, and then type the following at the DOS prompt:

```
scandisk /autofix /nosave
```

This command tells SCANDISK to check the drive for boo-boos and get rid of any that it finds. For more details about the SCANDISK program, check out Dan Gookin's *DOS For Dummies* (IDG Books Worldwide, Inc.).

Run a Virus Checker Program

Viruses are a threat, and you need to take action to prevent possible damage. Don't wait until a virus attacks your machine. Get a virus program, whether shareware or commercial, install it, and use it! (Chapter 11 discusses viruses in detail.)

We suggest that you run a virus checker every time you turn on your computer. Most of the available checkers give you the option to check at startup when you first install it. In addition, some newer programs run in conjunction with your other programs, providing continuous protection. Using this type of virus checker is a good practice, especially if you regularly download files from the Internet or other online services.

On the other hand, most virus checkers become quickly out of date as people produce new viruses. The programs need to be updated regularly, or after a short while, they cease to be truly effective. If you get a shareware program, remember to return to the site at which you got it at least once every three months and pick up any updates that you find. Often, commercial programs also offer free updates through online systems such as AOL and CompuServe.

Key things to remember about virus checkers include the following:

- ✔ Use a virus checker program every time you turn on the computer.
- ✔ Run a virus checker when you download a lot of files from the Internet or other online service providers.
- ✔ Update the virus checker program at least once every three months.

Chapter 16

Ten Useful Security Documents from the U.S. Government

- -

- -

*T*he government is us; we are the government, you and I.

— Theodore Roosevelt

The U.S. government provides many free security publications. Because the government developed the publications with taxpayers' money, they make these documents available to the public. You may have to send a request to the U.S. government directly, but these days, several of the documents are available online to everyone. (Appendix B shows you where to find these and other free security resources online.)

FIPS Publications

The National Institute of Standards and Technology (NIST), which is part of the Commerce Department's Technology Administration, partners with private industry to accelerate the development of high-risk, enabling technologies identified by industry as promising significant commercial payoffs and broad-based economic benefits. The agency's core mission is to promote U.S. economic growth by working with industry to develop technology, measurements, and standards.

NIST publishes the Federal Information Processing Standards Publications (FIPS PUBs) and issues them under the provisions of the Federal Property and Administrative Services Act of 1949, amended by the Computer Security Act of 1987.

FIPS PUBS currently include

- ✔ General publications
- ✔ Hardware standards and guidelines
- ✔ Software standards and guidelines
- ✔ Data standards and guidelines
- ✔ Computer security standards and guidelines
- ✔ ADP operations standards and guidelines
- ✔ Telecommunications standards

You can reach NIST's Computer Security Resource and Response Center (CSRC) by any of the following means:

- ✔ Emergency 24-hour hotline: 301-975-5200
- ✔ Anonymous FTP from host csrc.ncsl.nist.gov (129.6.48.87)
- ✔ Web site: http://csrc.ncsl.nist.gov
- ✔ Bulletin board system: 301-948-5717, 1, N, 8 300/1200/2400
- ✔ E-mail: CSRC@nist.gov
- ✔ Snail-mail:

    Computer Security Resource and Response Center
    A-216 Technology
    Gaithersburg, MD 20899

Guidelines for Implementing and Using the NBS Data Encryption Standard

FIPS PUB 74, April 1981

This standard provides guidance for using cryptographic techniques to protect sensitive or valuable computer data. You also need to read FIPS PUB 46-1 (*Data Encryption Standard,* January 1988) and FIPS PUB 81 (*DES Modes of Operation,* December 1980). If you are interested in the DES algorithm itself, you can find it in the *Data Encryption Standard. Modes of Operation* defines the four modes of operation (Electronic Codebook, Cipher Block Chaining, Cipher Feedback, and Output Feedback) for encryption and decryption. If you really have an interest in encryption, check out FIPS 113 (*Computer Data Authentication,* May 1985), FIPS 140-1 (*Security Requirements for Cryptographic Modules,* January 1994), FIPS 180 (*Secure Hash Standard,* May 1993), and FIPS 186 (*Digital Signature Standard,* May 1994) as well.

These resources are valuable for anyone considering the use of encryption. Chapter 13 discusses encryption in more detail.

Standard on Password Usage

FIPS PUB 112, May 1985

Though fairly old, this standard is still useful. It provides ten factors to consider when designing, implementing, and using access control systems based on passwords. The standard lays out minimum security criteria for these systems and provides guidance for selecting additional security for password systems that must meet higher security requirements.

This is the standard to get when you are trying to convince someone that three-character passwords that are changed once a year are not secure. You can read further about creating good passwords in Chapter 8.

NCSC Technical Guidelines and Reports

The National Computer Security Center (NCSC) publishes the Rainbow Series of security documents, which define the features of the Trusted Computer System Evaluation Criteria (TCSEC) and provide guidance for meeting specific requirements. You may have heard of the *Orange Book*, which defines security classes and provides the basis for implementing security in operating systems.

The NCSC also publishes academic reports, which provide an excellent perspective on major problem areas in computer security.

Glossary of Computer Security Terms, Version 1

NCSC-TG-004 (Victorian Green), October 1988

This glossary defines an initial set of computer security terms and is intended to promote the common understanding of the terms to foster meaningful communication.

This is a good resource to get so that you can talk the talk and walk the walk.

Computer Viruses: Prevention, Detection, and Treatment

C1-Technical Report 001, March 1990

This report discusses threats from viruses and tells how existing technology and security procedures can help. It reports on technical controls (for example, using virus software) and administrative controls (for example, controlling who can install software on your system).

The report also provides an analysis of the Internet Virus and examines the influence that the evaluation process (that is, the TCSEC) would have had on identifying vulnerabilities used during the attack. You can read about the Internet virus (actually, worm) in Chapters 11 and 12.

NIST/NBS Special Publications

NIST, formerly the National Bureau of Standards (NBS), also publishes special publications of general interest to computer users interested in making their computing more secure. In 1990, NIST established the Special Publications 800 series to provide a separate identity and to enhance the visibility of the Computer Systems Laboratory's expanded computer security program.

Security of Personal Computer Systems — A Management Guide

NBS SPEC PUB 500-120, January 1985

This publication provides practical advice on physical and environmental protection systems, data access control, integrity of software and data, backup and contingency planning, auditing, and communications protection. It provides references to other computer security sources, a self-audit checklist, and information about security products for personal computers.

Security for Dial-Up Lines

NBS SPEC PUB 500-137, May 1986

This publication provides ways to protect computers from intruders using dial-up telephone lines. It highlights hardware devices that can be fitted to computers or used with their dial-up terminals to provide communications protection for nonclassified computer systems.

The publication describes six different hardware devices and the ways you can use them to protect dial-up computer communications, and it discusses techniques for computer operating systems, system management, and administrative procedures.

Computer Viruses and Related Threats: A Management Guide

NIST SPEC PUB 500-166, August 1989

This publication provides general advice on managing the threats from computer viruses and related software and unauthorized use. It is geared toward managers of end-user or client groups and managers dealing with multiuser systems, personal computers, and networks, which means that it is not too technical.

Computer User's Guide to the Protection of Information Resources

NIST SPEC PUB 500-171, December 1989

This publication outlines the user's responsibility for information protection and provides security and control guidelines that you can implement. You also may be interested in the *Management Guide to the Protection of Information Resources,* NIST SPEC PUB 500-170, October 1989. The latter guide introduces information systems security issues.

A Guide to the Selection of Anti-Virus Tools and Techniques

NIST SPEC PUB 800-5, December 1992

This publication provides criteria for judging the functionality, practicality, and convenience of antivirus tools so that you can determine which tools are best suited to your environment.

An Introduction to Computer Security: The NIST Handbook

NIST SPEC PUB 800-12, February 1996

This publication provides a broad overview of the computer security field. It can help you to understand the basics of computer security by explaining important concepts, cost considerations, and interrelationships of security controls. It provides excellent reference material.

Chapter 17

Ten Useful DOS-Based PC Security Utilities

. . . .

In This Chapter

▶ Access control and write protection

▶ Password recovery programs

▶ True erasure

▶ Just for fun

. . . .

*Y*ou can get shareware and freeware programs for your personal computer in many places. As a PC user with access to the Internet, you should check out `http://www.jumbo.com/bus/pc/security/`. The Jumbo site includes references to over 49,000 freeware and shareware programs. Another good site is `ftp://oak.oakland.edu/SimTel/`, where many more DOS and Windows shareware and freeware programs reside.

Note: These addresses change over time, so if you cannot locate a site, use one of the many Internet search programs and look for the terms *freeware* and *shareware*. Examples of good search programs include Yahoo, Alta Vista, and Webcrawler.

If you choose to use any of the shareware programs, remember to send in your registration fee. These fees are typically only $10 or $20 and are well worth it. The freeware programs generally cost nothing, which is why they're called *free*ware.

If you can't find these utilities on the Internet, try America Online, CompuServe, or Prodigy. Perform a search on the terms *freeware* and *shareware* to find forums that discuss these utilities.

Access Control and Write Protection

Software in this section provides logon password control or password recovery software. (See Chapter 7 for more information about access control.) Logon control usually requires you to enter a special group of characters called a *userid* or *account,* followed by a password that identifies you to the software on the computer. Sometimes you forget your password. If you're fortunate, one of the programs in this section may be able to recover the password for you.

Front gate access

Thegate is a program intended to let you control who can access your DOS (not Windows) computer. It also creates a log of users, their passwords, start and finish dates and times, and time spent on the computer. This program may be useful for parents who want to monitor the number of hours their children spend on the computer. Each child can be given a password, and all activity on each password is logged. Parents can then review the logs each week and discuss what the child is doing. Look for a file called THEGATE.ZIP at one of the sites listed at the beginning of this chapter. Thegate is a DOS program and is not effective under Windows.

The program is freeware.

Windows monitoring

Mr Burns, shown in Figure 17-1, lets you monitor your Windows usage. You can see which programs your children are using and how long they spend on CompuServe or AOL. This program is also useful for individuals who want to track how much time they spend working on their word processor or playing games. The program runs in the background, generally unobtrusively. (The unregistered version tells you that it is running. Buying the license turns this message off.) Some of the data that Mr Burns collects includes the names and command lines of programs that are run (including the time they start and stop), which applications are active at any given time, the amount of time the computer is left idle, and the number of keystrokes used. This program comes with decent documentation (fairly rare in the shareware/freeware realm) and can be set up to run automatically.

The program is shareware.

Password generator

The Passgen program generates valid passwords of up to 25 characters. The program runs in Windows and appears to run fine in Windows 95. When started, it displays a screen with an almost overwhelming number of options.

The program creates passwords randomly, always generating a new combination of characters. It allows you to generate thousands of passwords at a time so that you can pick and choose ones that are easy to remember. Passgen gives you options to use numbers, special characters, and uppercase and lowercase letters when creating new passwords. The more variety you use, of course, the stronger the potential password. Users need to ensure that their system allows the use of all these options, however. For example, many security programs do not recognize the difference between uppercase and lowercase characters.

To use Passgen, double-click on the Password generator icon. A window like the one in Figure 17-2 appears. Select the options you want and press Execute. Pick a password that you can remember easily.

The program is shareware and works for 300 hours before you must remove or register and pay for it.

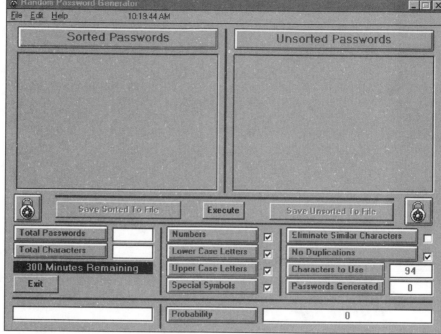

Figure 17-2:
The
Passgen
password
generator
program.

Keyboard locks

Sometimes you are in the middle of doing something on your computer and just have to get up to do something else. But you really do not want to leave your computer vulnerable to anyone who wanders by and decides to play with your files. The Windows program WDWSLOCK.EXE locks the keyboard until you return. The program also allows you to program-protect certain programs. This feature can be useful for controlling which programs your children can use.

To use the control, first you create a password by using the program called SETLOCK.EXE, and then you activate the lock at any time by running WDWSLOCK.EXE. After you set the keyboard lock, you can wander away from your PC. To control a program, you must change the Windows file that executes the program to run WDWSLOCK first.

For example, in Windows, click on the icon that runs the program you want to control. Next, choose File⇨Properties. Add **WDWSLOCK.EXE** before the current program name. This setup runs the WDWSLOCK program first. To be truly effective, you also need to protect the File Manager and other aspects of the system so that users cannot simply execute the program without using the icon or removing the locking program. Generous help files explain how to add these additional levels of protection in detail.

The program requires registration, because the shareware version displays the password! For $5, you may find WDWSLOCK useful.

A word of caution: These products stop the casual person from getting on your system, but they do not stop a determined attacker. In most instances, you can easily disable them or reboot from the floppy drive to obtain access. Therefore, do not rely on them for complete protection.

Password Recovery Programs

Have you ever forgotten a password? Everyone does at some time or other. If you are at work, you can just ask your security administrator for a new password and continue working. But what happens when you use passwords at home and forget them? In the following sections, we list a number of programs that can help you recover forgotten passwords in word processing and spreadsheet programs.

Microsoft Word Versions 1 and 2

If you use Word's password-protection feature and forget the password, help is available. Look for a file called WORDUNP.ZIP, which contains two programs, WINWU.EXE and DOSWU.EXE. The programs run either in Windows (WINWU.EXE) or in DOS (DOSWU.EXE) and create a new version of your document without the forgotten password. Run the programs by specifying the document that contains the password you've forgotten and the name of a new file.

In Windows, choose File⇨Run (or Start⇨Run in Windows 95) and enter the following: **winwu** *infile outfile*. Replace the word *infile* with the name of a file with a password you want to recover and *outfile* with the new name you want WINWU to create.

Microsoft Word Versions 6 and 7

If you use a newer version of Word for Windows, you need the file called WFWCD.ZIP. Within this file is a program called WFWCD.EXE, which is capable of recovering your forgotten password. We caution that this program typically works best with a data file containing lots of lowercase letters, such as a book chapter or recipe file. It may not work for a file that does not contain many alphabetic characters, such as a list of telephone numbers or a document that you produce entirely in capital letters. Run the program in DOS, specifying the document that contains the password you forgot. For example, to recover a file called BARRY.DOC in the DATA directory, use the following command:

```
c:>WFWCD c:\data\barry.doc
```

We ran the Windows version (just double-click on the program name) against a Word 7 file to show you what happens. See Figure 17-3.

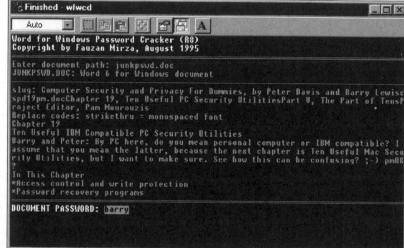

Figure 17-3:
Word for
Windows
Password
Cracker.

Corel WordPerfect 5.1

If you use WordPerfect rather than Word, you need the file called WPCRACK_A.ZIP. Within this file is a program called WPCRACK.C, which you can use to recover your forgotten password. A document file that comes in the .ZIP file explains the process fairly clearly. The author wrote the program specifically for WordPerfect 5.1, so it may not work with earlier or later versions.

Microsoft Excel 5.0

If you use a spreadsheet program such as Excel, you can protect certain spreadsheets by adding a password. As with word processing documents, however, people tend to forget the password months later when they need to revisit the file. The password recovery program for Excel is found in a file called EXCEL.ZIP. The program name is UN_EXCEL.EXE, and it runs under Windows 3.x and also on Windows 95.

This program has no documentation, so it may not work on all versions of Excel. Barry ran it against an Excel 7.0 file, and it did not work. A test with Excel Version 5.0 worked fine.

True Erasure

When you delete a file, you don't really delete it. On all DOS and Windows machines, you don't erase the file when you drag it to the Recycle Bin (Windows 95) or issue a DELETE command. The file remains available to anyone who uses a file utility to retrieve the file. All that happens when you throw a file away is that the *pointer* to the file disappears. If you really want to delete a file, you must erase it completely. Normally, you do so by overwriting your file with zeroes.

The ExoDel program completely erases your files so that almost no one can retrieve them. (The only way to literally make a file unrecoverable is to destroy the hard drive or floppy diskette. In Chapter 10, we list some companies that make it their business to help you recover files. And they are very good at it!) We often use this type of program when we provide diskettes to our clients. In this manner, we ensure that no customer data gets into the wrong hands.

ExoDel is a Windows 3.x-based program that features user-selectable and random-erase patterns. Being a Windows program, it is simple to use, but it strangely does not support drag and drop. You select the files you want to delete and then double-click to add them to the delete list. Then you simply press GO!, and ExoDel permanently deletes them. See Figure 17-4.

The program is shareware.

Figure 17-4:
The ExoDel
file deletion
program.

Just for Fun: Changing Your Windows 95 Recycle Bin

Just to show that we aren't complete nerds, following is a program that does not really add anything to security but is fun to use.

If you're a Windows 95 user, you know that when you delete a file, it is placed in the Recycle Bin. So if you accidentally delete a file, you can go to this folder and retrieve the file. But the Recycle Bin looks kinda boring after a while, doesn't it? You can replace it, however, with a much more fun idea: a toilet! This program is called TOILET.EXE and uses a sound file called FLUSH.WAV. Both are found in a file called TOILET.ZIP.

After you install TOILET.EXE, your plain old Recycle Bin takes on the shape of a toilet. When you place a file in it, you get a sound like a flushing toilet. Neat! (See? Even security people can have a sense of humor.)

The program is shareware. We found most of the shareware programs listed in this chapter on the Jumbo site mentioned at the beginning of this chapter. If you have trouble, use one of the search programs also mentioned earlier.

Chapter 18
Ten Useful Mac Security Utilities

In This Chapter

▶ Access control and write protection
▶ True erasure
▶ Virus programs and software auditing

*I*f you are a Macintosh user and don't know about the `ftp://sumex-aim.stanford.edu` site, you should. You can find most Macintosh freeware and shareware at this site, so take a visit. If you can't find one of the programs listed in this chapter at Stanford, hop over to `http://www.jumbo.com/bus/mac/security/`. The Jumbo site includes references to over 49,000 freeware and shareware programs. If you can't find these utilities on the Internet, try America Online, CompuServe, or Prodigy.

Access Control and Write Protection

In Chapter 7, you can read about access control. Software discussed in this section provides log-on password control or software write protection for a diskette.

BugOff

BugOff intends to keep unauthorized people from gaining access to your Macintosh while you're away. It provides a system startup password as well as a built-in screen saver with password dismissal (see the settings in Figure 18-1), which do not interrupt background processing.

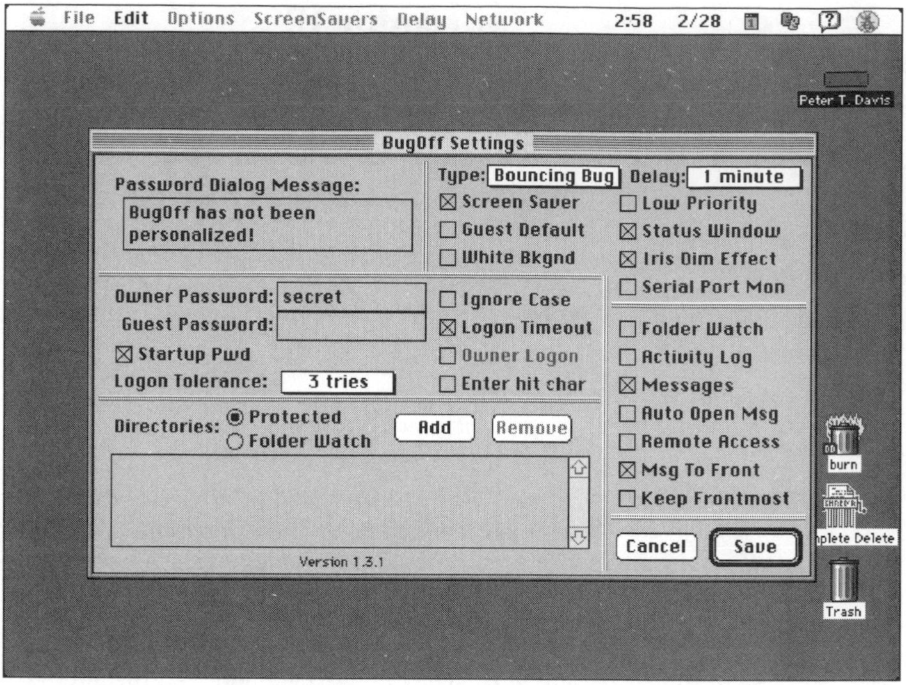

Figure 18-1:
BugOff
Settings.

BugOff allows for two passwords. The first password is the *system administrator,* or *owner,* which allows complete access to the system. The second lets users access the system with the exception of being able to open the preferences or having access to folders specified by the owner.

BugOff is freeware.

Firewall

Like BugOff, Firewall acts as the first line of defense from nosy people. It, too, is a screen lockout utility that provides a minimum level of security. To access your computer, you must enter the correct password in the password entry screen. After three incorrect login attempts, Firewall blanks the screen until you move the mouse or press a key and the system locks down for 60 minutes. Figure 18-2 shows the message after "lockdown" and the clock that counts down.

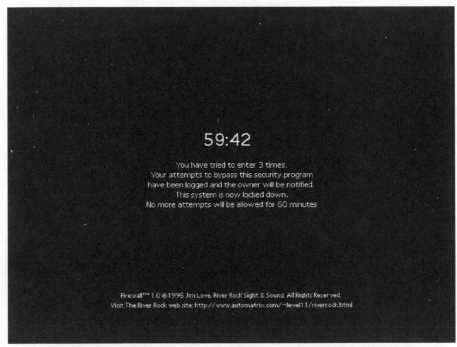

59:42

You have tried to enter 3 times.
Your attempts to bypass this security program
have been logged and the owner will be notified.
This system is now locked down.
No more attempts will be allowed for 60 minutes

Firewall™ 1.0 ©1995 Jim Love, River Rock Sight & Sound. All Rights Reserved.
Visit The River Rock web site: http://www.automatrix.com/~level11/riverrock.html

Figure 18-2:
Firewall
"lockdown"
screen.

In addition, Firewall logs start and quit time and date and lists all bogus password entries with the date and time.

Firewall is freeware.

PasswordMaker

PasswordMaker is an application that generates a valid six-character password given two keywords: a master keyword and your user name. Passwords currently comprise six numbers and lowercase letters, which should be friendly to most systems.

The program creates passwords by using a mathematical algorithm (not randomly) so you can always generate the password for a user name again as long as you use the same master keyword. As long as you use a good key, PasswordMaker generates completely different passwords even for very similar user names. This feature is useful for system administrators who regularly generate passwords for their users and need to reproduce the same password if it is lost or forgotten.

To use PasswordMaker, launch the PasswordMaker application. A window appears with two fields: Password Key and User Name. Simply fill in the Password Key field, fill in the User Name field, and click on the Generate button. Generating a password is shown in Figure 18-3.

Using this software definitely has its pros and cons. The main pro is that you can generate hard-to-guess passwords. The primary con is that the password that you generate is unpronounceable; however, you can regenerate it every time you need it by using PasswordMaker again.

PasswordMaker is freeware.

PowerLock

PowerLock, whose prime function is to prevent unauthorized access to your Macintosh, acts as a front door. It is similar in function to BugOff and Firewall. Easy to use, PowerLock is a startup application that you can completely configure and customize to suit your personal needs.

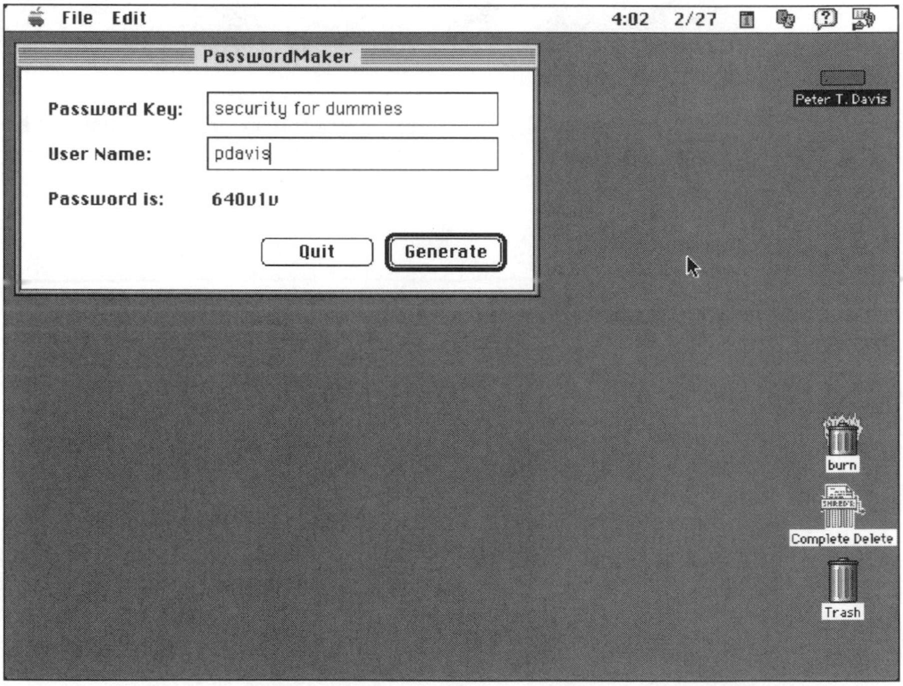

Figure 18-3:
Password-
Maker
window.

PowerLock provides some access control for your Macintosh. When you want to leave your system for five minutes to get a cup of coffee and not come back to find your kids playing yet another game (and forgetting to save your work), you can use PowerLock. When you're working on confidential material at work, you can also use PowerLock. The program is designed to prevent casual access to your files.

Like most access-control software, PowerLock starts when your Macintosh starts. You have three attempts to enter the correct password. After three unsuccessful attempts, PowerLock shuts down your Macintosh and, should your Macintosh support the feature, switches off the power — hence the name *PowerLock*. You know when any illegal attempts have been made, and a detailed log file records a wide variety of information. PowerLock also acts as or with a screen saver by displaying a color picture after 30 seconds of inactivity or shutting off the power after five minutes of inactivity.

When you first click on the PowerLock icon, you see the PowerLock *f*. Clicking on AutoLauncher provides the dialog box in Figure 18-4, where you click on Auto-Install. Select the desired security level (⌘+N) and okay it (⌘+W). Note the keys for FKEY and click on OK. Also, note where the PowerLock extension was placed and click on OK twice. After you do, you need to enter and re-enter your password. The next time you start your machine, you need to enter your password as shown in Figure 18-5.

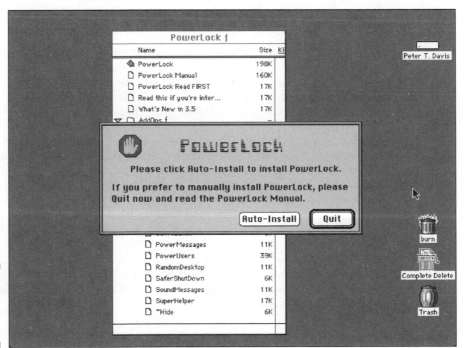

Figure 18-4:
PowerLock
install
window.

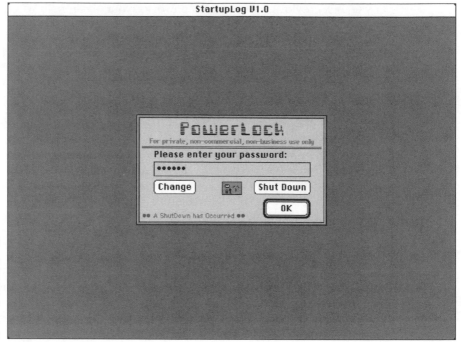

StartupLog U1.0

PowerLock
For private, non-commercial, non-business use only
Please enter your password:
●●●●●●
[Change] [🔒] [Shut Down]
[OK]
●● A ShutDown has Occurred ●●

Figure 18-5:
PowerLock
password
entry
screen.

SoftLock

SoftLock is a utility that lets you easily write-protect a disk by allowing you to lock and unlock disks using software. The software lock is part of the Macintosh operating system and is analogous to sliding the write-protect tab on a floppy disk. Locking lets you prevent a disk or file from being accidentally changed. A locked disk is sometimes called write-protected.

An advantage of SoftLock is that you also can lock a hard disk to prevent people from making changes to it. An optional password prevents the program from unlocking a disk until you enter the correct password.

Locking a disk prevents the disk from being changed in any way. Files cannot be modified or thrown away. When you have a disk that you want to read but never change, locking the disk ensures that files aren't modified accidentally.

The main window in Figure 18-6 has five buttons: Lock, Unlock, Eject, Drive, and Disk Info. To lock a disk, click on the Lock button; to unlock a disk, click on the Unlock button — simple and easy. When you lock a disk, SoftLock displays a lock symbol next to the disk's name.

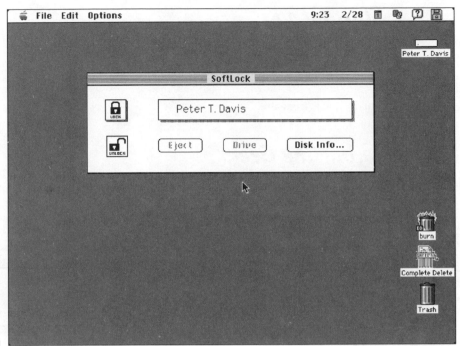

Figure 18-6:
SoftLock
window.

Sometimes you may want to prevent an unauthorized person from unlocking a disk locked with SoftLock, so you add a password as you lock the disk. To specify a password, choose the Set Password_ item from the Options menu. You must enter your password twice.

When unlocking a disk, SoftLock looks for this password and, when found, unlocks the disk only if you enter the identical password. A dialog box appears, asking you to enter the password. Type the password exactly as saved (including case), and the disk is unlocked.

SoftLock is not freeware; it is very economical shareware.

Floppy Unlocker

If you forget that floppy password, you may want to consider the freeware Floppy Unlocker, which locks and unlocks floppies and unlocks hard disks, without the password.

StartupLog

StartupLog simply adds a line to the end of a file log with the date and time that the program is run, and then it exits. When you put an alias of the program in your startup folder, you have a log of every system startup.

StartupLog is freeware.

Zorba "the Geek"?

Zorba also deters unauthorized users from using your Macintosh by demanding a password upon startup. See Figure 18-7 for the password dialog box, which masks the typed password characters. If you do not enter a correct password within three attempts, the program tries to shut down the system. The stored passwords are encrypted to prevent discovery by crackers using resource editors (such as ResEdit). All invalid and valid access attempts are stored in a log.

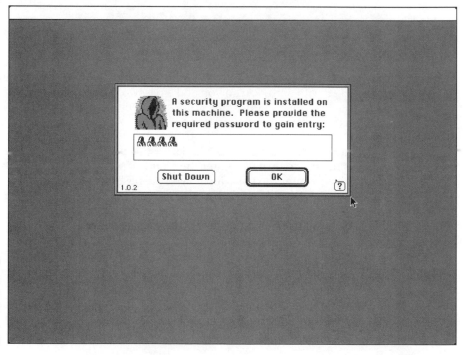

Figure 18-7:
Zorba's
password
dialog box.

Zorba can optionally warn you when more than 30, 45, or 60 days have passed since the regular password was changed.

Zorba also has an optional built-in screen saver that activates after 60 seconds of inactivity.

Zorba is freeware.

True Erasure

When you delete a file, you don't really delete it. On the Macintosh, you drag it to the Trash or do a delete from an application. This delete doesn't erase the file. In truth, anyone with a file utility can retrieve and use the file again. All that happens when you throw a file away is that the pointer to the file is lost. Therefore, when you really want to delete a file, you must completely erase it. Normally, you do this by overwriting your file with zeroes. We found two programs, Burn and Complete Delete, to completely erase your files so that no one (well, almost no one) can retrieve them.

Burn

No data security system would be complete without a way to destroy the original versions of a file after they are encrypted or to just protect files that you want gone. To ensure that people do not recover your data and cause you to get burned, you can use the Burn program. Burn is a file-destroying utility for System 7.*x* that prevents undelete utilities from recovering your data. Burn allows you to overwrite a file several times, so a snoop cannot recover it. You can let Burn select a random pattern for the overwrite or you can select your own pattern. In addition, Burn can erase free disk space, all with a convenient drag-and-drop interface. A benefit of Burn is that it erases files to the physical end-of-file instead of the logical end-of-file. The *logical end-of-file* is the character position following the last byte of meaningful information in a file. The last byte of physical storage space allocated to a file is the *physical end-of-file*.

Destroying a file or folder

You can overwrite files and folders by dragging them onto the Burn icon. The file or folder is overwritten a user-selected number of times with a user-selected pattern, then renamed, and then deleted. Both data and resource forks are deleted. A *resource fork* is the fork of a file containing the file's resources; it's usually called a resource file. A *resource file* is a collection of resources stored together as a unit on a disk. A *data fork* is the fork of a file containing the file's data, such as the text of a document. As a precaution, you need to confirm your intent to delete the file.

You can also destroy a file or folder by double-clicking on the Burn application and then choosing Delete from the File menu. The system prompts you to select an item for destruction.

Erasing free space on a volume

Burn allows you to erase the free space on your disks. This option is useful when you accidentally erased a sensitive file by using the regular Trash or when you deleted a file within your application. It is very safe because it creates a temporary file the size of the available free space on your disk, and then it "burns" that file.

To use this feature, choose Clean Disk Free Space from the File menu. Burn prompts you to select a volume to clean. After you select a volume and begin the cleaning process, a status dialog box shows the progress of the cleaning.

Burn is freeware.

Complete Delete

Complete Delete is another true erasure program that zeroes out the data and resource forks and then deletes the file. Figure 18-8 shows the description for Complete Delete. Clicking on OK, I'm through reading . . . presents a box such as that shown in Figure 18-9, where you select the file to delete completely. If you want to delete the file named Top Secret File, just select it and click on Open. You then need to reconfirm your intent to delete the file, as shown in the dialog box in Figure 18-10.

Virus Programs and Software Auditing

Three programs are included in this section. One provides simple information about the various types of Macintosh viruses. Another protects your system against viruses, and the third helps you find legal and illegal software on your system.

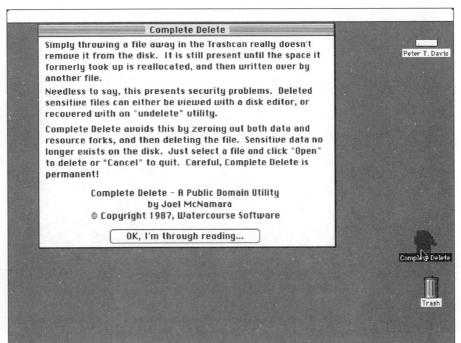

Figure 18-8:
Complete
Delete
description.

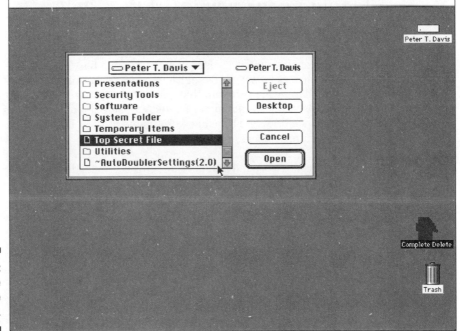

Figure 18-9:
Complete
Delete
window.

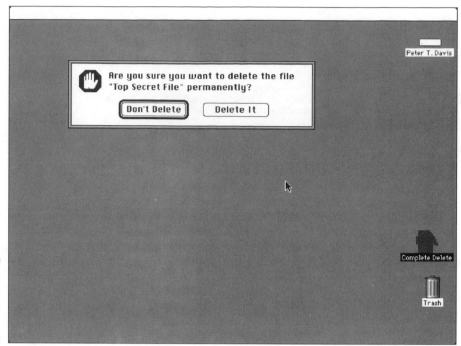

Figure 18-10:
Complete
Delete
confirmation.

Cleaning your system with a strong Disinfectant

As you are probably aware, viruses can cause great harm to your system. You can combat viruses by scanning your files, folders, floppies, and disks. Disinfectant is a useful freeware program that scans your resources and tells you when it finds a suspected virus. Launch Disinfectant, select a resource for scanning from the next window, and then click on Disinfect. After Disinfectant completes its scan, it returns the messages shown in Figure 18-11.

Should you decide to install Disinfectant, choose Install Protection INIT from the Protect menu. Restart your system, and Disinfectant continually scans your system and its resources for viruses.

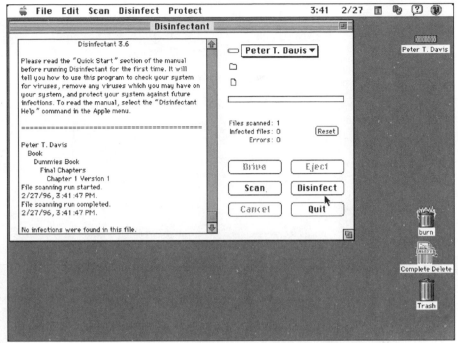

Figure 18-11:
The results
from
Disinfectant.

Looking up those symptoms with Virus Reference 2.1.6

Sometimes you need additional help understanding Macintosh viruses. If this is the case, you may want to get a copy of *Virus Reference 2.1.6* (see Figure18-12), which is an excellent HyperCard reference stack of Macintosh viruses.

Reviewing your software with KeyAudit

KeyAudit produces an audit of software assets to help you bring your system into compliance with software license provisions. KeyAudit saves its audit reports as tab-delimited text, which you can easily analyze with any spreadsheet or database program.

Double-click on KeyAudit and then click on the Audit button. All application programs found on local disks are presented in a list. Wait while KeyAudit reviews your system, and you see the window in Figure 18-13. Double-clicking on an application provides more information about it, as shown in Figure 18-14.

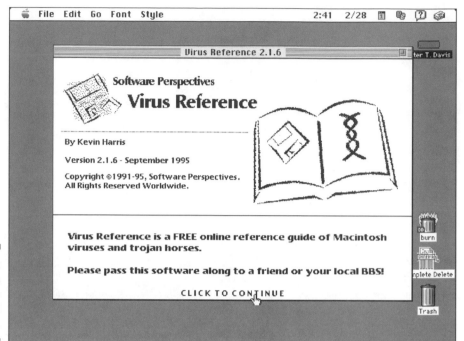

Figure 18-12:
Virus
Reference
HyperCard
stack.

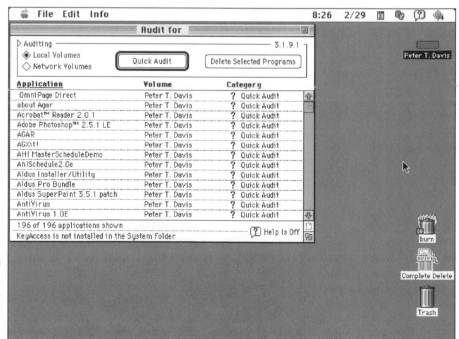

Figure 18-13:
KeyAudit
high-level
results.

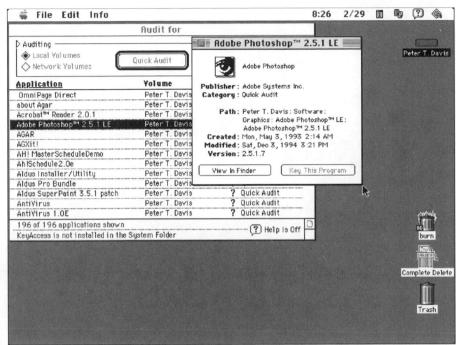

Figure 18-14:
KeyAudit
detailed
results.

A word of caution: These products stop the casual person from getting on your system, but they cannot stop a determined attacker. In most instances, you just need to reboot the system to get around the protection. But as they say, you get what you pay for!

Chapter 19

Ten DOS Security Commands

In This Chapter

▶ DOS security commands that you can use to protect your files

DOS is not the most secure operating system. In fact, it may be the least secure operating system. However, you can improve security on your system by using these ten DOS commands. Simply type them at the DOS prompt with the appropriate filename and options. If you're not sure of a command's syntax, type **help** at the DOS prompt, and you see information about all DOS commands.

For more information about using DOS commands, see Dan Gookin's *DOS For Dummies*.

ATTRIB

The ATTRIB command gives you an extra level of protection for data files. For example, `ATTRIB CIS.EXE +R` makes the CIS executable read-only. You can specify a file as *read-only* so that others cannot alter or delete it. You also can specify a file as *hidden* so that the file is not evident to casual snoopers. The Attributes feature exists on most operating systems. In fact, Microsoft probably borrowed heavily from UNIX for its DOS implementation.

This is another example where feeling secure may not be warranted. If you are a DIR aficionado, you know that you can type **DIR *.EXE /A**, and DOS displays hidden files. In addition, if you can't protect the desktop, then an intruder can just use the ATTRIB command to remove these attributes. And Windows 3.*x*'s File Manager and Windows 95's Explorer display *all* files!

BACKUP

The BACKUP command archives one or more files from one disk to another medium. You may want to try backing up and restoring from various mediums, such as floppy disks, tape, or digital audio tape (DAT). For example, to back up a file, type **BACKUP C:\SECRET\DOCUMENT A:**. (SECRET\DOCUMENT is the name of the file you want to back up for this example.)

CHKDSK

The CHKDSK command displays the status of the disk drive. It also provides information about used and unused memory.

You can use this command to aid in determining whether changes occur in your environment from one day to the next. When you run a regular report by using CHKDSK, you can determine whether significant portions of your memory are being used suspiciously (a potential virus), or whether programs suddenly are taking up more memory (also a potential virus).

COPY

When the name of the file to which you have chosen to copy (the destination file) already exists, the COPY command overwrites the file (that is, the data), making it unrecoverable.

This command is dangerous if people don't know what they're doing, but crackers also can make an innocent-looking batch file destroy an entire disk by inserting a COPY command.

However, you can use the COPY or RENAME command to hide a secret file. Using the command is as simple as typing **COPY SECRET.DOC PBR1V2.DLL**. (SECRET.DOC is the name of the file you'e hiding.) So many DLLs are on your system that it is unlikely that anyone would think to look here.

You may want to include the following COPY variant in the top ten commands, too.

XCOPY

You can use the XCOPY command to reproduce the contents of an entire disk onto a target disk. If the target is unformatted, this command formats the disk. The contents of the target disk are completely overwritten, including the volume name. DOS offers no way for mere mortals to recover existing data. However, the NSA (National Security Agency), CSIS (Canadian Security & Intelligence Service), or Mossad still can recover your data unless you do your overwrite about 13 times.

DELETE

This command marks the entry for your file in the File Allocation Table (which is the filing system for DOS) as erased, without actually removing the file. Really removing the file takes a lot of time because accessing a disk is excruciatingly slow. The mark signals to DOS that the area that was once your file is available for use. The data still is intact until the system writes to the disk, or if you are lucky and the system doesn't write to where your data was previously stored. A new file may only partially overwrite your data. However, you can use recovery utilities to get your data back. Check out Chapter 14 if you want to understand the concept of true erasure.

ERASE

This is the most dangerous DOS command, in that it overwrites data with zeros and completely removes the possibility of recovery. Hopefully, you follow our advice from earlier chapters and make backups for your data before you use this command.

On the flip side, if you use ERASE to overwrite the secret file on which you just used PGP (see Chapter 13) to send to your coworker, then a snooper can't recover the file.

FC

The FC command compares files on your disk. This command is handy when you want to determine whether anyone has altered or modified your files or infected them with viruses.

FDISK

This command creates partitions, changes partitions, and deletes partitions on a DOS disk. The command simply segments one disk into two or more logical disks. Then you can password-protect a partition.

FORMAT

This command formats the disk in the specified drive, writing zeros and ones to the surface of the drive. If data existed before you issued the FORMAT command, it no longer exists. Again, you can recover your drive when you overwrite only once. If you accidentally issue the FORMAT command and overwrite data, stop what you're doing, take your computer to your local "Mom and Pop" computer shop, and see what it can do for you.

RENAME

The RENAME command changes the name of a file. A common hack involves doctoring the COMMAND.COM or renaming other .COM or .EXE files so that the COPY command calls one of the destructive commands such as DELETE or ERASE. This hack causes users to actually destroy their files. This is why backing up all disk files, saving directories, and password-protecting all desktops is important.

On the flip side, you can use RENAME to hide sensitive documents. (See the "COPY" section earlier in this chapter.)

Chapter 20

Ten DOS and Windows Programs and Files to Protect

*Y*ou can probably think of many programs and files that belong to you that you want to protect: your favorite recipes that you painstakingly typed into that recipe program; all those personal letters (does anyone write letters anymore?); homework assignments.

In addition to the files that you create, a bunch of files make your life really, really miserable if you lose or accidentally change them. You need to consider these files when setting up your backup program. (You *are* setting up a backup program, right? If not, go back and read Chapter 10.)

In this chapter, we show you how protecting a few of DOS and Windows files can make your life a heavenly experience. Many of the files mentioned here are technical in nature, and although we do our best to describe them, please back them up anyway, even if you don't really understand their function.

By backing up all these files, you can always recover from an accidental deletion. Of course, you should always try the DOS UNERASE command first. But if this command doesn't work, your backups come in very handy. These files take up very little space, so backing them up does not take up a significant amount of disk space.

If you have a tape backup device (explained in Chapter 23) and back up both the DOS and WINDOWS directories entirely, just add the first two files in the following list to your backup program to make a complete backup.

CONFIG.SYS

When you start up your computer, DOS looks at this file first. The CONFIG.SYS file explains the wondrous hardware that you have on your system, like your CD-ROM drive, sound card, and modem, in terms that DOS can understand. You usually find the CONFIG.SYS file in the root (or first) directory on your hard drive. (The hard drive is usually your C:\ drive.)

AUTOEXEC.BAT

DOS also uses this file every time you start up your computer to carry out whatever commands you type at the command prompt. The *.BAT* part defines the file as a *batch processing file,* or a file that runs programs or DOS commands for you. You can always find the AUTOEXEC.BAT file in the root (or first) directory on your hard drive.

Your DOS system can start up without the CONFIG.SYS or AUTOEXEC.BAT file, but when it does so, you do not have access to any of the extra hardware on your system, and things may not appear normal to you. For example, if your machine starts Windows every time you power up, a command in the AUTOEXEC.BAT file tells it to do so. Without this file, Windows does not start automatically. (Windows 95 users need to be aware that neither this file nor the CONFIG.SYS file is completely necessary. Windows 95 has other ways to determine what's on your system, so you may not need to back them up. If you run any DOS games, however, you can be assured that these files are going to be used; so in that case, you need to back them up.)

IO.SYS and MSDOS.SYS

You cannot see these files on your system, which makes backing them up pretty tough, right? Wrong. These files are a part of the MS-DOS operating system. They are hidden because the average person really has no need to know much about them — and if you can't see them, you'll leave them alone. Leaving them alone is good, because DOS can't run without them.

When your system starts up after you press the power on switch, a part of the system tells the computer to find these files. If they can't be found, you get this message: `Non-System disk or disk error - Replace and strike a key when ready`. You may have seen this message before, because it comes up if you forget and leave a diskette in your floppy drive.

IBMBIO.SYS and IBMDOS.SYS

IBM PC-DOS uses these files. They are also hidden from casual view. IBMBIO.SYS and IBMDOS.SYS work in the same way as the MS-DOS files IO.SYS and MSDOS.SYS. Which ones you have depends on which version of DOS you bought when you purchased your PC.

You can find out which version of DOS you have by using this command:

```
VER
```

You can view hidden files on your system if you really want to by using this command:

```
DIR /a:h
```

COMMAND.COM

After the system finds those .SYS files, it tries to find this file. If it does, all is well, and your familiar DOS prompt appears. If it doesn't, you get an error message. This file contains a list of some of the commands that DOS lets you use. For example, the DIRECTORY (DIR), DELETE (DEL), and DATE commands are in this file. Without the file, DOS doesn't know what to do when you type these commands.

WIN.COM

This is Windows. Cool! When you type **win** at the DOS prompt, this program starts and brings you those pretty little window boxes. (You must have Windows already installed on your system for this command to work.) Much better than a blank, dark screen with C:\> on it, isn't it?

WIN.INI

You can pronounce it either "win.eye-n-eye" or "win.in-ee" — either is acceptable. This file contains a bunch of technical stuff that Windows uses to control all the programs that you install. For example, this file defines which background wallpaper and screen saver options you use.

SYSTEM.INI

Another Windows file, this one contains even more technical stuff. It lets
Windows know where the software for the mouse is and what kind of mouse it
is. Lots of things called *drivers* tell Windows all about the hardware you use,
from your keyboard to your monitor.

.GRP and .INI

This section doesn't relate directly to one file. .GRP and .INI are the extensions
for a whole bunch of files in the WINDOWS directory of your hard drive.
Windows uses these files to set up your desktop and your programs.

You find a .GRP extension for each window on your desktop. For example, in
your WINDOWS directory, you find MAIN.GRP, APPLICATIONS.GRP, and many
more. One exists for each group that you have defined. The .INI files are small
files that describe your applications to Windows so that it knows what to do
when you start up a program. Each time you create a new window or add a new
program, another .GRP file and another .INI file get added to the WINDOWS
directory.

Chapter 21

Ten Ways to Secure Windows 95

● ●

In This Chapter

▶ Securing Windows 95

● ●

*I*n 1995, Microsoft delivered Windows 95 from the promised land. We thought that because the operating system was new, security would be an integral part of the product. Well, it is and it isn't. Windows 95 provides some security features, but they are a far sight from what one might expect from an operating system today.

Windows 95 provides the following security measures:

- **Unified logon prompt:** Log on once to all networks you want to use. When you turn on your PC with Windows 95 installed, the system prompts you for your password. This password unlocks any other passwords you have to use to log on to Microsoft (say, Windows NT Advanced Server) or Novell (say, NetWare 3.*x* or 4.*x*) networks.

- **User-level or share-level security:** Protect shared resources by password or an access list specifying your authorities.

- **Password caching:** Passwords stored in a password list. Windows 95 uses these stored passwords when you request a network, application, or file that requires a password.

- **Password list editor:** View and delete the contents of your password list files.

Unfortunately, with the exception of Windows NT, the overall security in Windows has not kept up with the value of the data that you are storing on your system. All other versions of Windows, including Windows 95, have one or more gaping holes that can put you at risk of accidental access or intentional snooping.

As we explained already, nothing can completely stop a determined attack, but you can take some steps to improve the security of your Windows 95 system by controlling some of the most egregious problems. In this chapter, we introduce ten ways to secure Windows 95.

Cutting a Startup Disk

Microsoft, as well as we, strongly recommends that you create a startup disk during Windows 95 setup. Clicking the Yes, I want a startup disk [recommended] button and doing the diskette shuffle is easy. Should you have any problems upgrading from Windows 3.*x* (and you just might), you can always use your startup disk to get back into Windows, do diagnostics, make changes, and reboot.

If you did not create a startup disk when you installed your system, you can still create one. Select the Add/Remove Programs option in the Control Panel and then click on the Startup Disk tab. Click the Create Disk button, and the system prompts you to insert a floppy in drive A:. As the message says, you need one diskette to create your backup disk.

Boot Bypass

Even if you know only a little about computers, you can make a floppy disk and use it to get your system running. If your computer security depends on safeguards that load and run after you initially boot the machine (such as a password-protected screen saver or the Windows 95 login password), you're vulnerable. A cracker can bypass your security and change your accounting records, delete your address book, or just browse through the information on your system.

To prevent unauthorized access to your system, physically protect your system (lock the room it is in), use the keyboard lock and remove the key, and use the BIOS settings available on newer machines to prevent booting from a floppy drive (A:) or to enable a power-on password. Refer to Chapter 8 for information about BIOS settings and power-on passwords.

Psst — The Password Is Cancel

You probably think that Windows 95 has access control built right in. When you boot Windows 95, you see the Welcome to Windows dialog box, which prompts you for a user name and password. This means that your system is secure, right? Wrong! Try clicking on Cancel or pressing the Escape key the next time you start Windows. The password dialog box closes, and you see the default desktop. The default Windows 95 login box tells Windows which user profile settings to load, and Windows unlocks the encrypted file containing the rest of your passwords, such as the ones you use to open your Exchange Inbox, connect to a NetWare or Windows NT network, or log in to your Internet account.

If your risk analysis shows that access control is an issue, you may want to download the improved password caching Dynamic Link Library (DLL) from Microsoft at `http://www.microsoft.com/windows/download/ mspwlupd.exe`. When you start the MSPWLUPD program, you must click on the Yes button to confirm your desire to update the password list library. When you click Yes, the software automatically installs and takes effect after you restart your computer.

You may also want to open the Passwords applet in Control Panel, click on the User Profiles tab, and then click on Users can customize their preferences. This step allows you to set your logon settings and access privileges differently than the default Windows 95 logon.

Next, use the Windows 95 Policy Editor, found in the Resource Kit, to define what each user of your system can and cannot do. Each logon can have its own set of privileges and access to different files. You can severely limit what a default logon can do.

Password File Lists

Windows 95 stores passwords for resources in a password list file (.PWL). This file stores passwords for the following:

- Your screen saver on a computer running Windows 95 that is protected by share-level security
- Applications that are password-protected
- Windows NT logon passwords
- NetWare servers

The password list is stored in the WINDOWS directory on the local computer. Each resource typically has its own password. The password file is encrypted.

To secure your passwords for other applications, open the WINDOWS folder, search for a file with the password extension of .PWL, and delete the file. When Windows 95 prompts you to enter new passwords, make sure that you have not checked the Save Password box. Saving your password is a sure-fire way to ensure that someone will steal your identity when he or she gets onto your PC.

You also can use the Passwords applet to change the passwords for your screen saver or your network server, for example.

You can disable password caching (that is, saving to the .PWL file) by using the System Policy Editor.

Share to the World

When you installed Windows 95, you may have clicked the I want to be able to give others access to my files option, as well as the TCP/IP networking protocol option to access the Internet. If you did, you may inadvertently be sharing your files with people all over the world. To Microsoft's credit, its Internet Explorer looks for this condition when you install it and offers to turn off File and Print Sharing for the TCP/IP protocol.

Examine your Control Panel TCP/IP properties in the Network applet to make sure that File and Print Sharing is unchecked in the Bindings tab dialog box. To do so, follow these steps:

1. **Choose Control Panel from the Start menu.**

2. **Double-click on the Network applet.**

3. **Scroll in the window down to TCP/IP and highlight it.**

4. **Click on the Properties button.**

5. **Select the Bindings tab.**

6. **Uncheck File and print sharing for Microsoft networks.**

Using Explorer, right-click on each drive you have and set up a password for each drive with the Sharing menu. To do so, follow these steps:

1. **Choose Explorer from the Programs menu in the Start menu.**

2. **Highlight the drive that you want to password-protect (for example, the C: drive).**

3. **Click your right mouse button.**

4. **Choose Sharing; then click on Shared As.**

5. **Decide how you want to share and enter a password.**

More Sharing Than You Intended: Windows 95 File and Printer Sharing Security

Windows 95 also has a potential security problem with file and printer sharing. If you use the File and Print Sharing option to share files with other users on a network, you may be affected. This option is not enabled by default, so you are not at risk unless you manually enable it. To determine whether File and Print Sharing is enabled, double-click on the Network icon in the Control Panel. Then click on File and Print Sharing. If either entry is checked, you have enabled File and Print Sharing (which one is enabled depends on which box you checked).

Your environment must meet both the following conditions:

- ✔ You configure your machine to share files and printers with other users on a network by using File and Print Sharing for NetWare Networks. (This option is not turned on by default.)

- ✔ You enable remote administration or install Microsoft Remote Registry Services. (These options are not turned on by default.)

Should your environment match the one just listed, another user on the network can gain read-only access to your computer after the administrator logs off the machine until you restart your computer. To correct this problem, Microsoft has issued an updated driver for File and Print Sharing for NetWare Networks (available at `http://www.microsoft.com/windows/download/vservupd.exe`). The free, updated driver ensures that only valid users have access to the computer's drive. Typically, these valid users are individuals who have the authority to update the computer's configuration.

Very Public Mail

In Windows 95, by default, anyone can walk up to your machine, enter his or her password, and potentially gain access to your private e-mail stored in Exchange, the "universal inbox" that comes with Windows. Even if you entered a password to associate with your old e-mail when you converted to Exchange, you're still vulnerable to intrusion. The Exchange inbox is available to anybody on the desktop, so unless you have some other way of preventing people from getting to the desktop, you have a problem.

You should turn on base security (see the password discussion in the "Psst — The Password Is Cancel" section). Then go to Exchange's Tools⇨Services menu, select the Personal Folder file (or whatever you call it), and click on Properties. Then click on Change Password and enter a password that is different from your login password. Now both your e-mail and your basic desktop are safe from the casual snooper.

Recovering the Registry

The Windows 95 Registry provides a database for storing system and application configuration data. The Registry is roughly analogous to the .INI files in Windows 3.x, with each key in the Registry similar to bracketed heading in an .INI file and with values similar to entries under the .INI headings.

When Windows 95 starts, it backs up the Registry by copying the current SYSTEM.DAT and USER.DAT files to SYSTEM.DA0 and USER.DA0, respectively. Should Windows 95 fail to start, you can copy the backed-up Registry from the last successful startup over the current Registry. This method recovers the last successful settings after a system failure.

Also, you can export, import, or re-create the Registry by using either the Windows-based version of Registry Editor or the real-mode version on the Windows 95 emergency startup disk.

To export or import Registry files, use the Export and Import commands from the Registry menu.

Use REGEDIT /C with extreme care, and only when you are sure that the specified .REG file contains a complete image of the Registry. Also, the Resource Kit does not provide sufficient information to guide you through the process of editing a .REG file, so we recommend that you edit a .REG file only under the guidance of a product support representative.

If you need help, call Microsoft technical support department at 206-635-7000 in the United States or 905-568-4494 in Canada. If you do not have the number for your country's Microsoft Support Network (it should be in your *Introducing Microsoft Windows 95* manual), call your Microsoft product vendor.

Controlling Panels

You set up your personal computer just the way you like it, and then the kids start using it. But they tend to mess things up, especially your favorite configuration. One way to prevent this problem is not to have certain icons in the Control Panel. How do you accomplish this feat? Well, you can edit the CONTROL.INI file in the WINDOWS directory. Use the Notepad application to open this file. Look for the [don't load] section (it should be first). If you can't find this section, just type it at the top of the file. Add **<cpl file >=no** for every icon you want to disable. Replace **cpl file** with the .CPL file associated with the particular icon.

Note: When you disable the icon, the system maintains the current settings. All you're doing is removing the icons for the particular applet from the Control Panel window so that no one can go in there and change your settings. If you want the icons back, you need to remove the **<cpl file >=no** statement from the CONTROL.INI file and then restart your machine.

Table 21-1 lists the .CPL files for each Control Panel icon. For example, to disable the Add/Remove Programs icon, add **appwiz.cpl=no** to the CONTROL.INI file. Save the CONTROL.INI file and then restart your computer.

Table 21-1	.CPL File Control Panel Icons
Filename	*Icon*
ACCESS.CPL	Accessibility Options
DESK.CPL	Display
MODEM.CPL	Modems
NETCPL.CPL	Network
MMSYS.CPL	Multimedia and Sounds
SYSDM.CPL	System and Add New Hardware
TIMEDATE.CPL	Date/Time
PASSWORD.CPL	Passwords
INTL.CPL	Regional Settings
JOY.CPL	Joystick
APPWIZ.CPL	Add/Remove Programs
MAIN.CPL	Fonts, Keyboard, Mouse, and Printers
MLCFG32.CPL	Mail and Fax
WGPOCPL.CPL	Microsoft Mail Postoffice

Share-Level (In)Security

When a computer is running Windows 95 with File and Printer Sharing Services, other people can connect to shared printers, volumes, directories, and CD-ROM drives. To protect these shared resources, Windows 95 provides share-level security. With share-level security, you can provide the correct password only to people who need access.

The problem with this security is that it is like the old Clairol commercial — you tell two people, and they tell two people, who tell two people, and before you know it, everyone knows the password. If you suspect that a security problem exists, you have to change the password and give the new password to legitimate users. Obviously, this situation is problematic. You should avoid share-level security like the plague. It just cannot be done easily and effectively.

If you insist on using share-level security, then protect your directories. You can share a directory and hide it from the Network Neighborhood browsing list by adding a $ to the end of the directory's name (for example, PRIVATE$).

Chapter 22

Ten Viruses and What They Do

• •

• •

*T*he following list is just a small sample of the over 6,500 known viruses. Get yourself a copy of Kevin Harris's *Virus Reference* (Software Perspectives) for Macintosh or Patricia M. Hoffman's *Virus Information Summary List — VSUM* for DOS or Windows to learn more about the various viruses and Trojan horses out there.

Generally, you get these viruses from diskettes or from files that you download from bulletin board systems, commercial online services, or the Internet. Chapter 11 talks about the various ways you can avoid or get viruses. A proactive practice is best to prevent viruses, but just in case you have been less than vigilant, this chapter describes some common viruses and their symptoms to help you recognize them.

Boza

Derivatives: Bizatch

Platform: Windows 95

Type: Malicious. Boza, a nonresident appending virus, infects .EXE files.

Some terminology is necessary to your understanding of viruses. First, *malicious* means that the virus means you harm. Other viruses are *benign,* or *mischievous,* and just annoy you. Others are *malignant* and can destroy your system or its components.

Second, *nonresident* means that the virus does not reside in memory but instead attaches itself to an executable waiting for execution.

Symptoms: Boza infects up to three .EXE files in the current directory. If it cannot locate and infect three files within the current directory, it moves to the parent directory (or one directory down) and attempts to infect more files located there.

Removal: Reinstall infected programs from trusted, clean diskettes.

Brain

Derivatives: Brain-B, Brain-C, Clone, Clone-B, Nipper, Pakistani, Pakistani Brain

Platform: DOS

Type: Malicious. Brain is a resident boot sector infector and infects disk boot sectors by moving the original contents of the boot sector to another location on the disk, marking those three clusters as bad in the FAT and then writing the virus code in the disk boot sector.

A *boot block* consists of the boot record and the boot sector. A *boot record* is a short machine-language program that tells the programs in read-only memory (the bootstrap program — the system literally "pulls itself up by its boot-straps") where to look for the boot files (IBMBIO and IBMDOS.COM, or the corresponding Microsoft programs). The boot record is created when you use the DOS FORMAT command. A boot sector includes the version of DOS, the names of the boot files, and some basic error messages. *FAT* is the *file allocation table* and is the filing system for DOS. It is the catalog, defining the directory and file structure, and contains the files' addresses. Changing any of these signifi-cantly affects the operation of your system.

Symptoms: Brain changes the volume label to (c) Brain; on some systems, this label is found in sector 0, where the system stores its boot record. The virus takes up between 3K and 7K of RAM.

Removal: Use McAfee's CleanUp, Fridrik Skulason's F-Prot, McAfee's MD Boot Virus Disinfector (Mdisk), or Symantec's Norton Anti-Virus (NAV). Alternately, use the DOS SYS command to overwrite the boot sector on the infected system diskettes or hard disks.

Dark Avenger

Derivatives: Amilia, Black Avenger, Boroda, Diana, Dark Avenger 1801, Dark Avenger-1693, Dark Avenger-1799, Dark Avenger-1813, Dark Avenger-C, Dark Avenger-D, Dark Avenger.1E, Dark Quest, Eddie, Evil Men, Kang Yong, Mercury, PS!KO, PS!KO-1459, PS!KO-1687, PS!KO-1800, Rabid Avenger, Sneaker, VAN Soft

Platform: DOS

Type: Malicious. Dark Avenger, a TSR, infects .COM, .EXE, and .SYS files. A TSR (terminate and stay resident) program remains in memory and is activated again by an interrupt. On your system, you might use hot keys to start another program. In this case, you are using an interrupt. So Dark Avenger lies dormant until an interrupt wakes it up. For example, the timer interrupt happens many times per second. Dark Avenger maintains a counter in the disk's boot sector and randomly overwrites a sector on the disk after every 16th infection.

Symptoms: Dark Avenger infects .COM, .EXE, and overlay files, including COMMAND.COM. It installs itself into system memory, becoming resident. Infected files increase in length by 1,800 bytes. The Dark Avenger virus contains the phrase "The Dark Avenger, copyright 1988, 1989," as well as the screen message `This program was written in the city of Sofia. Eddie lives_. Somewhere in Time!`

Removal: Use McAfee's CleanUp, Fridrik Skulason's F-Prot, or Symantec's Norton Anti-Virus (NAV), or delete all infected files.

Jerusalem

Derivatives: 1808 (EXE), 1813 (COM), Arab Star, Black Box, Black Window, Hebrew University, Friday the 13th, Israeli, Jerusalem B, Jerusalem-C, Jerusalem-D, Jerusalem DC, Jerusalem-E, Jerusalem-Polish, Jerusalem-PLO, New Jerusalem, Oscar, Russian

Jerusalem is thought to have been based on the Suriv 3.00 virus, even though Suriv was isolated after the Jerusalem virus.

Platform: DOS

Type: Malicious. Jerusalem, a parasitic virus that attaches itself to other legitimate programs, reduces free memory and is a terminate-and-stay-resident virus. It may delete files.

Symptoms: Jerusalem is a memory-resident generic file infector or TSR. It infects .BIN, .COM, .EXE, .PIF, .SYS, and overlay files when executed. .EXE files may grow every time you run them. You should find a system slowdown. Friday the 13th and Black Window may delete files as well.

Removal: Use McAfee's CleanUp, Fridrik Skulason's F-Prot, Symantec's Norton Anti-Virus (NAV), or MicroCom's VirexPC, or delete all infected files.

Joshi

Derivatives: Happy Birthday Joshi, Joshi-B, Stealth Virus

Platform: DOS

Type: Malicious. Joshi is a resident boot sector or master boot sector infector.

Symptoms: Joshi resides in memory after infection. It takes about 6K of system memory, and total memory shows as 6K less when you use the DOS CHKDSK command. On January 5 of any year, the virus hangs the system and displays `type Happy Birthday Joshi`. You cannot use the system again until you type **Happy Birthday Joshi**. You may experience problems when attempting to access programs or data files on write-protected diskettes.

Removal: Use McAfee's CleanUp, McAfee's MD Boot Virus Disinfector (Mdisk), or Symantec's Norton Anti-Virus (NAV).

Michelangelo

Derivatives: None

Platform: DOS

Type: Malicious. Michelangelo infects the floppy boot sector and the master boot sector.

Symptoms: Michelangelo becomes memory resident, decreasing total system memory and available free memory by 2,048 bytes. It infects floppy boot sectors when loaded and the hard disk master boot sector when you attempt to access a file on the hard disk. Michelangelo activates on March 6, at which time it formats the system hard disk by overwriting it with random characters from system memory.

Removal: Use McAfee's CleanUp, Fridrik Skulason's F-Prot, or McAfee's MD Boot Virus Disinfector (Mdisk).

nVir (strains a and b)

Derivatives: Hpat, nFlu, AIDS, MEV#, nCAM, prod

Platform: Macintosh

Type: Malicious. nVir infects the System file first, and then Finder, DA Handler, and any launched applications.

Symptoms: nVir causes system crashes and may cause files to disappear. Your system may beep when loading applications or at random times. If you have MacinTalk in your System Folder, strain b says `Don't panic`.

Removal: Use Symantec's Anti-virus for Macs (SAM) or reinstall the system files.

SCORES

Derivatives: N/A

Platform: Macintosh

Type: Malicious. SCORES infects the System file first, waits two days, and then infects an application every three and a half minutes.

Symptoms: SCORES adds invisible files called Scores and Desktop_ (where _ is a space) to the System Folder. Your system may crash, and you may experience printing problems. Infected files increase in size by 7K. You may also experience insufficient memory. SCORES changes the icons for the Note Pad and Scrapbook to generic document icons.

Removal: Use Symantec's Anti-virus for Macs (SAM) or reinstall the system software.

Stoned

Derivatives: 1991 Boot, Deunis, Donald Duck, Hawaii, Marijuana, New Zealand, Rostov, San Diego, Sex Revolution, Smithsonian, Stoned II, Stoned Mutation, Stoned-16, Stoned-AT Love, Stoned-Collor, Stoned-Mexican

Platform: DOS

Type: Malicious. Stoned infects the boot record and reduces total memory size and free memory.

Symptoms: Stoned and its derivatives infect the hard disk master boot sector and damage directory or FAT information. During the boot process, you may see the message `Your computer is now stoned` or `Your PC is now Stoned!` After infection, Stoned infects diskettes as you load them.

Removal: Use McAfee's CleanUp, Fridrik Skulason's F-Prot, McAfee's MD Boot Virus Disinfector (Mdisk), or Symantec's Norton Anti-Virus (NAV).

Word Macro 9508

Derivatives: WinWord.Concept, WW6, WW6Macro, Prank

Platform: Microsoft Word 6.0 for DOS, Macintosh, OS/2, and all versions of Windows (including Windows 95)

Type: Mischievous, in that it won't destroy your system or its components.

Symptoms: The Word Macro virus changes macros in some Word files and templates and may alter file types. As previously mentioned, virus authors usually write their prizes for a particular operating system, such as DOS. The macro virus is different because it was written for the Word application, which runs on different operating systems and can spread across platforms. The virus adds AAAZA0, AAAZFS, Payload, and FileSaveAs macros to the available global macros.

Removal: Download free virus software from `http://www.microsoft.com` and run it.

Chapter 23
Ten Useful Backup Devices

*W*e try very hard to get you to realize that you need to back up your data. To badly paraphrase a copyright slogan, copy to that floppy! In this chapter, we show you a few of the more popular backup devices and list some of our personal pros and cons.

Remember one thing when buying a backup device: No matter which device you buy, you're likely better off than not buying anything. So don't fret unnecessarily over what to buy — doing so only lets you put off the decision.

Which is the best backup device? The one you use regularly! You can find most of the following devices at your local computer retailer.

Our apologies in advance to any vendors who may feel snubbed by not being included here. First, there are too many devices to talk about. Second, we may not know about you or your product. (Send us an e-mail, and we'll consider inclusion in future editions. You can reach Barry by using this address: lewisb@cerberus.com.) Third, things are changing so fast that we are concentrating primarily on the tried and true.

A final note: By the time this book is printed and distributed, much will likely have changed. This field is growing so fast that keeping up is impossible. For example, both SyQuest and Iomega have 1GB storage devices coming out to replace the 100MB to 130MB devices that they currently sell. These devices are expected to be priced around $600, which could easily mean that by this time next year, they may be in the $200 to $300 range. Things change that fast.

HP Colorado T1000

Hewlett-Packard Colorado drives have been around for some time. Although this vendor offers a large number of popular and inexpensive models, we focus on this model because it is inexpensive and provides up to 800MB capacity per cartridge by using data compression. *Data compression* is a process in which special software (included with the backup software) removes all the spaces in your file, such as those you see in a normal sentence, to reduce the amount of data that it needs to back up.

HP has a full line of tape backup models, including higher priced models offering even more backup capability. (The company says that it is the world leader in tape backup, so you should find its products competitively priced.) We found the internal T1000 to cost about $175, with tapes priced at about $20.

If you have Internet access, check out Hewlett-Packard's Web page at `www.hp.com:80/cms/index.html`. Type the address exactly as shown, because this directory takes you directly to the HP tape backup page and bypasses many other HP products, such as printers.

HP Colorado T1000e

If you have more than one computer, buying one external backup device is less expensive than buying individual internal devices for each machine. These devices are great for home offices with a desktop and a laptop computer or for company departments with many individual, non-networked machines.

This model is essentially the same as the T1000. It plugs into the parallel port, however, making it ideal for quick backups. (You don't need to have someone install it inside your machine.) All you do is install the software on each machine you want to back up. Then just back up the first machine, unplug the T1000e, move it to another machine, insert a different tape, and run the software again.

This device costs only slightly more than the internal model and uses the same tapes. We have seen it advertised at $199. You can find information about this model at the same Hewlett-Packard World Wide Web address as the T1000.

Conner TapeStor

This unit has also been around for some time and is a proven, inexpensive backup solution. It comes in a variety of models, such as the 420 and 850. The numbers give you an indication of how much data they can back up in compressed form.

These models are internal, meaning that you must install them inside your computer before they can work. Conner was recently bought by Seagate, the popular hard drive manufacturer. What this change will do to price or performance we do not know; however, the firm is large and solid, and we expect that it will continue to enhance the Conner line of tape backup devices.

We found these drives to be priced competitively, with the TapeStor 420 at about $150 and the TapeStor 850 at $210. You can find tapes for about $20.

Look for Conner on the Internet at `www.conner.com/floppy-minicartridge-serie.html`. As with HP, these Web sites are large, so we are providing a more direct address so that you can go straight to the backup products. Over time, you may find this site moved to Seagate's Web page, which is at `www.seagate.com`.

Iomega Zip

These nifty little units are so popular that finding them in the stores when they were first introduced was difficult — they sold out that fast. For around $200, they provide 100MB of data capacity on cartridges that look much like diskettes, only a little bigger. The cartridges cost about $20 each.

If you buy a Zip drive that connects to the parallel port (where your printer usually connects), you can move the drive from machine to machine. This model is slower than one with a permanent connection, however, because the printer port isn't designed for really high speed.

Using these devices is a good way to share large files with friends or associates. If you use a computer at work, you can also use these devices to bring work home, as you may often have files that are too big to fit on a diskette. We think that people like the Zip drives largely because they store a lot of data and resemble the diskettes that people are accustomed to using. Be aware, however, that they are not as fast as other backup devices, so backups take a little longer. This slowness is usually not a problem if you configure the software to run the backup at night or first thing in the day.

Iomega Jaz

If you have larger storage needs, look for these 1GB models to hit the streets soon. You can expect these drives to have similar speeds as your regular hard drive, which significantly reduces your backup times. In fact, the company claims that its Jaz drives are faster than most hard drives.

These devices are much more expensive at around $600, but they have the advantage of providing unlimited hard drive capacity as well as full backup capability. Imagine hooking up one of these drives, purchasing a few cartridges, and having more storage space than you could possibly want. (At least for now, that is. We can remember when having a 20MB hard drive was a really big deal. How times change!) The only downside to these drives for the average user is cost. Although the drive itself is not that expensive, the cartridges are expected to cost about $100 each. If you decide to purchase one when they arrive, remember to use more than one cartridge for your backups. Don't put all your eggs in one basket, even if they fit!

If you have Internet access, check out Iomega's Web page at www.iomega.com.

SyQuest EZ135

These guys have been selling Winchester drives for a long time. The company now offers the EZ135, which appears to be a direct competitor to the Zip drive. SyQuest EZ135 drives cost around $230, and cartridges cost about $20 but hold 135MB of data — slightly more than the Zip cartridge for about the same price.

Like other drives, you can purchase a parallel port version if you own more than one personal computer, although using a parallel port version is slower. This drive, however, is significantly faster than the Zip, so if speed is an issue, this device may be the one for you. It is quick enough that you can use it as a spare hard drive by storing little-used files on a tape, which you can insert when you need it.

If you have Internet access, SyQuest's Web page is at www.syquest.com.

SyJET 1.3GB

This device is the latest offering from SyQuest. In addition to a 1.3GB cartridge, you can purchase a less expensive 650MB cartridge — you decide what size is appropriate for your backups. This model comes as an internal unit that you need to install before use. Like other drives, however, you can use it externally if you purchase the parallel port conversion kit that SyQuest offers. These drives are being priced at $500, with cartridges costing about $95.

These drives are fast, effective, and truly inexpensive when you consider what they offer. If you are thinking of upgrading your hard drive for a bigger size in addition to getting a tape backup device, consider the SyQuest 1.3GB, which easily backs up your new hard drive with its gigabyte-size storage capacity.

Panasonic PD/CD-ROM Drive

We could never end this chapter without including at least one CD-ROM drive. These drives are really neat and can store more data than you can shake a stick at.

This device recently received a *PC Magazine* Editor's Choice award. These drives cost around $650 and offer around 650MB of storage on cartridges that cost approximately $60. In addition to providing backup capability for your data, the drive can be used as a standard four-speed CD-ROM drive to play music or run CD software.

PC Card Devices (PCMCIA)

For notebook computer users, the new PC card devices offer really, really small backup options. If you follow computer news, you see less and less of the term *PCMCIA* and more of the term *PC Card*. PCMCIA stands for *Personal Computer Memory Card International Association* and is a mouthful even for technical people, who also have a hard time remembering what the six characters are. PC Card was coined so that everyone could pronounce and remember the term!

These small cards are available now as backup media and can hold from about 170MB to 500MB of data. They are expensive, however, at $500 or more for each card. The advantages of size (they are little bigger than a credit card) and convenience (you can use them as secondary storage and get hard drive performance when retrieving the data) may be enough for some people to consider using them. Barry will certainly be keeping a close eye on these devices, because size and weight become important when one travels extensively like he does. You can find these devices from vendors such as Calluna and Integral Peripherals.

You can find Calluna on the Internet at `http://www.ppcp.com/calluna.htm`.

DVD (Digital Video Disk)

The latest in the area of backup devices is a thing called DVD, or Digital Video Disk, which increases the amount of data that a CD can hold by 100 times. DVD is a new standard being endorsed by all the major vendors. The big advantage is that these drives hold somewhere in the neighborhood of 5GB to 8GB of data, which enables you to place a complete movie on one disk the size of a music CD. Yikes!

DVD devices are very expensive at the moment, but they are going to push down the current price of CD-ROM drives, making them even more economical. Expect to see DVD devices break the $1,000 mark by the end of 1997.

Part V
Appendixes

The 5th Wave — By Rich Tennant

"WE SORT OF HAVE OUR OWN WAY OF PREDICTING NETWORK SECURITY BREACHES."

In this part...

This part contains information for those readers who hunger for more. Here you can find lists of publications and Internet sites that discuss computer security in more detail, sources of security software and products, a glossary of computer security terms, and a list of common security acronyms and abbreviations that you can use to impress your friends and coworkers.

Appendix A
I Want to Learn More

*T*his book just scratches the surface of information security in general and personal computer security specifically. You may want to try some of the resources listed in this chapter to broaden your knowledge.

Useful Online Resources

Many hardware and software companies use online services to exchange e-mail, provide current product information, and distribute updates. In some cases, you may find a forum on AOL, CompuServe, or Prodigy devoted to your particular brand of hardware and software. Otherwise, you may have to surf the Internet looking for information about your system. If you're just looking for software or other security products, see Appendix B for a helpful list of Internet sites and vendor information.

You can also find sources of general security information online. One forum on CompuServe especially worth mentioning is the National Computer Security Association (GO NCSA). This forum offers information on Security Awareness Day, viruses, and security magazines, among other topics.

You can enter a NCSA chat room for online discussion of such topics as information warfare, operational security, viruses, and cryptography. Or you can browse one of their libraries for infromation about any one of the following topics:

✔ Ethics

✔ Security magazines

✔ Viruses

- ✔ Disaster recovery

- ✔ Encryption

- ✔ PC/Mac/LAN security

- ✔ UNIX/Internet security

- ✔ Telecommunications/PBX/Cellular security

- ✔ Laws/Regulations/Policy

- ✔ Electronic commerce

- ✔ OPSEC/Information warfare

- ✔ Auditing

- ✔ Corporate intelligence

- ✔ Cryptography

- ✔ Security management

As you can see, this forum is quite detailed. It offers something for everyone interested in security, even for those with the most individual of preferences. You probably didn't realize that information security is so specialized!

Of course, you can always surf the Internet for security information, too.

Search Engines

Sometimes when you are on the Internet, you know that plenty of information on the security topic you are interested in is available, but you don't know where to find it. In that case, point your browser at one of the following search engine Web sites. When the search engine asks you for a keyword, just type the topic you're interested in, and the search engine finds Web sites that contain information about the subject:

ALIWEB Search Form

```
http://www.cs.indiana.edu/aliweb/form.html
```

All-in-One Search Page

```
http://www.albany.net/allinone/
```

CUI W3 Catalog

```
http://cuiwww.unige.ch/cgi-bin/w3catalog
```

CUSI Services

```
http://pubweb.nexor.co.uk/public/cusi/doc/list.html
```

Internet Table of Contents

```
http://nearnet.gnn.com/gnn/wic/internet.toc.html
```

The Lycos Home Page: Hunting WWW Information

```
http://lycos.cs.cmu.edu/
```

The Open Text Index

```
http://www.opentext.com/
```

SavvySearch

```
http://www.cs.colostate.edu/~dreiling/smartform.html
```

TradeWave Galaxy

```
http://galaxy.einet.net/
```

WebCrawler Searching

```
http://webcrawler.com/
```

World-Wide Web Search Engines

```
http://www.amdahl.com/internet/meta-index.html
```

The World-Wide Web Virtual Library: Subject Catalogue

```
http://www.w3.org/hypertext/DataSources/bySubject/
         Overview.html
```

The WWWW - WORLD WIDE WEB WORM

```
http://www.cs.colorado.edu/home/mcbryan/WWWW.html
```

Yahoo! Search

```
http://www.yahoo.com/search.html
```

Mailing Lists

The following addresses are for some of the more interesting security mailing lists. These mailing lists are great sources for the most current security information available. To get a comprehensive list of security mailing lists, send e-mail to info@iss.net with *send index* in the message, or pick up a list at either http://iss.net/ or ftp://iss.net/pub/.

Alert

Alert provides information on the following topics:

- ✔ Security product announcements and updates
- ✔ New-found vulnerabilities
- ✔ New security frequently-asked-question files (FAQs)
- ✔ New intruder techniques and awareness

To join, send e-mail to request-alert@iss.net and in the body of your message (not in the subject line), type **subscribe alert.**

Best of Security

This list offers security information from many sources (including other mailing lists, newsgroups, conference notes, papers, and so on). If you read only one mailing list, you should read this one.

To join, send e-mail to best-of-security-request@suburbia.net and in the body of your message, type **subscribe best-of-security.**

CERT (Computer Emergency Response Team) Advisory

CERT is devoted to Internet advisories. This list is a must for anyone connected to the Internet or using any version of UNIX.

To join, send e-mail to cert@cert.org and in the body of your message (not in the subject line), type **I want to be on your mailing list.**

Computer Privacy Digest

A forum for discussing the effect of technology on privacy.

To join, send e-mail to `comp-privacy-request@uwm.edu` and in the body of your message (not in the subject line), type **subscribe cpd.**

Computer Underground Digest

This list covers many issues concerning the computer underground.

To join, send e-mail to `listserv@vmd.cso.uiuc.edu` and in the body of your message (not in the subject line), type **subscribe cudigest.**

Cypherpunks

The cypherpunks list is a forum for discussing personal defenses for privacy in the digital domain.

To join, send e-mail to `majordomo@toad.com` and in the body of your message (not in the subject line), type **subscribe cypherpunks.**

INFSEC-L Information Systems Security Forum

INFSEC-L discusses information systems security and related issues.

To join, send e-mail to `listserv@etsuadmn.etsu.edu` and in the body of your message (not in the subject line), type **subscribe infsec-l your-name.**

Phrack

Phrack is a hacker magazine dealing with phreaking (telephones) and hacking (computers).

To join, send e-mail to `phrack@well.com` and in the body of your message (not in the subject line), type **subscribe Phrack.**

PRIVACY Forum

The PRIVACY Forum covers both technological and nontechnological privacy-related issues (with an emphasis on the former).

To join, send e-mail to `privacy-request@vortex.com` and in the body of your message (not in the subject line), type **information privacy.**

Risks

Risks is a digest describing many of today's technological risks.

To join, send e-mail to `risks-request@csl.sri.com` and in the body of your message (not in the subject line), type **subscribe.**

Virus

Electronic-mail discussion forum for sharing information and ideas about computer viruses, including virus sightings, virus prevention (practical and theoretical), and virus-related questions and answers.

To join, send e-mail to `listserv@lehigh.edu` and in the body of your message (not in the subject line), type **subscribe virus-l** *your-name.*

Virus Alert

This is the place to share urgent virus warnings with other computer users.

To join, send e-mail to `listserv@lehigh.edu` and in the body of your message (not in the subject line), type **subscribe valert-l your-name.**

USENET Newsgroups

The Internet has the equivalent of bulletin boards where people post messages and others respond to them. These online bulletin boards are called *USENET newsgroups.* Over 14,000 different newsgroups exist, each devoted to a different topic. You're sure to find one that tickles your fancy (and we mean that quite literally). On USENET, you can subscribe to a variety of security-related newsgroups, including the following:

```
alt.2600
alt.2600.moderated
alt.cellular
alt.cyberpunk
alt.dcom.telecom
alt.hacker
alt.hackers
alt.hackers.cough.cough.cough
alt.hackers.malicious
alt.os.multics
alt.phracker
alt.privacy
alt.privacy.anon-server
alt.privacy.clipper
alt.security
alt.security.index
alt.security.keydist
alt.security.pgp
alt.security.ripem
alt.society.cu-digest
bit.listserv.security
bit.listserv.virus-l
comp.dcom.telecom
comp.privacy
comp.risks
comp.security.announce
comp.security.misc
comp.security.unix
comp.society.privacy
comp.virusde.
comp.security
misc.security
sb.security
sub.security
sura.security
uwo.comp.security
```

Useful Publications

Many security-related periodicals are available. Some are free if you qualify; you have to inquire with the publication to see whether you or your organization are eligible for a free subscription. Also check out the various PC magazines, which frequently feature security-related stories. Following is a list of useful publications to get you started:

Publication	Phone Number
Computers and Security	011-44-865-512242
The Computer Law and Security Report	212-989-5800
Computer Security Digest	313-459-8787
Consumertronics	505-434-0234
Datapro Research	800-328-2772
EMC Technology	703-347-0030
Full Disclosure	708-395-6200
Hactic	011-31-20-6001480
InfoSecurity News	508-879-7999
Intelligence Solutions Newsletter	800-877-9138
International Journal of Intelligence	212-737-7923
International Privacy Bulletin	202-544-9240
Internet World	203-226-6967
Monitoring Times	704-837-9200
PIN Magazine	301-652-9050
Privacy Journal	401-274-7861
Security Book Catalog	800-366-2655
Security Insider Report	813-393-6600
Security Magazine	708-635-8800
Security Management	703-522-5800
Security Technology News	301-340-7788
Telecom and Network Security Review	800-435-7878
Virus Bulletin	011-44-235-555139
Wired	415-904-0660
2600: The Hacker Quarterly	516-751-2600

Some of these publications are also available online.

Helpful Organizations

The following list gives you the names of organizations that are directly concerned with or have Special Interest Groups (SIGs) dealing with computer security:

American Society for Industrial Security (ASIS)
1655 N. Fort Meyer Drive, Suite 1200
Arlington, VA 22209

Association for Computing Machinery (ACM)
Special Interest Group on Computers and Security (SIGCAS)
11 W. 42nd St.
New York, NY 10036

Association for Computing Machinery (ACM)
Special Interest Group on Security, Audit and Control (SIGSAC)
c/o Steve Clemons
Norfolk Southern
8 N. Jefferson St.
Roanoke, VA 24042-0006

Association for Information Management (AIM)
7380 Parkway Drive
La Mesa, CA 92401

Association for Systems Management (ASM)
P. O. Box 38370
Cleveland, OH 44138-0370

Association of Contingency Planners (ACP)
P. O. Box 73-149
Long Beach, CA 90801-0073

Business Resumption Planners Association (BRPA)
P. O. Box 1078
Niles, IL 60648-5078

Business and Industry Council for Emergency Planning and Preparedness (BICEPP)
P. O. Box 9457
Newport Beach, CA 92658

Computer Emergency Response Team
Software Engineering Institute
Carnegie Mellon University
Pittsburgh, PA 15313-3890

Computer Professionals for Social Responsibility (CPSR)
P. O. Box 717
Palo Alto, CA 94301

Computer Security Institute (CSI)
600 Harrison Street
San Francisco, CA 94107

Data Administration Management Association (DAMA)
152 W. Northwest Highway, Suite 103
Palatine, IL 60067

Data Entry Management Association (DEMA)
101 Merrit, 7 Corporate Park
Norwalk, CT 06851

Data Processing Management Association (DPMA)
505 Busse Highway
Park Ridge, IL 60068-3191

Disaster Recovery Institute
5647 Telegraph Road
St. Louis, MO 63129

Information Systems Audit and Control Association (ISACA)
P. O. Box 88180, 300 Schmale
Carol Stream, IL 60188-0180

Information System Security Association (ISSA)
401 North Michigan Avenue
Chicago, IL 60611

IEEE Social Impact Group, Computer Security
1730 Massachusetts Ave.
Washington, DC 20036-1903

International Information Systems Security Certification Consortium, Inc. (ISC2)
P. O. Box 98
Spencer, MA 01562-0098

MIS Training Institute
498 Concord Street
Framingham, MA 01701

National Centre for Computer Crime Data (NCCCD)
904 Daniel Court
Santa Cruz, CA 95062

National Computer Security Association (NCSA)
10 South Courthouse Avenue
Carlisle, PA 17013

National Institute of Standards and Technology
National Computer Systems Laboratory
Technology Building B-64
Gaithersburg, MD 20899

Useful Books

A plethora of books about computer security are available. The topic has heated up because of interest in the Internet and the many stories circulating about poor online security. (We haven't included any Internet security books because that's a whole other ball game.) You may want to add the following titles to your bookshelf:

Computer crimes and espionage

BloomBecker, Buck. 1990. *Spectacular Computer Crimes.* Homewood, IL: Dow Jones-Irwin.

Cornwall, Hugo. 1987. *Data Theft.* London: Heinemann Professional Publishing Limited.

— — — .1991. *The Industrial Espionage Handbook.* London: Random Century.

Farr, Robert. 1975. *The Electronic Criminals.* New York: McGraw-Hill.

Hafner, Katie and John Markoff. 1991. *Cyberpunk: Outlaws and Hackers on the Computer Frontier.* New York: Simon & Schuster.

Icove, David, Karl Seger, and William VonStorch. 1995. *Computer Crime: A Crimefighter's Handbook.* Sebastopol, CA: O'Reilly & Associates.

Schwartu, Winn. 1991. *Terminal Compromise.* United States: InteriPact Press.

Stoll, Clifford. 1989. *The Cuckoo's Egg.* New York: Doubleday & Company.

Crackers and hackers

Cornwall, Hugo. 1988. *Hacker's Handbook III*. London: Century Hutchinson Limited.

Landreth, Bill. 1989. *Out of the Inner Circle*. Redmond, WA: Tempus Books.

Levy, Steven. 1984. *Hackers*. New York: Doubleday & Company.

Raymond, Eric, ed. 1991. *The New Hacker's Dictionary*. Cambridge, MA: MIT Press.

Sterling, Bruce. 1992. *The Hacker Crackdown: Law and Disorder on the Electronic Frontier*. New York: Bantam Books.

Shimomura, Tsutomu with John Markoff. 1996. *Takedown: The Pursuit and Capture of Kevin Mitnick, America's Most Wanted Outlaw, By the Man Who Did It*. New York: Hyperion Press.

Encryption

Bamford, James. 1982. *The Puzzle Palace*. New York: Houghton Mifflin.

Denning, Dorothy E. R. 1983. *Cryptography and Data Security*. Reading, MA: Addison-Wesley.

Kahn, David. 1983. *Kahn on Codes*. New York: Macmillan Company.

— — —. 1967. *The Codebreakers*. New York: Macmillan Company.

Lysing, Henry. 1974. *Secret Writing*. New York: Dover Publications.

Schneier, Bruce. 1994. *Applied Cryptography: Protocols, Algorithms, and Source Code in C*. New York: John Wiley & Sons.

Security and control

Alexander, Michael. 1996. *The Underground Guide to Computer Security*. Reading, MA: Addison-Wesley.

Bacard, Andr. 1995. *The Computer Privacy Handbook*. Berkeley, CA: Peachpit Press.

Canadian Institute of Chartered Accountants. 1991. *Managing and Using Microcomputers.* Toronto: CICA.

Cobb, Stephen. 1992. *The Stephen Cobb Complete Book of PC and LAN Security.* Blue Ridge Summit, PA: Windcrest Books.

DeMaio, Harry B. 1992. *Information Protection and Other Unnatural Acts.* New York: AMACOM.

Forester, Tom and Perry Morrison. 1991. *Computer Ethics: Cautionary Tales and Ethical Dilemmas in Computing.* 2nd ed. Cambridge, MA: The MIT Press.

Rothfeder, Jeffrey. 1992. *Privacy for Sale.* New York: Simon & Shuster.

Schneier, Bruce. 1995. *E-Mail Security: How to Keep Your Electronic Messages Private.* New York: John Wiley & Sons.

Tiley, Ed. 1996. *Personal Computer Security.* Foster City, CA: IDG Books Worldwide, Inc.

Viruses and worms

Cohen, Fred. 1984. *Computer Viruses: Theory and Experiments.* Proceedings of the 7th National Computer Security Conference: 240-263.

Deloitte Haskins & Sells/Information Systems Security Association. 1989. *Computer Viruses.* New York: DH&S.

Fites, Philip, Peter Johnston, and Martin Kratz. 1989. *The Computer Virus Crisis.* Toronto: Nelson Canada.

Hoffman, Lance J. 1990. *Rogue Programs: Viruses, Worms and Trojan Horses.* United States: Van Nostrand Reinhold.

Kane, Pamela. 1989. *V.I.R.U.S. Protection.* New York: Bantam Books.

Lundell, Allan. 1989. *Virus!* Chicago: Contemporary Books.

McAfee, John and Colin Haynes. 1989. *Computer Viruses, Worms, Data Diddlers, Killer Programs and Other Threats to Your System.* New York: St. Martins Press.

Stang, David J. 1990. *Computer Viruses.* Washington, DC: National Computer Security Association.

Well, these references should keep you busy. After all that reading, hopefully you'll still have time to implement all the good things you discover.

Appendix B

Sources of Personal Computer Security Software and Products

A cornucopia of information is available on every conceivable topic within the field of security; all you have to do is find it. We take some of the hassle out of that search by providing you with a starting point.

First and foremost, we provide you with the address for the Software Publisher's Association. The SPA can help you with information about copyright laws and answer your questions about copyrights. That Internet address is

```
www.spa.org
```

Security Sources on the Internet

The Internet provides thousands and thousands of security references. We have packaged the addresses of a few into a legible listing to give you a head start. Remember, Web pages come and go at a horrific pace, so please don't blame us if you find that some of these references are no longer available.

Space does not let us provide descriptions for all the sites, so you need to do some exploring if you are looking for information about a specific topic.

Finally, don't forget to register and pay any necessary fees for software you download.

DOS security software

www.ibm.com/	IBM's home page
www.jumbo.com/bus/dos/security	Truly large collection
www.cs.purdue.edu/coast/archive/index.html	University archives
ciac.llnl.gov/ciac/ToolsDOSSystem.html	CIAC U.S. Department of Energy

Windows 3.x security software

www.microsoft.com/	Microsoft's home page
www.jumbo.com/util/win/security/	Largest collection anywhere
www.coast.net/simtel/win3/security.html	Security archives
www.jumbo.com/util/win/virus	Antivirus software

Windows 95 security software

www.jumbo.com	Largest collection anywhere
www.win95.com	One-stop Windows 95 site
www.netex.net:80/w95/windows95/	Unofficial Windows 95 archive

Macintosh security software

www.apple.com/	Apple's home page
www.jumbo.com/bus/mac/security/	Great Mac collection
misbss20.larc.nasa.gov/security/4.0/macdef.html	Antivirus software
www.vector.net/~elstech/macman.html	Mac Manager (desktop security)
hyperarchive.lcs.mit.edu/HyperArchive.html	MIT's HyperArchive of Mac stuff

`kaos.deepcove.com/pacificbyte/ _virus/virusaps.html`	Mac antivirus tools
`www.stanford.edu/home/ computing.html`	Tons of stuff from Stanford University

General interest and all platforms

`tile.net/vendors/ allbyproduct.html`	Dan Kyburz's vendor list
`www.rsa.com`	RSA encryption
`www.phys.unsw.edu.au/~pec/amiga/`	PGP for the Amiga computer
`world.std.com/~franl/pgp/pgp.html`	The PGP site
`misbss20.larc.nasa.gov/security /4.0/sectools.html`	UNIX programs (COPS, Tripwire)
`first.org/software/`	NIST UNIX tools
`www.cs.purdue.edu/coast/ archive/data/category_index.html`	All kinds of software
`www.jnt.ac.uk/newsfiles/ janinfo/cert/JANET-CERT/ SOFTWARE.html`	UNIX and network security tools
`www.ultranet.com/~lomicka/ good.html`	Backup utility for Atari computers

Just for fun

`www.odci.gov/cia`	The CIA
`www.fbi.gov`	The FBI
`www.awpi.com/IntelWeb/ Canada/CSIS/index.html`	Canadian Security and Intelligence Service (CSIS)
`ntrk923.htmllonezone. com/CDROM/SOFT/`	Voice print software

Security Vendors

Like Internet sites, vendors of security products are springing up all over. We include some of the more well-known vendors in the following list. The vendors provide a range of security products, from access control to encryption.

We provide you with the product and company name and, where known, an Internet address and telephone number. Web addresses and product availability change frequently, but this information was accurate at the time we wrote this book. We do not advocate any one vendor over another.

Product: Power protection equipment
Personal computer power surge and UPS
Vendor: American Power Conversion
Telephone: 401-789-5735
Internet: www.apcc.com

Product: Antitheft devices
Personal computer anchors and tie-downs
Vendor: AnchorPad Products
Telephone: 800-626-2467

Product: Enterprise Access Control (EAC)
Personal computer access control software
Vendor: Axent Technologies Inc.
Telephone: 801-224-5306
Internet: www.axent.com/

Product: Password Coach
Password generation software
Vendor: Baseline Software
Telephone: 800-829-9955

Product: Surge protection and UPS
Personal computer power surge and UPS
Vendor: Best Power Technology Inc. (Canada)
Telephone: 800-356-5794

Product: DiaLOCK and SecurED
DOS and Windows security control software
Vendor: COM&DIA
Telephone: 415-595-8782
Internet: www.com-dia.com/

Product: VirexPC and VirexMac
            Virus protection software
Vendor: Datawatch Corp.
Telephone: 508-988-9700

Product: Central Point Anti-Virus
            Personal computer antivirus software
Vendor: Central Point Software
Telephone: 503-690-8090

Product: F-PROT Professional
            Antivirus protection software for most platforms
Vendor: Command Software Systems Inc.
Telephone: 407-575-3200
Internet: www.datafellows.com/

Product: Windows and Mac security software
            Security software tools for Windows and Mac machines
Vendor: Kent*Marsh Ltd.
Internet: www.kentmarsh.com/KMLProducts/KMLProducts.html

Product: Antitheft devices
            Physical protection devices
Vendor: Globus Systems Inc.
Telephone: 800-538-4701

Product: Empower
            Access control software for Macs
Vendor: Magna
Telephone: 800-80-MAGNA

Product: Antivirus software for Mac, DOS/Windows, and OS/2
Vendor: McAfee
Telephone: 408-988-4004
Internet: www.mcafee.com

Product: PC/DACS
            Personal computer access control software
Vendor: Mergent International
Telephone: 203-257-4223
Internet: www.mergent.com

Product: Microsoft Office
            Microsoft Office home page; Microsoft Word security fixes
Vendor: Microsoft Corporation
Internet: www.microsoft.com/kb/softlib/office/office.htm

Product: Dr. Solomon's Anti-Virus Toolkit for DOS, Windows, and OS/2
Antivirus software
Vendor: OnTrack Computer Systems Inc.
Telephone: 800-752-1333
Internet: www.ontrack.com

Product: Encryption Software
Vendor: RSA Data Security Inc.
Telephone: 415-595-8782
Internet: www.rsa.com

Product: Stoplight
Evaluation copies of security control for Windows 95, Windows
3.*x*, and OS/2
Vendor: Safetynet
Internet: www3.gti.net/safety/evals.html

Product: *PC Magazine* on the Web
Vendor: Shareware authors
Internet: www.zdnet.com/pcmag/pcmag.htm

Product: PC-Sentry
DOS-based security tools
Vendor: Solid Oak Software
Internet: www.raiorg/~solidoak/pcsinfo.htm

Product: Norton Anti-Virus
Antivirus protection software for most platforms
Vendor: Symantec Corp.
Telephone: 800-441-7234
Internet: www.symantec.com/avcenter/index.html

Product: ThunderBYTE Anti-Virus Utilities
Antivirus protection software for most platforms
Vendor: ThunderBYTE
Telephone: 800-667-8228

Product: The Software Labs One-Stop Shareware Shop
Vendor: Various authors
Internet: www.softwarelabs.com

Product: Encryption
A commercial version of PGP
Vendor: VIACRYPT
Internet: www.ljextra.com/ltpn/pSecurity_Encryption.html

Product: LockTite
DOS and Windows access control
Vendor: Virtual Designs Inc.
Internet: www2.linknet.net/vdi/lockt.htm

Product: Watchdog
Personal computer access control
Vendor: Fischer International Systems Corp.
Telephone: 800-237-4510

Product: Diskette and PC cover locks
Protect internal components of your computer
Vendor: Z-Lock Manufacturing Co.
Telephone: 310-372-4842

Appendix C
Glossary

- -

access

Your right to perform activities on a computer such as read, write, or delete files and information. The ways and means by which you physically store or retrieve data and communicate with and make use of resources on a computer system.

access control list

A matrix of users, programs, or processes and the types of access that can be performed across that matrix.

access control mechanisms

Hardware or software features, operating procedures, management procedures, and various combinations of these resources designed to detect and prevent unauthorized access and to permit authorized access to a system.

accident

Something that occurs by chance or is unexpected. Often an unfortunate event that happens due to carelessness or unforeseen events.

account

Another word for the ID you use when logging on to a computer. See also *userid*.

accountability

The quality or state that enables your actions to be traced so that you may be held responsible.

algorithm

A step-by-step procedure, usually mathematical, for performing a specific function such as a PIN verification or an encryption.

ASCII (American Standard Code for Information Interchange)

The language used to decipher the meaning of yes/no (or 0 and 1) bit combinations. For example, 01000010 is the character B to a computer. Used by almost all UNIX, DOS -based PC, and Mac machines.

attack

To commit security violations such as masquerading and modification.

audit

The process of making and keeping records that document specific events.

authenticate

To verify the identity of a person or process.

authorize

To grant the necessary permissions so that an intended action can be performed. For example, we can *authorize* you to read a file but not to change the information.

availability

The quality of being available for use at any given time.

backup

A copy of a disk or of a file on a disk. Making a spare copy of a disk or of a file on a disk is called *backing up.*

backup procedures

The provisions for recovering lost data files and programs and for the restart or replacement of a system after a system failure or other similar disaster.

bit

An abbreviation for *binary digit,* the smallest unit of information that a computer can hold. The value of a bit (1 or 0) represents a simple two-way choice, such as yes or no, on or off, positive or negative, or something or nothing.

boot

To start up by loading the operating system into the computer. Starting up is often accomplished by loading a small program that then reads a larger program into memory. The program is said to "pull itself up by its own bootstraps," hence the term *bootstrapping* or *booting.*

breach

A break in the system security that lets a person or program access the resources on a computer that the person or program is normally not allowed to access.

brute-force attack

A computerized trial-and-error attempt to decode or guess passwords by trying every possible combination. Also known as an *exhaustive attack*.

bug

An error in a program that prevents the program from working as intended. The expression reportedly comes from the early days of computing, when an itinerant moth shorted a connection and caused a breakdown in a room-sized computer.

bulletin board system (BBS)

An electronic system that supports communication via modem among computers. Typically, a bulletin board system supports public and private electronic mail, uploading and downloading of public-domain files, and access to online databases. Large, commercial bulletin board systems, such as CompuServe and GEnie, can support many users simultaneously; smaller, local boards permit only one caller at a time.

byte

A unit of information comprising eight bits. Computers use a language called ASCII to decipher all these little yes and no components into usable information.

callback

A procedure established for identifying a computer that is dialing into another computer system. Typically, the callback device disconnects the calling computer and re-establishes contact by calling the first computer back.

catalog

The name for a list of files stored on a disk. Sometimes also called a *directory*.

central processing unit (CPU)

The brain of the computer. The microprocessor that performs the actual computations in machine language. CPUs today are typically really small, about the size of an eraser.

channel

An information transfer path within a system. May also refer to the mechanism by which the path is effected.

character

Letters, numbers, or symbols that you type on your keyboard. This whole book is composed of characters.

checksum

Digits or bits of information totaled according to arbitrary rules and used to verify that data has not been changed.

chip

Slang for a silicon wafer imprinted with integrated circuits. Often used to mean the central processing unit (CPU).

clear text

Information that is in its readable state (before encryption and after decryption). If you can make sense of it, it's likely in clear text.

communication link

An electrical and logical connection between two devices. On a local area network, a communication link is the point-to-point path between sender and recipient.

communication program

A program that enables the computer to transmit data to and receive data from computers through the telephone system.

compromise

The loss, misuse, or unauthorized disclosure of a data asset. Your cellular telephone conversation with the boss can be compromised (listened to) by anyone who has a radio scanner.

computer

The part of your system that contains the CPU and does all the thinking. Some people refer to all the system parts (the monitor, keyboard, hard drive, and so on) as the computer.

confidentiality

Ensuring that data is disclosed only to authorized persons.

configuration

The total combination of hardware components (the central processing unit, video display device, keyboard, and peripheral devices) that forms a computer system. Also, the software settings allowing various hardware and software components of a computer system to communicate with each other.

crash

A malfunction caused by hardware failure or an error in a program.

criticality

A condition in which noncompliance results in serious harm. Indicates your dependence on the information.

cryptoanalysis

The steps and operations performed in converting messages (cipher) into plain (clear) text without initial knowledge of the key employed in the encryption algorithm.

cryptographic system

The documents, devices, equipment, and associated techniques that are used as a unit to provide a single means of encryption (enciphering or encoding).

cryptography

Transformation of plain text into coded form (encryption) or from coded form into plain text (decryption).

cryptology

The field that includes both cryptoanalysis and cryptography.

damage

Impairment of the worth or usefulness of information.

data

Uninterpreted information. Processable information with the associated documentation. Your cash receipts are the data that your financial program works with to manipulate into reports.

database

A collection of information organized in a form that can be readily manipulated and sorted by a computer user. Also, short for *database management system*.

database management system

A software system for organizing, storing, retrieving, analyzing, and modifying information in a database.

database server

A special server that manages the database and fulfills database requests in a client/server database system.

data diddling

Unauthorized alteration of data as it is entered or stored in a computer.

data integrity

Verified correspondence between the computer representation of information and the real-world events that the information represents. The condition of being whole, complete, accurate, and timely.

data leakage

The theft of data or software.

data protection

Measures to safeguard data from undesired occurrences that intentionally or unintentionally lead to modification, destruction, or disclosure of data.

data security

The result achieved through implementing measures to protect data against unauthorized events that lead to unintentional or intentional modification, destruction, or disclosure of data.

data storage

The preservation of data in various data media for direct use by a computer system.

decipher

To convert, by use of the appropriate key, cipher (encoded or encrypted) text into its equivalent plain (clear) text.

decrypt

See *decipher.*

deficiency

A weakness in organization, administration, programs, or machines that results in threats to information.

deliberate

Intentional, willful (presumably to do harm).

destruction

Rendering an asset ineffective or useless. Making something a recognizable loss; for example, damaging a file to the extent that it must be recovered from backup storage or re-created manually.

digital

A system based on discrete states, typically the binary conditions of on and off.

digital transmission

A communications system that passes information encoded as pulses. Microcomputers use digital transmissions.

directory

A pictorial, alphabetical, or chronological list of the contents of a disk. A directory is sometimes called a *catalog*. The operating system uses it to keep track of the contents of the disk.

disclosure

An act or instance of revelation or exposure. A disclosure can be obvious, such as the removal of a tape from a library, or concealed, such as the retrieval of a discarded report by an outsider or disgruntled employee.

disk

A storage device in which data is recorded on a number of concentric circular tracks on magnetic media.

download

To transfer a file from a large computer system or BBS to a personal computer. *Uploading* is the opposite operation.

eavesdropping

Unauthorized interception of data transmissions.

encipher

To convert plain (clear) text into unintelligible form by employing a cipher system.

encrypt

See *encipher*.

exposure

A quantitative rating (in dollars per year) that expresses an organization's vulnerability to a given risk.

file

A labeled collection of related information stored on magnetic media such as diskettes and hard drives.

file server

A computer that provides network stations with controlled access to shareable resources.

fraud

A deliberate deception perpetrated for unlawful or unfair gain.

hacker

A computer enthusiast. Also, one who seeks to gain unauthorized access to computer systems.

hardware

In computer terminology, the machinery that forms a computer system.

identification

The process of a computer recognizing who you are, typically through the verification of your userid or account.

information

Data that has meaning to someone. Includes input, output, software, data, and all related documentation.

input/output (I/O)

The process by which information is transferred between the computer's memory and its keyboard or peripheral devices.

integrity

Freedom from errors. The characteristic that data is changed only in a specified and authorized manner.

intruder

Someone who attempts to gain illegal access to your computer.

I/O device (input/output device)

A device that transfers information into or out of a computer.

key

In cryptography, a sequence of symbols that controls the operations of encryption and decryption.

key generation

The creation of a key or a set of distinct keys.

local area network (LAN)

A communications system that uses directly connected computers, printers, and hard disks and allows shared access to all resources on the network. Each component usually resides within close proximity to the other components, such as within an office building or department.

logic bomb

Malicious action, initiated by software, that inhibits normal system functions. A logic bomb takes effect only when specified conditions arise.

logical access

Access to the information content of a record or field.

logical access controls

Specific actions taken to allow only authorized persons to access computer data. Typically, such controls are implemented by using special software designed to manage this task.

log on

The process of accessing a file server or computer after physical connection is established. Entering your userid and password is the usual method of accessing a secured system.

microcomputer

A general term referring to a small computer that contains a microprocessor. In this book, you can use the term interchangeably with *personal computer.* It differentiates large computers (more memory and faster processors) from smaller ones, although the distinction is disappearing as microcomputers grow larger and more powerful.

modem

A technical term for the thing that lets you dial up another computer or access CompuServe and AOL. It allows two computers to transmit data back and forth.

modification

Changing an asset (a file or data) so that the form or quality of it is different. A file can appear intact and may be perfectly usable, but it can contain erroneous information.

network

A collection of interconnected, individually controlled computers, printers, and hard disks, plus the hardware and software used to connect them.

operating system

Software that controls the internal operations (housekeeping chores) of a computer system. Operating systems are specific to the type of computer used. MS-DOS, UNIX, and System 7.5 are examples of operating systems.

password

A set of characters given to or created by a user that are entered into a system for authentication purposes. A protected word or secret character string used to authenticate the claimed identity of an individual, resource, or access type.

penetration

Successful unauthorized access to a system.

peripheral

Any device used for input/output operations with the computer's central processing unit (CPU). Peripheral devices are typically connected to the microcomputer with special cabling and include such devices as modems and printers.

permission

A particular form of allowed access: for example, permission to read as contrasted with permission to write.

physical security

Protection of assets achieved through the implementation of physical devices such as tie-downs and case key-locks.

plain text

Text you can read without needing to decipher it. The text in this book is an example of plain text.

privacy

Your right to control or influence what information related to you may be collected and stored, by whom it may be collected and stored, and to whom that information may be disclosed.

privileges

A term used to describe the granting or refusing of the use of certain system functions that can affect system resources and integrity. System managers grant privileges according to the user's needs and deny them to restrict a user's access to the system.

processing

A systematic sequence of operations performed on data.

protocol

A set of characters at the beginning and end of a message that lets two computers communicate with each other.

read

A fundamental operation that results in the flow of information only from an object to a subject.

recovery cost

The cost associated with restoring data, systems, or an organization to what it was prior to an event.

resource

Any function, device, or data collection that may be allocated to users or programs.

risk

The potential for a given threat to occur within a specific period. The potential for realization of unwanted, negative consequences of an event.

risk analysis

An analysis of system assets and vulnerabilities done to establish an expected loss from certain events based on estimated probabilities of the occurrence of those events.

scavenging

Randomly searching for valuable data in a computer's memory or in discarded or incompletely erased magnetic media.

security

Protection of all the resources on a computer system.

sensitivity

The characteristic of a resource that implies its value or importance and may include its vulnerability.

separation of duty

A principle of design that requires two or more people to authorize an event. Bank tellers use this principle when they call the supervisor for verification when you deposit a large amount of money.

server

A computer that provides specific services to other computers (called *clients*). Servers can be file servers, disk servers, or print servers.

sneaker

A computer professional who seeks to test security by attempting to gain unauthorized access to computer systems.

software

Programs and routines that are loaded into a computer system: for example, virus utilities, the operating system, and programs like Word and Lotus Symphony.

telecommunication

The electronic transfer of information via telephone lines from computer to computer. See also *bulletin board system* and *modem*.

threat

One or more events that may lead to either intentional or unintentional modification, destruction, or disclosure of data. An eventuality that, should it occur, leads to an undesirable effect on the environment.

Trojan horse

A program purporting to do useful work that conceals instructions to breach security whenever the software is invoked.

user

The individual who is accountable for some identifiable set of activities in a computer system. In other words, you!

user group

A computer club in which computer users exchange tips and information, publish a newsletter, support a local BBS, and listen to sales pitches from vendors at meetings. A meeting of like-minded individuals who practice information sharing. GUIDE, SHARE, DECUS, ISSA, and EDPAA are examples of user groups. (See Appendix A for a list of user groups.)

userid

The characters that you use to identify yourself when logging on to a computer. (For example, Lewisb is Barry's userid.) The userid is typically followed by a password.

utilities

Useful programs that allow you to rename, copy, format, delete, and otherwise manipulate files and programs.

virus

A program, usually a Trojan horse, that copies itself into programs and your computer's memory and affects the system by showing a malicious message or sometimes deleting your data.

vulnerability

A weakness in a system or program that can be used to violate the system's expected behavior.

WAN (wide area network)

Computers connected over longer distances, such as between separate buildings.

wiretapping

Monitoring or recording data as it moves across a communications link such as the telephone system; also known as *traffic analysis*.

worm

A program that distributes itself across one or more systems, perhaps exploiting weaknesses in that system.

write

Using your computer to create or change information. A fundamental operation that results in new data.

WWW (World Wide Web)

The term given to all those wonderful home pages you visit in our book. Really just a fancy document.

Appendix D
Computer Security Acronyms

• •

ACF	Access control facility
ANSI	American National Standards Institute
AOL	America Online
ASCII	American Standard Code for Information Interchange
BASIC	Beginner's All-Purpose Symbolic Instruction Code
BIA	Business impact analysis
BIOS	Basic input/output system
BIT	Binary digit
BMP	Bitmap
BSA	Business Software Alliance (antipiracy organization)
CAAST	Canadian Alliance Against Software Theft
CAAT	Computer Assisted Audit Technique
CD-R	Compact disc recordable
CD-ROM	Compact disc read-only memory
CERT	Computer Emergency Response Team
CIA	Confidentiality, integrity, and availability
CMOS	Complementary Metal-Oxide-Semiconductor
COPS	Computer Oracle and Password System (UNIX security tools)
CPU	Central processing unit
CRC	Cyclical redundancy check
CSE	Canadian Security Establishment
CSI	Computer Security Institute (a for-profit business)
DAT	Digital audiotape
DBMS	Database management system

DCE	Distributed Computing Environment
DEA	Data Encryption Algorithm
DES	Data Encryption Standard
DOS	Disk operating system
EDI	Electronic Data Interchange
EDP	Electronic Data Processing
FIPS	Federal Information Processing Standards
FTP	File Transfer Protocol
GIF	Graphics Interchange Format
GSSP	Generally Accepted System Security Principles
HTML	HyperText Markup Language (used to create web pages)
HTTP	HyperText Transfer Protocol
IDEA	International Data Encryption Algorithm
ISACA	Information Systems Audit and Control Association
(ISC)2	International Information Systems Security Certification Consortium
ISSA	Information Systems Security Association
JPEG	Joint Photographic Experts Group
LAN	Local area network
MAC	Message authentication code
MIME	Multipurpose Internet Mail Exchange
MIT	Massachusetts Institute of Technology
NCSC	National Computer Security Center
NIST	National Institute of Standards and Technology
NSF	National Science Foundation (U.S.)
NT	New Technology
PEM	Privacy Enhanced Mail
PGP	Pretty Good Privacy
PIN	Personal identification number
POP	Post Office Protocol
RAM	Random access memory

RAS	Reliability, availability, and serviceability
RFC	Request for comments
RFI	Request for information
RIPEM	Riordan's Internet Privacy-Enhanced Mail
ROM	Read-only memory
RSA	Rivest, Shamir, and Adleman
SAC	Security, audit, and control
SANTA	Security Analysis Network Tool for Administrators
SATAN	Security Administrator Tool for Analyzing Networks
SMTP	Simple Mail Transfer Protocol
SPA	Software Publishers Association (antipiracy organization)
SSL	Secure Sockets Layer
SSO	Single sign-on
TCB	Trusted computer base
TLC	Too little control
TSR	Terminate and stay resident
UPS	Uninterruptible power system (supply)
WWW	World Wide Web

Index